MW01482950

RESONANCE KINESIOLOGY
A WORKBOOK

To Osho for getting me started and to everyone who explored
the boundaries of knowing while we worked together, and
to Philippa and Christine for their encouragement and support in
the creation of this book, thank you.

RESONANCE KINESIOLOGY
A WORKBOOK
by Linda Christie

Understanding Energy
The Science of Working with Loving Light

BOOK ONE The Way Forward

BOOK TWO The Earth Book

First published 2005 by Linda Christie,
Tighnabruaich, Struy, Beauly, Inverness-shire IV4 7JU

Resonance Kinesiology
A Workbook

ISBN 0-9552042-0-8
ISBN-13 978-0-9552042-0-3

Printed by Nevisprint Ltd, Scotland

Disclaimer

The work I do is for people who want to progress, to move forwards in life and feel fulfilled at the end of their lives. This endeavour contains a risk: with more awareness you are more vulnerable, more open to falling off the path, and this has to be understood as a calculated risk before any such adventure is embarked upon.

You cannot achieve a spiritually aware state without opening to all that is, without looking deeper into the realities of the universe. If this is understood you will understand that to work with the material contained in this book you will have to take responsibility for yourself and that the author and publisher cannot be held responsible for your actions or for the outcome of any work carried out under this guidance.

A NOTE TO THE READER

This book is the result of twenty-three years of working with people and exploring my own inner world. It was hard to figure out why so much distress and pain was focused within my heart and feelings, and this question spurred me on to look deeper. Kinesiology was a great tool, it helped me find what was true, what conjecture, and led the way to uncovering the real causes of so much pain here on earth.

Resonance has a lot to show us about how our life works or doesn't work. At a basic level, when you meet someone you really connect with it is a great feeling; when you are oppressed by your relationship or your boss, what is this reflecting back to you about your own inner state, your relationship with yourself? That like attracts like seems to be a fundamental law and is the basis of the idea of resonance. We all hold many negative resonances within us that we are unaware of; these can be cleared, and the rest of the story is then up to us.

We are blissfully ignorant of the interaction between the different levels of reality, but resonance operates all the way down the dimensions, and here in our third-Density reality on earth we have the opportunity to clear the chaff from the wheat once and for all, to identify and let go of the "stuff" that is holding us trapped. It is not all doom and gloom, we hold many abilities that can naturally develop as we look deeper.

A NOTE TO THE READER

We are not used to looking within when there is a problem. Kinesiology is an easy method to use on yourself or others. By using muscle testing to ask the body directly for yes or no answers, it bypasses the mind so the truth is not corrupted by our prejudices and we can trust what is happening in realities beyond our everyday experience of life.

To use the book, muscle test through the contents pages to find which section or sections you need to work with. Refine your enquiry to a page, a paragraph, maybe even a sentence and look around the subject: like clues in a detective mystery you will collect vital pieces of information which, if put together, will give you a clear picture of what to do next.

Each session with others or working on yourself need have no fixed aim or agenda. To watch the the process unfold is fascinating as often a deeply held issue or trouble is gently brought to light and solved by an unusual and indirect manner; making it easier to see, understand and accept through the skill of the universal love that hides behind all loving enquiry into the truth. The marvel that unfolds is often of great value and deep significance as it offers not only a cure for the problem but understanding of its history and its future potential in the scheme of things. A life can be a repeating nightmare of narrowing beliefs and confining structures or it can open out, give joy and fulfilment and that is the aim of all true enquiry.

I have found this work so much help both to myself and others and wish only to share that which has worked for me with you the reader. I wish you well with your adventures within, knowing that a new world that can delight and amaze you lies beneath the surface of everyday life.

Linda Christie
Tighnabruaich, November 2005

A NOTE TO THE READER

Resonance is one way of saying similar to, and in harmony with something. The more there is a connection the closer the frequencies are, and these connections and hidden agendas are the focus of this work. Some resonances are positive, give you peace and contentment and a strong feeling of self worth. The negative connections and resonances are more tricky, have often lain in wait to trip up new ventures, and now, if identified, can help you move forwards with greater ease and speed.

The resonances of energy on this earth are often expressed by colour or sound frequencies that can be used to release exactly the precise energy form that needs to be deleted from your internal computer. With experience you can see and feel what is true and of the core of your being, and what is not and is an overlay from the experiences of the personality both in this life and others.

Take time to look at this book; it holds information on how to move forward with truth, without the overlays of people's beliefs and ideas about what is best for themselves and others. Kinesiology, when worked with correctly, is a tool to uncover what is real and true and needs attention. This way you can heal the hurts, cleanse the energy body and clear a way forward for further growth and awareness.

BOOK ONE
THE WAY FORWARD

Understanding Energy
The Science of Working with Loving Light

HOW TO USE BOOK ONE

Prepare for this work, do some form of kinesiology so you feel comfortable with the process of muscle testing before you begin using the book as a tool for balancing yourself. Certain techniques can be used by anyone when they feel fit, but the real purpose of this manual is to use it with muscle testing; then it can pinpoint the problem and the correction can be sought, and checked, easily. Take time with the basics and the rest will follow. The contents of the first book are around balancing the Self, understanding how energy works, and becoming familiar with the different levels and issues you may encounter. When you feel confident with the process of muscle testing - and this to start with is most usually taught and learnt in pairs - the deeper levels of kinesiology can be accessed. It will be hard but not impossible to use the book through intuition and feeling what is needed. Dowsers too can use their method of pinpointing the issue to be looked at. All are valid, but muscle testing is the quickest and best route forwards.

This step then is just a beginning, and the first book, *The Way Forward*, is dedicated to the basics of an understanding of the method. When this becomes second nature, and easy to use, progression to the second book, *The Earth Book*, is then possible. To be involved in the second book without this preparation will lead to distortion and confusion, for the basics have to be in place before you can move deeper. It will take time to do this work but, if done openly, it will bring much joy and understanding to its users.

THE WAY FORWARD
CONTENTS

CONTENTS

11

CONTENTS

CONTENTS

Headings in bold indicate practical instructions.

13

WRITING FROM DIFFERENT LEVELS

The levels are one way of explaining the difference in the approach and feeling around much of the writing in this book. Linda is on one level, the Third Density or 3D, and feels and thinks as a human, in a human way and in a human context. The information she can access comes from much higher levels, her Higher Self and beyond, and from this higher level there is an overview of life on Earth and beyond. From this wider perspective, out of time, you can see the issues around free will and the lessons each individual is faced with. This insight can help growth and evolution towards Loving Light and the expression of love on Earth: compassion.

In this context, the messages that end with the words *We love you* come from another level, first of the Self and then from a wider experience, beyond the limitations of Self. The higher the frequency and level, the greater the melting and fusing of energy, so that individuation is quite different from the experiences you have within an earthly life of incarnation. So see the perspectives as being different but with a single aim. The human perspective is hands on, immediate, intense. The message through the Higher Self is cooler, more distant but more in touch with the real issues and ideas that spring from beyond the limitations of life on Earth. This wider and higher frequency is where humanity is heading. Humanity itself is part of the energy of the Higher Self, of its truth and its real nature or core. Insight does not come from outside the Self in the form of a message from another entity or being, but is from within the being, translated and transmuted through the heart and mind. In this way words and thoughts become intelligible and accessible to others on Earth. This is Linda's purpose: to act as a transmitter of love and Light down to this level of being expressed as human, here on Earth.

The levels are part of yourself, remember that. Some parts you can access easily through the mind, other parts of the Self are more difficult to access, more subtle, more specific to a certain frequency not easily contacted on Earth. You can enjoy the contact with this frequency, have an insight into your truth and access real strengths. You can experience a feeling of being at one with creation that is difficult to obtain on Earth. It gives an overview into your own life and the life of others that breeds compassion and understanding. This will help with your own responses to difficulties in life, both internal and external, and those responses of others that are hard to bear. We love you.

Channeling from Linda's perspective

The process for me is a happy one. I always feel calmer, more centred, and, whatever the content of the message, more in touch with reality. The words are difficult to find sometimes, as if I recieve an impulse, a broad thought, that then has to be translated through my mind into words and English that can be understood by others. This part of the process produces some strange grammar, long sentences with lots of adjectives, all searching around for the precise meaning of the impulse being given. It is hard sometimes to focus on these words as the process moves so fast. Take care. Do not put too much emphasis on each word but look deeper at what the overall meaning might be.

GUIDE TO TERMS AND WORDS USED IN THIS BOOK

The need for help and guidance in the use of names within the book is because there is an overflow of meaning to be held by the very narrow concepts given to these words; they can be made larger, can be expanded, or new words can be invented. Right now it may be easier to expand and clarify the meanings given to known words, and this is expressed in the following pages.

The self for instance can mean many things, from the everyday definition of myself, my life, my understanding and knowledge of my own separate personality and being, to a wider, larger sense where the whole being is referred to, the parts of the being that are not readily accessible in everyday life: the higher frequencies of the totality of being, of the knowledge of other times, other lives, and other levels of reality; and also the lower frequencies, the levels of the body memory, of understanding not accessible to the conscious mind.

 So all these additional meanings are signified by a capital letter at the beginning of the word. The smaller, more everyday usage of self has no capital and refers to the everyday understanding of the word. With this clarity an understanding of the concepts and instructions within the book will be easier to understand and use. We love you.

Before reading this book take time to look through this guide and understand the meanings given to some everyday words that can have many nuances and levels. The word Earth, for instance, covers many, many levels and in this book it often refers to the energy of the Earth, the core of consciousness, the Logos of this planet, the energy of Gaia. Take care with this and all will follow easily.

EARTH

It is the central point, the core, that humanity needs to relate to, not the periphery, the surface, which is the expression of the Earth's energy. You need to go deeper in many senses, deeper to the core of its loving presence, deeper to the form beneath you: the anchor, the connection downwards from the first chakra, down to the roots of existence in physical form for you here, incarnate on Earth. This will help you to open more clearly, in a more grounded way, so you can contact other frequencies in safety.

For the Earth there is also a point of change, of take-off, and this too is what you need to relate to, the higher frequencies of the Earth's energy. This is important now and can help the Earth's periphery and peoples to change within its own energy field.

Much will change on the periphery in the next few years: weather, health of plants and planet, strange and unexplained events. This will all be easier to bear if you can contact the source of the being, of the Earth at her core. This will help you.

DENSITIES AND DIMENSIONS

Dimensions are subdivisions, areas within one band of experiencing, different facets all related to one whole experience. You as humans live in your bodies as three-dimensional, third Density beings. Within this band of third Density (3D) lie many other beings, many in spiritual realms, unseen by your eyes; many also in form, again unseen by your eyes. They exist on other frequencies within this main band of experiencing. As other people experience life differently from you, so other beings on third Density experience life in different ways from you. They exist in other dimensions, some higher in frequency, some lower but all existing within the same band of influence.

Other bands, other Densities also exist. Some are closer to you, others on higher frequencies are inaccessible to all but a few humans, as the range of frequencies exists outside of the human level of experiencing. However, whether it is through sight, feeling or touch, you can feel on a much wider band many higher Densities. Sixth and even seventh Density are available to the Will, so clearing this sensing mechanism within the third chakra of your physical being is important.

Other Densities, and the dimensions that lie within them, can impinge on this third Density with ease. It is as if a pack of cards believes it can operate outside of the people who play the game. With awareness you can see the bigger picture of many levels of being, some scary, some loving. This in some ways is a choice, a benevolent or malevolent universal energy that plays the cards. To look at this issue is important now, for you need to feel where you stand, and make contact within the self to many other higher and lower levels of existence, to see and feel your importance and your part in the game of existence. The cards are black or red; humanity too has to find its suit and colour so it can proceed forwards.

So now we have Earth, Densities and dimensions. We have to look at ourselves. What levels do we inhabit? What experiences do we have that move us out of our 3rd Density level and help us to explore? First this exploration covers other dimensions of 3D and then a wider and lesser known field of experiencing that needs to be reconnected. Other parts of the Self exist in other, higher Densities. These need to be reconnected not as masters, not as game players. You are not the helpless victim, a card in someone else's game but you realise you are the being who plays, you are the cards and the table.

A Spiral of Densities

A spiral of Densities forming one complete octave of experiencing, originating from and returning to the Source.

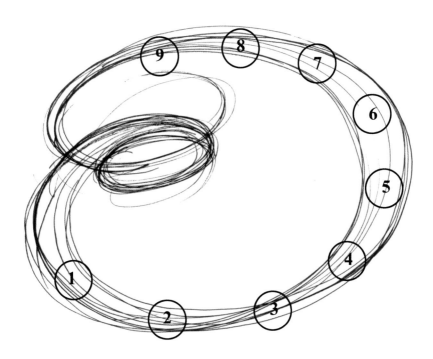

The fact is that All is One and that each level of experiencing has its place within the whole. It is meant to be like this, this progression, it is not a mistake or a punishment but a learning, growing experience for each soul that embarks on the exploration of life in form.

This can be in many places other than Earth but these places exist on different frequencies and cannot be seen by human eyes, except by a few who see beyond the limitations of human sight. This ability can be developed now too, but you need to feel how to operate, how to move with such a being. Do you open and move forwards, or shut down and retreat? To make these simple movements, it is important to feel the power of love and sureness of your own spirit and its inner strength. This ability is the first step, so look within first and only secondly for other beings. This is the best way forwards.

So to the Earth. The Earth has much to offer humanity but you have to look now beneath the surface of reality, to the energy that lies beneath, within the light of the core of existence. We love you.

THE BODY

The body is the vehicle, the method of transmission of energy so you can individuate as one unique consciousness in form. The body gives you the opportunity to be aware of a level of being that is also unique to this time, this place. The body has originality and unity behind its being and expression. It is chosen as the one point of departure for other levels of being. This is a very important step and so much is done, from other Densities and dimensions, to allow this force to incarnate again and again. Each consciousness is given a body to inhabit that can serve it during a lifetime: it is a precarious process, many accidents happen, so all is not always as it was intended, as it was hoped it could be. But nevertheless, each incarnation is an opportunity to grow in love and if this occurs all is well, and progress, however slow, is made on a larger, wider scale. The physical form: you are familiar with its use, you are less familiar with what it embodies. It is these internal areas that we look at next.

THE SPIRIT

The spirit is the incarnating energy source that comes through the being, through the spine into each incarnation. It has a greater or lesser effect upon a lifetime due to the contact, the awareness and the consciousness the being has regarding its own energy, on the level of truth and compassion for all. There is one point of departure for all on Earth: to learn to grow, to contact this spirit energy and to make peace with the intentions of the whole, to care for the body/mind/spirit as a unity, as a total being incarnate in a body. No seams, no fragments, each part meshing together within the whole of the physical form or body. This gives the best chance for the body, mind, spirit to learn and grow in awareness and finish the karma of many previous lives and grow strong in love and compassion for self and others.

THE WILL

The Will can inform the spirit. It is the feeling centre, the input mechanism that gives tone, gives information to the consciousness incarnate. If it is working well, it gives true information about outer events, not clouded by doubts and fears. If confused, it can instil a deep fear of expression within human beings so they feel stuck and unable to move and go forwards. This deadlock is the point that many on Earth find themselves in at this point. It is a time to reclaim the Will energy and find its strength and use, for only when this Will energy is reclaimed can a being move forward to the Light.

THE MIND

The mind is the all-pervading sensing mechanism that is tied to the Will through the heart. The mind is of a higher frequency, but also, because of its inherent structures, it is often more corrupted, more at peace with itself when it follows a rule laid down by itself so it does not have to think or feel how to operate in a new way. These new ways feel risky for the mind which tends to follow regular pathways. The mind is the seat of the personality level. It can also hold the input of the higher Mind, the expanded levels of consciousness, so it covers a wide range, a huge level of expression. Much of its true nature is hidden to the conscious mind. This unconscious level needs to be explored and with the higher Mind this can be done. The higher can inhabit the lower and shed light on the hidden levels of the personality and subconscious that need to be acknowledged to move forwards in truth. We love you.

KINESIOLOGY

Kinesiology is the wellspring, the centre, the skill that is the key to much work, much deep clearing. It can be a fountain of knowledge or a tool for deception and misuse. It depends, like all tools, on the user. It can open the doors to other levels, other realities,

Densities and dimensions, in a loving heart. For an open being Kinesiology can be the way forward to a new understanding, a new feeling of All That Is.

The method of dowsing is old. The application and the use of it can fit the present time. So for now, you have to see Kinesiology as a link to all aspects of your being, body, mind, heart and soul. The method is simple: a yes/no, by the movement of fingers, the relaxing or holding of small muscles that can connect to a far deeper level of the Self. The focus for the questioning is important, the openness to the answer the next priority. You have to be impartial yet intuitive, clear on what you need to ask. It is no good asking about food sensitivities if the problem and issue are energetic. Only by looking deeply will you find the truth.

Systems can guide you, but reality needs to take you by the hand and show the way forward for you, not for another. You have to be brave, forge your own path and this can be daunting but rewarding. Kinesiology is a key to many levels: use it wisely and it will open the doorway to your own movement forwards, your own joy and expression of self in this life on Earth.

Kinesiology is the beginning of all exploring in this book. It is a check, a measure of the truth of any situation, so you can evaluate what you are checking at each stage of the process, to assess the problem and check that the work has been completed and the energy has changed. Also use how you feel to judge if any clearing work is complete. Sometimes there is another level you need to explore and look at and too hasty a conclusion can leave the job half done, the real issue still hidden and needing attention.

There are many different forms of Kinesiology available today and from these you can learn the basic principles. Many of these forms of Kinesiology deal with 3D life alone and do not look deeper. The beauty and simplicity of this way of working is that you can delve deeper into consciousness and reality by slowly uncovering the different levels – first within yourself, your earthly being and then beyond, into other realms, other Densities. Being sure and confident that you can obtain the truth is an important first step, so learning a structure, a system, can be helpful to start with. Later on, you can use your own system and develop a method that suits your own abilities and interests. Kinesiology courses are available at the Centre of Light and in many places around the world. With practice you can be sure of your own inner being and feel in contact with your vertical connection.

THE VERTICAL CONNECTION

This is the link with the Higher Self and with the Earth Star chakra beneath the feet. Once established this link can expand so you can touch a level of unity both above, on higher frequencies (called in this book the Creator Being level) and below, to the core of consciousness of the Earth itself. This connection is what holds you strong in your being on Earth. If you can become aware of the many differing levels of reality within your own being, you are free to move at will, to enjoy and explore whatever level is appropriate at the time.

Other beings can connect more easily with you in a loving way when your connection is clear: no longer do you reach for another to dull the pain of separation from your totality. So, the healing of human consciousness is the result of this reconnection to one's totality. This connection has to be a conscious choice and decision: it does not just happen or come through another, although the love and energy of another can catalyse your desire to open the heart and feel for your truth within the self. The master/pupil relationship is just one step on the road to co-operation between levels and Densities so a true loving connection can manifest in all you do on Earth and beyond.

KINESIOLOGY: TWIDDLING

Twiddling is an easy method of checking within yourself for the truthful answer to a query. It leaves you free to explore anywhere, at any time, and although the thumb and fingers are a handy tool and easy to use, any muscle system within the body will do. In many methods of Kinesiology the arms are used. An outstretched arm , when gently pressed, locks and gives a YES response. A weak muscle, when pressed with a similar gentle pressure, relaxes and falls to your side giving a NO response. The form you choose to use must fit with your body and life. It may take a little practice working with others before you feel confident to work alone, but this can come in time.

To disengage from the mind and centre in the heart is important, and here meditation and other methods of integrating the self are helpful. This book will help you make this step and consolidate a way of aligning the self that will uncover many imbalances and offer the opportunity to focus on your inner being. With time, the Higher Self can communicate directly through the body, opening the door to deeper working and more understanding of the nature of consciousness and reality. We love you.

TWIDDLING

YES

NO

A SIM - STRONG INDICATOR MUSCLE

A strong indicator muscle gives a yes response in a muscle test, usually on an outstretched arm. If you have difficulty getting clear answers check first that you are not dehydrated. Pull a few hairs so you slightly raise the skin from your body and at the same time check on a SIM; if it's weak, drink at least one glass of water. Check the SIM is now strong. Subconscious fear can also be a problem; check both switching and blocking, standard procedures in Kinesiology. Eight deep breaths can also bring balance.

MUSCLE TESTING FOR A SIM

THE WISDOM OF THE BODY

The body is the form you take when you incarnate on Earth; it is the vessel that expresses the energy from your source and totality that seeks to incarnate here on Earth and express itself in a physical form. Over many years, many lifetimes, you have refined and reduced the energies that make up your totality so that you can return, slowly but surely, to your source, to a oneness of being that holds all the many parts of your being in a pattern of symmetry. Like the fractals in a leaf, the total being forms a complex and beautiful pattern that resonates and sings a song of itself out into the Universe. You are learning to combine the many elements of your physical forms and being here on Earth, so you can mirror this harmony, this expression, down into a physical life here on Earth.

Whether the pattern is this way or that way is not so important, it is the fact that it makes a pattern, a harmonious note, with all parts fitting together. Like a jigsaw, you first have to find the pieces, and then fit them together to make a picture. The picture is your true Self, the pieces the many aspects of yourself you can relate to in a physical body: the mind, the emotions, the heartfelt feelings of love and the physical expression of all these, the actual physical body. The body with all its mystery and delicate balance that needs so much care from your total being to stay grounded and at one with itself. It is as if a plant needs light and constant attention so that it can flourish. In a way you are watered by energies that flow into you from your total being or source. These energies flow through you and nourish you, keeping your energy in a constant state, so you do not feel so disconnected from the whole that imbalance and death can ensue. At times these links become tenuous; in sickness or in mental disturbance, these flows are often interrupted and much damage to the physical form can follow.

Within the physical form lies the nugget, the core, the central communication to this source energy. The spine is the first point of access for this flow of energy from the source, and through the top of the head, the flow energises and moves through the intricate, whirling energy centres within the chakras of the body. These centres are numerous. The main chakras align from front to back around the spine but numerous others regulate this flow of chi, or energy, to every part of the living organism so it is sustained and fed. Your role on Earth now is to become conscious of this fine, vital energy and become aware of its source, so you can bring more of the higher into the lower. This higher and lower is not outside of yourself, these ideas are only words to help express a truth about frequency, around high and low as energy states. So all frequencies are here and now but some are more accessible than others. The food you ate last week is not accessible to you easily. Where is it? Some eliminated, the waste products, and some assimilated, integrated into your physical form so it can no longer be found. This is how these higher energies are read by you. You can feel energy as health but you cannot see where it comes from, cannot understand the source, and see only the miracle of the physical expression as the source of your being: the heart, the breath, the aliveness of a living person. When you die what happens? Parts, like the food, are eliminated. The essence of your being returns to Source, taking with it the energies it needs to incarnate again. If you are true to your Self you weigh little, float to the correct frequency for you, the correct point of melting and return for you at that time. The heavier the load, the more likely the being is to reincarnate, to start again the process of being and experiencing that makes up another lifetime here on Earth.

There are many who identify with the spirit alone, many with the body; but denial of any part of you as sacred is a mistake. All has its place, has its function in the scheme of things and the body itself can be the tool to bypass the limitations of the mind and its reasonable approach to life. Here, through the body, is a straightforward, direct link to the source of your being, to the higher frequencies that are part of yourself, part of your knowing and wisdom that has incarnated here and now as you.

You are aware of your personality, your likes and dislikes, and seek to feel the comfort and security of the safety that comes from being solid, carefree, and at one with all that happens around you.

You look for many solutions to this denial and it is easy to find others who will offer to guide, to show you a path, back to yourself. They can help and inspire and show you a path but you have to walk, to move, to explore and this feels so hard, so unjust that some effort is needed to find out who you are. It's obvious, is it not? But is it? You are aware of so much, there is more. Look deeper and you will find it, this flow we talk of that holds you secure in an incarnation. It can hold you securely, consciously holding you in a larger framework: the knowledge and light of the total Self. This experience of returning, of becoming whole, is the most important task for all human beings at this time.

The Earth supports from beneath, provides you too with a flow of energy that supports your life here on Earth. But if you're not aware these flows will seem to diminish, and the experience of health and wholeness will seem more difficult, more tricky. This is because you have to become responsible for who you are, lean directly on your energy flows, tap into them, harness the love you hold so that you can move on. The flows are vast and immense, they circle the globe and the human body too, an enveloping energy structure that is in a delicate balance. Each person, each one who can hold these high frequency flows makes it easier for others to follow. What is unusual can become normal. As you have taken the mobile phone into your lives so you can communicate on many different levels and frequencies, if you choose to make this effort.

It is best to start at the beginning, learn the basics about yourself with the help of your own body, mind, spirit and heart. Experiment, become more of a feeling person, less of a thinking being, and this will help you. The pull in your world is to become more reasonable, more logical and ungrounded. This will not help you make this step so beware of spending all your time in logical thought, it will not aid you in the process of contacting subtle energy within. You have to sit, take time, take care of your inner world first, and all will follow. We love you.

INNER DEVELOPMENT AND THE WISDOM OF THE BODY

Like hill walkers unprepared for a change in the weather, we open to higher frequencies, unaware of the reality of higher dimensions. If we depend and look to others on this higher level for guidance, while denying our feelings, we can be in big trouble. We need to feel the quality of this guidance: does it feel like going home, loving and gentle, or does it tell you what to do? Co-creation is the signature of the love inherent on the Light path. Love and respect should exist between levels, a mirror of the inner love and respect for the Self.

This warning is to help you become aware that everything you meet on the path may not be helpful to you. Feeling is important, when choosing whether to open and melt with another being, or stay centred within. This is true on any level. Everything changes so quickly now and what seemed OK last week may be different today. Not all the high-frequency energy a human being can contact is of the Light. The Dark path also offers insight and understanding, and without the ability to feel clearly you are unaware of the implications of the invitation offered. This offer is not wrong nor is it going to disappear while we live in form on Earth. We each make the choice which path we wish to follow. There is no judgement from above as to our decision, it is purely a personal choice for each individual to make about how they wish to evolve. Ultimately all beings return to Source. The question is which path to take forwards, up through the Densities.

Many who intend to open to the Light fall unwittingly under the influence of the Dark path, due to their lack of inner integration and acceptance of the Self. If you feel fear around your own inner darkness, this is a powerful resonant energy with the fear and 'power over' energy offered by the Dark path. Often this fear is subconscious and only a faint feeling of separation and unease will manifest into conscious awareness. Beings on the Dark path from higher frequencies are not ugly but appear as light beings, and the wisdom offered is true from their perspective but leads you towards the path of love of Self for Self. The truth of this offer is easy to detect by feel. You learn discernment through building a connection and communicating to all levels of the Self. A path of development designed by your own source can bring you easily to an enlightened state: all parts of the Self working together with full understanding of the strengths and weaknesses of the total being, a being that exists on many Densities and dimensions.

Often, people do not recognise the pull and feel of unloving Light. Without feeling, you are vulnerable to the attraction of bright, unloving Light that also offers insight from higher dimensions. When there is resonant fear and denial held within your body, this blockage to the free flow of energy resonates with the structures of power and fear inherent in the Dark path. While living in form on Earth we cannot avoid this invitation of the Dark as we make our choice of path forward. We have to face this choice if we wish to progress, for we are built out of duality on a deep level, and have experienced light and dark, good and evil, victim and victimiser, over many lives. However, if we can accept our personalities and inner feelings, both positive and negative, we then lose our resonance with unloving Light and naturally feel at home in the soft, gentle warm Light of the unity of All. You need to follow your heart and feelings to proceed on a path to the Light, you cannot use the limited understanding of the mind alone. To be clear what our feelings are trying to tell us, after centuries of denial, is a difficult task. An accurate method of contacting the many levels of the Self can be a great help in developing confidence and awareness of our inner being.

Kinesiology, with its many disciplines, offers clear methods of communicating with these many levels of the Self. Slowly a realisation of what may be possible, through this simple method of communicating through the body, is opening the doors to many levels of consciousness. The body is a useful ally in our spiritual progression and can give us insight into what is hidden from our conscious awareness, both within the Self, and outside in the world. There is a way that we can live in harmony with ourselves, the planet, and other people. In our efforts to create this reality we often misconstrue the meaning of love and loving relationships. The old ways do not work, as if no rules apply anymore. We get confused and unsure about how to respond and react to life, hesitating when making decisions. What is the right way forward, the best solution, both for others, and ourselves? Seeking help from the outside can take us away from our own centre and knowing, making us needy and unable to judge what is right for us. This giving away of personal power and responsibility often takes groups with good intention towards the Dark.

Kinesiology is a great leveller in development groups. It can uncover the truth, if you are brave enough to look for it, and when others bring different pieces of the jigsaw into the picture, these do not contradict each other. There is a harmony in human life which, as we become more used to listening to our inner knowing, develops our own inate abilities. There is a bigger picture, the problem is our minds rebel, sure that they know best. When we can listen to our inner wisdom and realise it takes time and effort to begin this inner dialogue, we will move quickly to our own right place within the universe, where true security can be found.

THE VALUE OF LIFE IN FORM

The openings to the sky and the Earth are new. Let them come and discover the inner peace from the connection now. The trees are waiting, watching for the new, waiting for the old to fade away, to disappear now. To go onwards, there has to be a period of letting go. This is hard. It will in many ways be hard on Earth for the next few years. Much buried fury, much hate, much violence surfacing from the subconscious and the Will. Much hatred directed at others, not owned, not accepted. Much violence put by one man, one human, upon another.

In time this turmoil will change too when all evolves to another space, another Density. The reckless abuse of the physical form will not be able to continue: only the thoughts and feelings and heart will be in operation, not the body. The body is a gift, it is worth remembering this in these difficult times. Only with a body can you feel in such a direct, tangible, physical way. Only in this form can you touch and melt with another in physical contact. This may seem a small and obvious point, but in the bigger scale of evolution it's this loving connection that is the glory and the strength of the physical experience in human form. So use it wisely. You can overpower, you can hurt and harm, you can love and open, and experience the joy of touch and contact.

All this is important in these last few years. We cannot tell you when this transformation will come. It will be in a blink of an eye, not a long, drawn out time of change, where you can plan and plot where and what you are, and want to be. It will be an instantaneous transformation that will leave all on Earth new and fresh, waiting to develop in its new forms. Yes, the 3D experiencing has been given a special place within the universe and it is now at a moment of completion; so use this time to explore all its facets before you have a different experience in another Density.

Those that move to 6th Density will experience a change but it will be a soft, flowing, moving experience. This is not a test, not a sifting by judgement, more a movement to what is home, what is appropriate. Only fear, and lack of awareness of what the soul holds here on Earth, will stop and mar the process. The sleepers sleep, the awakened move on, it's very simple. The asleep have a choice to make, if not now, later, if not later in another form that is not of Earth as we know it. Forget your fears and explore the Self and all will be well. We love you.

PICKING UP THE VIBRATION OF OTHERS

The world outside, the world of everyday life, is in turmoil, is in confusion, is in flux. Few are there to hold an inner peace and strength and those that can are a little weak at this time. To protect the bud of a flower in winter is sensible and thus it is with you too, to protect the inner life for it is a little vulnerable.

That does not mean that you cannot communicate or enjoy your fellow humans but you have to be aware of the interfaces of energy patterns that occur through unprotected exposure to others. Like a sponge, you all, to a certain degree, are picking up the vibration of others. This is O.K. if you have the chance, time and space to discharge these. If not, an interface of energy occurs, an intermingling one with another that is not appropriate as you attempt to lift the body's vibration and rate of expression on the 3D. You are vulnerable because you are all in process, half and half, still not one thing or another. Soon the cement will set firm and the need to protect so much will disappear. This will come soon so do not fear this time of retreat and vulnerability. It will pass. We love you.

SEPARATION AND THE ROLE OF THE MIND

When I first started channeling I was unsure how this amazing process worked. I still perceived the messages and guidance I received as coming from outside myself; as a connection to loving and wise beings that needed my efforts to be in a meditative space to make the contact possible. It has taken many years to realise that my original perspective was an illusion. The first, shaky contacts with the Higher Self become integrated into your Earthly being through practice and time. Channeling does not come from outside the self but inside, from a part of the self that is always there, if we wish to make contact through the heart and are open to listen. In time we can approach higher frequencies.

It is worth remembering that the Higher Self of most human beings exists on sixth Density. Mediums in the past have contacted beings outside of themselves, not always on frequencies as high as the sixth, their spirit helpers being of human origin, living closer to the Earth. This process is different, is a melting and merging with one's own truth and being: a step that will begin the building of a vertical connection through the human body up to the Higher Self and Creator Being and down to the Earth. This connection is the beginning of the process of Ascension. The following channeling helps to explain the contact from a higher perspective and the importance of clearing and cleaning our human energy field.

THE ILLUSIONS OF SEPARATION: CAN WE COMMUNICATE WITH OUR OWN HIGHER FREQUENCIES AND NOT LOOK OUTSIDE OURSELVES FOR LOVE AND SUPPORT?

We have to be able to combine with you somehow, unknowingly, we do not have to have your conscious attention. It is helpful and necessary for you to give yourself time to be alone, to be here, but it is not necessary for us. We come when we are needed, when we feel you need us to be there and we protect you at all times, not just when you are on the cosmic phone. It is like this, this relationship. It is there always. Just as you are at one with your body on this plane, on another dimension we are at one in truth. We are part and parcel of the same energy field, the same matrix, the same knowing, so this idea of separation is really false and is not actually a problem, except in your own minds. This filter can cause you all problems. You have believed yourselves as alone, as lost, and these imprints have to be removed. They are deep within the universal energy body of mankind. He has not known the joy of union with his own energy, let alone anyone else's in the universe, and so all this stuff around separation is carried by you all the time.

This is going to be changed and slowly those willing to make this move will start to come together, come into line and work to help each other through this part of your growth. It is therefore not wise to allow other energy fields that are not apparent to you, are unable to focus their attention on this transformation, to continue to upset the energy fields of those who are starting to balance themselves more completely. It will soon occur that the lessons that are coming forward will push all to re-evaluate their place within their lives. What is coming soon is a sort of knowing that will aid all who are open to it to see more closely what they need, what they want.

What is the difference here, these two forces of need and want hold you all prisoner. For the needs are basic, the wants extra, coming from another space altogether, coming from lack, lack of love both from outside and inside. Lack of love for self, first, lack of love for others is also part of this but first clear the self. It is going to be easy to progress forwards when love is a constant motivating force within, not just there as a larger picture constructed by the mind and its extraneous wants and desires. The mind causes you to focus on these desires and not the real problems that hold you back. You want this or that or the other, it does not matter what, it's just the energy put outwards, flowing outwards to receive a response from energies that are less than wholesome. These energies are forced to be there because of this pull towards those that literally call this stuff to them. You have to see now that the deeper energies within man are giving him the purpose he needs, are giving him the push he needs to look. It will be hard for many to look within when all is drawn into such a difficult arena with so much going on that seems to be relevant, then irrelevant, depending on which part of the mind you are looking from. The mind itself can only guide itself forwards with energy from a deeper level of the being. It needs to feel the source, spirit need, not its own wants and desires that cloud this deeper cause and effect process. You are all part of one energy: all mankind has the potential to rise above the separation, the pain, the confusion he feels inside.

THE ROLE OF THE MIND

The primary role of the mind is to collate, to diffuse, and to give out the commands to the body. It is an apparatus that has its roots in another dimension, its place in another space than this Earth. It helps to keep the mind, body and spirit in a working trio, it is part of the process, and it loves and gives to the component parts under its rule. The mind loves and gives to the body, it loves and gives outwards to others, it holds the essence of the Source within it. The mind needs to be part of the process of enlightenment, it needs you to be able to give it love for it cannot become part of another Density unless it is loved and used with love. It needs to be made aware, it needs to let go of its past, it needs so much from people but they are not using it correctly, they are using it as a means of escape from its truth, and here you have the problem. The fear, the resistance to being clear, to looking more deeply, holds people stuck and this stuckness is inherited, it goes on and on like a wheel. The karma held in the mind and the body cannot be freed until the mind too accepts its own grace and lets go of its past. The process can be done slowly or in an instant, it is up to the courage of the person concerned.

Here is a constant, a constant being, here is the truth of the One to be brought forward now. Let it be seen that all is going to be fine. Let it be heard and all will be well. We love you.

Energetically the mind is a structure and is often seen as the chief stumbling block on the path to enlightenment. To drop the mind sounds good and certainly the Dark energies' fondness for structure makes the mind especially vulnerable to distortions of the truth. However there is another side to the story. From a higher perspective the mind, along with all other parts of the Self, needs loving acceptance for true evolution to follow.

WORKING WITH COLOUR

COLOUR AS A METHOD OF CONTACTING HIGHER FREQUENCIES OF THE SELF, TUNING IN AND PROTECTION.

Each person will have a particular colour, a particular frequency they can tune into to contact their Higher Self and Creator Being. This energy needs to be rooted into the Earth beneath the feet, contacting first the Earth Star chakra, about eighteen inches (45cm) beneath the feet, and then the crystal light at the Earth's core.

Using a SIM, a colour can be found to use at a particular time. As you progress, the colours may change and a wider spectrum can be used of different colours for different occasions. The most common colours are purple, blue, green silver, gold and pink although other specific colours or combinations of colours may be appropriate.

To start with, it's best to visualise a beam of colour from above you, moving down around you and into the ground. With practice, you can see or feel the beam move within the body and radiate outwards. These colours can also act as a protection, allowing you to feel clearly what is happening around you in the world whilst protecting you from negativity.

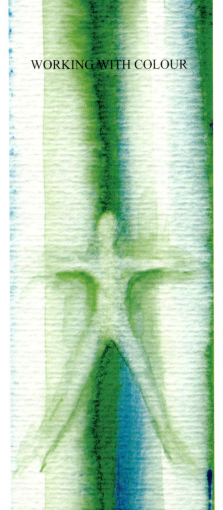

Little and often is the best method of working with these colours. Five to ten minutes, each morning and evening and before you start any healing work, is enough.

The more you work at it, the clearer the colour and the connection will become. At times you may not see the colour at all. This does not mean it is not working. Some people may have to feel if they are tuned in.

POLARISATION TO LIGHT AND DARK AND FILTERS IN THE MIND

We come to tell you that today all the energies of differing points of view are colliding and bringing their energies to bear on this planet. The forces of good, the forces of the Dark, all come to see which angle, which side, which place, which position each person is in. What will happen, what will result from this is that the energies will even out. Those that can bear the weight of the change, the progression, will be led faster towards people, situations and to that part of themselves where the knowledge of what they need to know and grow will become apparent.

Those that choose not to listen to the inner prompting to sort themselves out now will fall into blame, they will desist from making attempts to struggle to free themselves further. This denial and blame is common, accentuated by the increase in the high-frequency energy reaching Earth, and the many people not listening now will find it increasingly difficult to understand what is going on around them. The karmic processes will soon speed up and with the acceleration many will be unable to understand what is happening to them. It is easy to stand back and see this happen but not easy to understand the swings and falls when life is pushed and pulled around you and all begins to look chaotic and unsure. Those that can remove the filters, the stuckness of karma, will see with clarity and will be able to repair so much of the stupidity that has called a halt to the processes of growth for all the living beings around this Earth.

This Earth longs to express the many forms she holds within her. If one is removed and released into a realm of non-form, those that are here in form have to hold the levels, the vibration, the experiencing of each of these beings that are not able to incarnate. Those beings that are here hold the keys that transform this state of affairs so that a new flood of natural events can unblock this system and free all living forms to be able to flower again. The forms will differ, the shapes take on a new matrix, but the essence of the living stuff of life will still flow strong and sure into a new form. Those forms of the old way will be released and let go of. They will find a balance, a place within the new in a new form. Nothing is ever lost but the changes will be sudden and occur so strangely that many will feel they cannot cope with such a transformation.

First let it be said that those that give and love and trust need not fear. This change is going to be a beautiful sight, the landscape new but inviting and offering a new start to many beings in spirit. Hold yourself clear of any sort of worry about all this. The change will come in time, and for now love what is here for the essence is always the same. The trees bear fruit, the fruit contains the seed, the seed grows. The tree is the same but the shape may be different as it adapts to a new environment. It is the same but it looks different: do you see why the filters have to go? To see the truth you have to be clear, in truth you can see the essence and in this true form nothing is lost, it is always there. If this is not the case, the filters distort and all is seen through the karmic rubbish you hold, accelerated and expanded as the awareness expands. This is the problem, for that which is negative within each one of you, as it expands, clouds the glass. Each little piece of your mirror needs to be searched and cleaned so you can see what is in front of your eyes without fear and with the ability of seeing the truth of this reality.

We are able to show you a glimpse of all that will become of all. It is like a fairground, a fairground where everyone is playing with their favourite event. Let us see. If you are drawn to one sort of event, you get to like it. The big wheel becomes a favourite and once known, what was scary becomes a pleasure. Slowly you try everything. There are favourites, special treats that shock and thrill you. Holding this image, imagine the fair being engulfed in a huge cloud of rain and swept over by many differing energies. These turn everything upside down and make it difficult to see. Everything is still working but no one is sure what's happening. Slowly, someone will dare to try an event out, even though it looks as if it won't work and never could again. Surprise: it does and instead of being a bore it has a new dimension to it. It goes underground, and then up and over to a height not known before. The big wheel has become a mega-big wheel and no-one is sure what to make of it. Those that jump in will be surprised at the enjoyment they can have. But those that see it as frightening, especially if they were insecure to start with, will want to go home, to leave the fair and be off to a new space. They will find it possible to do this, the choice is theirs and somewhere they will know if the big wheel is for them or not.

Fairgrounds are visited by many. Who will wait to try all the different events is another question. Most will only explore their favourites. This is not a good idea right now; explore them all, try them all, see the possibilities of all types of life, alone, with others, in communities. You have to see for yourself, but to be stuck with a fear or complex about any option is a dangerous thing. It might just get bigger, blow up into a mega-big wheel, and then what can you do? Surrender to it? If there is fear, this is not possible. Acceptance comes only with love, love of others and mostly love of the Self. One has to be OK with one's Self at all times. Pleasure and pain, all dimensions have to be acknowledged, and then all will spin and move freely and whatever is asked will be an easy move because that which could hinder has already been dealt with when it was not too hard to accept.

We love you all and hold you in much love. We do not wish to see you or anyone suffer an unnecessarily painful entry to this new dimension. So we pressure you to try to move, to give you the time to express and leave behind all the fears you have collected on your way through life incarnate. Give yourselves love, don't be afraid here, it is going OK, all is working, you have time to release what needs to be released, time to look at the rest of the fair before you will be asked to surrender to this great energy. Give yourselves the space that is for yourselves; it's not much to do, just being, watching and witnessing what is around you. Let go of your fears, we watch and wait. We love you.

It was a revelation to me that human beings have a choice to make. My Christian upbringing with its emphasis on good and evil seemed far away from the meditation and spiritual life I experienced. Opening to oneness, to Light, held no fear, no possibility of opening to dark or negative energies. My teacher warned that much could happen on the path and we needed protection. Many are innocent and unknowing, I had no idea what this could mean. Now I am older and wiser and the choice we all face, between love of Self given to others, the Light path, and love of Self given to Self, the Dark or negative path, is going on around me all the time. This is how it has to be if humanity is to evolve. We need to live in separation to play the game of free will and experience duality: a fact that needs acknowledging with no judgement on the choices of others. Better to move on at this time than to sit on the fence of third Density.

To polarise to the Light we need the Will and the heart to be involved. The Will is the emotional feeling centre based in the third chakra. Reclaiming our lost Will energy seems to be the main reason for our earthly experiences, and now the pace is hotting up. The experiencing of third Density is drawing to a close and the Will energy desperately tries to move, to be felt. This is fine if it is accepted, if personal responsibility acknowledges unpleasant feelings and accepts them without blame. Too often judgement and blame enter the picture and denial ensues.

Empowering the connection to higher frequencies without the participation of the Will energy creates denial within the being. This choice polarises you to the Dark path, more often by default than design. The personas of victim and victimiser are the play of third Density dualistic life and now they have to be transcended, not by pretending we are not affected by others' actions but by dealing with the personality's responses and reactions effectively and without blame. Many of the techniques in the following chapters help you to stay in balance and look at the truth of what you see around you without judgement or denial.

WATCH AND FORGIVE THE SELF

Go slowly, go carefully and concisely with all this changing of energy and frequency. Be still and know yourself for what you are, for what you will be. Be calm, be collected and sure in yourself for the future is bright and clear. Do not fear for the Earth, for the world, for its peoples and, most of all, for your Self. Remember the wholeness of all things, the oneness of all things, the conception and decay on the material plane of all things. Let these changes come and go within and without. Watch the destruction and let it be, watch the growth and let it expand. Watch the despair and give it compassion, watch the love and awakening and give it your strength. Watch all things and remain witness to the Self, to the innermost Self of the soul of the being you are part of and is part of you. This will give you the strength and love for the Self to go on.

Forgive the Self when it feels right, for mistakes made in the past, for judgements put upon the Self by the Self, for hurts caused by the Self to the Self and others and, most of all, forgive the Light for leaving you in darkness. Forgive the Self for the fall from love and Light in creation so long ago by the choice to deviate, and help and hold secure all consciousness that needed to experience in form the feelings of aloneness and separation to grow in love of the All in One and Self.

Let this all pass slowly from you, let it go and grow for now is the time to expand and move forwards at a pace. It will come overnight when you are asleep, when you are not consciously aware, the call to move on, to move forwards. Let these times pass like a twinkling of an eye and let yourself be part of the One. We hold you in love and Light. The Angels and helpers of the Light path beings, we love you.

ENERGY WORK, LEARNING TO BALANCE

The following methods can all be used to correct the basic energetic imbalances. When people start this work they may have to express, either verbally or by working with the body, emotions and feelings that have been long repressed. There is often judgement about these feelings and only when they can be accepted as feelings, not good or bad, but just understandable feelings, can they then be dealt with more esoterically using visualisation. Colour and sound play a vital part in the process.

This early expression of emotion is not to be left out as it is an important step to losing the fear of negativity that is so much a part of human conditioning. Acceptance of the inner Dark and love for the Self is the first, basic stage when we have to accept our own denied feelings of rage, anger, hatred, and the myriad ways we respond with fear to situations and blame ourselves or others for events.

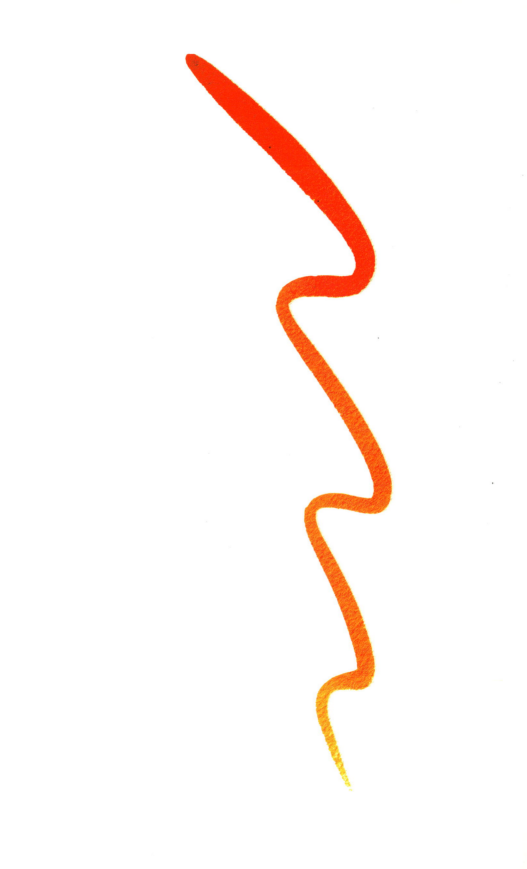

ENERGY FLOWS WITHIN THE HUMAN BODY

The flows of energy within the human body are vast; they flow from one side to another, from top to bottom and from down to up. They all have to be balanced to flow properly, all have to be rightfully expressed to give the entity (the human being) its correct energetic bodyweight to withstand the flows of energy from around it, from beneath and above it. Gravity and other forces play a part in this as well as other forms of energy you are not familiar with. The flows around you, around each one of you, vary and change day by day. These flows, like everything else, are not static, and a build up of a certain flow that is not being expressed and released can cause disharmony and a sort of static charge that stops it being expressed. It is held rigid, it is held and cannot be freed. As the block starts to pinpoint a particular flow, a particular piece of the body, other forces come into play.

The energy field reflects within the body's physical structure. The tissues, the organs start to respond to an imbalance and express it within their own cellular structure. This blockage is then manifesting on many levels and has to be cleared on many levels; hence the need for many avenues of work, of therapy, to clear these blockages. But primarily, it is on the energy level that these blockages have their roots. Why does this happen? Why does the energy get stuck here, there or anywhere? It is held by thought: not by conscious thought but by thought on a much deeper level that has its roots in response to a certain issue, a certain set of feelings or experiences. These factors give rise to repeat patterns, and so these energy blocks tend to be stuck in a place on an individual for lives at a time and have to be consciously released at some point for the whole to clear and become healthy and whole. Wholeness and oneness are in truth the same.

The body seeks wholeness, seeks health, seeks ecstasy, seeks love. It responds to these messages from the mind too but is often so weighed down by the detritus, the muck of the past, that a positive response is impossible here and all looks difficult, stuck and immovable. This is not so, but the root of each problem has to be found before true progress can be made. Therefore clearing these blocks takes time, not on a linear level but on a true level of being. You can only allow so much negativity to be felt, to be expressed, to be released at one sitting. The body is incarnate, is vulnerable and needs you to work through all this with love and with ease. Then you can adjust these flows to bring optimum energy to each person, an energy flow that corresponds to them, to their matrix and so refreshes them and keeps them light. We love you.

FIVE COLOURS

Another way to balance emotions is by using stress release while looking at the five colours from the five elements. The Emotional Stress Release points are situated on the forehead about half way between the hairline and the eyebrow. With the first two fingers, hold the shallow indentations on each side of the forehead. These indentations align with the centre of the iris above each eye. The five colours run in a cycle as follows: red, yellow, white, blue and green. A positive emotional balance around the colour is indicated as + and the negative of the emotion out of balance is indicated as -. The following is a basic guide to the emotional energy around the colours.

RED   + joy - hysteria
YELLOW + compassion - depression
WHITE   + grief you can deal with - grief you can't handle
BLUE + fear you can deal with - fear you can't handle
GREEN + harmony - anger

To Test

Collect objects of the five colours, preferably from nature, that you can hold comfortably. Check on a SIM for weakness when you look at each colour in turn for a few minutes. The colours should be checked in the order red, yellow, white, blue and green.

To Correct

If you find a weak SIM on any colour, hold the ESR points on the head while you look at the colour for a few minutes. Re-test and continue until the SIM is strong. Move around all the colours until they are all strong. A simple method of using this technique involves holding your ESR points and looking at each colour in turn for approximately five minutes.

You can use the colour combinations of red and yellow, yellow and white, white and blue, blue and green and green and red followed by red and white, white and green, green and yellow, yellow and blue and blue and red. Test if you need ESR on the combinations as well as the single colours.

MEDITATING IN THE NATURAL WORLD

If you wish to face yourself honestly and find your inner truth, meditation in the natural world will give you the deepest connection to unity outside of the Self you can find on Earth, if you are open to this contact. Outside in nature, you are relating to something without a mind input and thought process: a reality that is not a human creation. In nature, you can touch and sense an expanded awareness and maybe, if there is fear, being away from a mind-orientated human reality can help you to feel safe, let go and look within.

It's not a complicated process to meditate in nature: walk or sit down, maybe a bit of both, preferably alone, so you are not distracted by words and the need to communicate from the mind. Choose a place you like. This doesn't have to be a major expedition: a favourite tree, the garden or a walk by the river will do. Be open to what you see, let the mind drop and bring yourself into the here and now. Look with the wondering eyes of a child and every time the mind gets pulled into past and future, gently come back to the present. If you feel drawn to a particular spot, sit and go within. Keep your eyes closed and just feel yourself and where you are at. Let the emotions go. If there is pain, release it. With anger the same, express it and let it go so you can come back to yourself.

Make experiments, sit with the trees, look at the sky, watch the water flowing by, touch the grass, the rocks, the leaves, and feel. Usually our hands are doing, not feeling, so it's a positive change to have a sensory contact with no mental input. You can feel the consciousness within nature: the rocks are alive, the clouds, the sea, everything, and you can even feel it breathing. If you open to nature it will respond and return your love with joy. The relationship is co-creative, you give and nature responds, and there is no forcing. Nature is gentle and will relate to you on whatever level you wish to participate. If you choose to perceive nature from a 3D perspective of separation, this is what you will see but there is more, and the mirror of reality can reflect the truth of our unity and interconnection to the whole. The intelligence of the universe operates at all levels of being and this shines through the contact.

Meditation is a state of stillness centred in the heart. In trying to describe this state many words have been used that can lead you astray. Nothingness, no mind, emptiness are concepts that suggest the mind is not there at all. In fact, in meditation there is a shift of focus to the heart so that the mind is not the centre of attention and gently hums away in the background. While you are in form, the mind will never completely stop. There will be points of stillness but you cannot maintain this state on the 3D. Within the stillness, communication is possible and an exchange on the deeper levels can develop, firstly to your own Higher Self and Source, and also to the Devic kingdoms. Children can naturally have this contact but, for many reasons, it is broken. So the experience of being at one with nature can have a very real feeling of going home to a familiar state.

Many people approach nature with good intentions and the structures and pathways of the past. Many old structures, such as Shamanism and Celtic ritual, are valid pathways but can hamper rather than help if they become an overlay and distortion that keeps you separated from the truth of here now. It may be better to carve your own path, uncluttered by any tradition, and let the rituals and meaning develop through your own experience. We love you.

MEDITATIONS IN THE NATURAL WORLD

SKY MEDITATION

Make yourself comfortable, lying down if possible, so you can see the sky easily. Look with awareness at the sky and the infinite empty space above. Close your eyes and, when you feel ready, look within and feel this immense inner space. When you wish, open your eyes again and look at the sky. Open and close your eyes until you can feel the mirror of the internal and external space start to melt. The purpose is to feel the vastness of your own interior space.

WALKING VIPASSANA

The basis of Vipassana meditation is to develop the witness, the inner watcher that can observe the workings of the inner being. Often the breath is used as a focus, but this awareness can also be developed while walking. Go to a place in nature where you feel comfortable and can enjoy the surroundings. Go alone and walk slowly with awareness, noting everything around you. Stay in the here and now, looking and feeling. Bring yourself back to present time if your mind should start to wander into the past or future. If you walk with awareness you will see the Light within the forms of nature, the trees, rocks, plants and feel their loving presence. In this environment your heart can open easily as you melt into the loving reality of natural forms.

Do this exercise when it feels appropriate and do not force it with your mind. On some days the energy is low on Earth and your task will be harder.

NOT TWO

Whenever you feel judgement setting in about reality, repeat silently within the mantra **Not two**. This mantra can be a great help to break the ego's judgement of others and of situations you come across. Try it at work or when you are with people you find difficult to be with. It really helps to gain a deeper perspective on what is happening and makes 3D life easier and more playful.

"Not two" can be difficult and a bit daunting to use when looking at someone you see as Dark and destructive, but as loving darkness is the only way beyond it, at least with this mantra you will become more aware of your prejudices and judgements about life.

CONNECTING WITH THE HEART

Spending time sitting quietly outside on your own can help you to connect with your heart and your own internal feelings. By watching the movement of water you can more easily let go and by focusing your attention on the sounds you can hear around you in nature, you can focus within more easily.

This focusing on water, its sound and movement, takes you away from everyday life and the mental stress you may be feeling. It is important at first to focus your attention completely on the water. Watch the flowing movement it makes and concentrate on the gentle sounds you hear. When you have focused your attention in this way, close your eyes and feel within. Focus on your heart chakra and feel what is actually going on there. If you feel the need to release any particular emotion, do so but do it gently. This is a gentle meditation, which helps you to let go of the mind and focus on the heart with clarity.

USING COLOUR IN VISUALISATION

We ask humanity to draw to itself the feelings of love, of connection, first to themselves then to the outer energies of love and light that circulate this planet. Colour is one source, one gateway of movement for man. Within the world there is much to learn from colour. Here you can see the forms held in place through time and space and synchronicity with colour used as the balance, the gate, the opening to that realm. The colour pulses hold a certain energy that feeds the form so that it can incarnate on a certain waveband of being. This colour work will change, will grow in importance as the openings to the source energies start to happen.

Colour is one way of connecting; another is through the inner stillness, the quiet of the mind, the release from the mental turmoil. Here work needs to be done to clear the past patterns, the duality set within the mind of good and evil, light and dark, judgement and blame, both for oneself and others and God for getting us into this mess to start with.

These thoughts run riot in the subconscious mind of man and create havoc, not only in thoughts but in the manifestation of the thought, the everyday life, the experiences of now. To release these hidden messages to the Self takes time and a certain degree of dogged determination for here much is uncovered that is unpleasant, unkind, unthinkable, and to face this is hard for humanity.

We ask each one, each person that believes in the rightness of love, of Light and energy flowing freely, to take time and look before they call forth too great a degree of higher energy. For here, without care, the subconscious mind can escalate all that is negative and unclean and as this is hidden, it can cause problems for the person, either in ill health or madness and disruption. The fear, from the inner being, of this reality holds many stuck firmly in a comfortable and static state. As energy cannot remain static now, some change will have to happen. This will be seen as disease, as disruption, as decay of the fabric of everyday society and yet within this will be a new flowering of those that are willing, are able to rise and look at that which is hard to face within.

We are able, through our connections on Earth, to communicate and give to many messages of hope, of encouragement, of love and these can be given now to anyone who seeks to begin this process. See yourselves as open, as available to the Light. Visualize the opening of the heart, let it expand and grow and give out the energy of love which you bring to it, both from the Earth beneath your feet and from the sky also, from above. Pull these two separate energies together and fuse them within the heart. Open to this new energy of love combining with the heart and see the fluid movement of energy start to flow again, to grow again and give back to the Earth, to the sky, what it so wants and needs itself: love. This is what can heal, can save, can transform this world and give it the grace again to renew itself on a higher, wider vibration than before. These days grow even nearer when this change of vibration, of energy will occur and we ask all that care to work, work to clear, work to open the heart and love themselves first. In this way all will proceed with ease and grace.

To those that are in keeping, in alignment with the soul's purpose, let them come together now and free themselves to rise together. Now is the time when much can be achieved so do not be deceived by outside events on this Earth. Much is being shaken free and loose but within this turmoil on the outer planes of existence, some new energy, some new happening is taking form. Relax into yourselves, into the love that surrounds you and bring forward, each one of you, the inherent abilities you each have to change and grow and give to yourselves, to others the love you hold within. We love you and wish you well in your journey from one dimension to another.

Fear not that all is not well on this Earth. It is OK, it moves as it should towards completion. We love you. The Angels of Light.

VISUALISATION

Let them sit and open, open to the oneness within all beings. Let them feel the love within life as a total expression of all that there is on this and many worlds.

Let them open to a light above them, see it and focus on it and let it shine downwards, downwards and inwards to their own heart. Their own heart can expand and glow and feel the comfort of this bright light from above.

See then the colours within this light beam, the gold, the white, the blue and the many colours that are held within it. Let it shine down, down now through the being, down through the feet and into the earth, deep into the earth like an anchor holding you steady.

This shaft of light, anchoring you and holding you firm so you can explore within yourself and see the many facets of the Self, the Self lit up by the strength of the beam from above. See the darkness within and let the light shine upon it and heal the old hurts and wounds. Open to the light more and more and feel its presence within the soft, the gentle light of love and help from above you.

DENSITIES AND DIMENSIONS

Dimensions are facets of expression, layers of knowing, in which beings form themselves to experience different levels of being, of evolving and growing. The dimensions of this Earth cover many of the lower fields of expression and the Earth now struggles to raise herself, and the beings incarnate upon it, to a higher level of vibration, a higher dimension. All beings in form on Earth will feel the effects of this rise, this raising of the awareness and can use this movement to grow and evolve if they wish to. The choice, the matter of whether this offer is taken up, is the responsibility of each individual being. The reflection of each person's, each being's choice, will create the reality, the dimensions they see and perceive life from.

The 4th Density is the next step for most of the beings alive on Earth at this time. The movement forwards is one towards a more loving, a more heart-centred existence where the balance of energies, for those on the positive path, will be centred in the heart. Below the heart you have the physical centres, the chakras one, two and three that govern the physical life, the emotional life, the Will, the feeling states that you all experience. On top of this are the higher, finer centres of chakras five, six and seven; these relate directly to the expression of spirit, the being's true source of connection to its soul. These finer centres need the input, the experiencing and perceiving of the lower centres through the emotions and feelings, to function properly. This cannot occur while the dead weight, the old flotsam and jetsam of past times, past lives, lies unexpressed around the chakra centres of each human form.

Now the push, the rush to release this unwanted material, so that a gentle, graceful slide into the higher and finer vibrations now starting to hit the Earth can help all those willing to rise with these energies to find a true connection to their own source energies. To achieve this, people need to be in contact with their true feelings in each and every situation, so they are guided by the Will, the feelings. The body's response to all situations gives a true and accurate picture of reality to the soul, the spirit, the higher finer centres within. This can occur within each person within the next few years.

At this time too other energies, other forms of being will also be able to inhabit this Earth from within, not outside, the human form, so that yet higher dimensions can proclaim their joy and love upon this Earth and guide and help those that struggle to free themselves from the mud of the 3rd Density.

Density, the Densities you all live in, the expression, the colours, the waves of perception, these are all tied into the Density of origin. Colours are Densities, are feelings, are spaces that construct, within their differing energy fields, different dimensions of space and time. Differing realities can occur within the expression of different Densities. We use this term loosely to include all ranges of shape, colour, form and sound that inhabit the universe. They arise in a progression, a movement, a cyclical movement from oneness, from the whole, out into the form of colour and downwards into more complex, more varied forms, the fall into matter that occurs as each spirit chooses this experience. The results, the outcomes of its experiencing within form can begin at any point, can take any movement but once the progression has resumed back to source, back to the oneness, whatever movement has occurred since then, the resuming of the original loop will always recur.

Nothing gained can ever be lost, no movement back to the source can ever be polluted, although by free will on this Density, the 3rd, you can waver, you can move within the confines of your freedom to choose the experiences that the being needs for its own evolution. Each path, each passage forwards can be by the long route or the short. It is of no matter in the end as all experiences are ones of evolution; even those that seem to be of the darkness can help to evolve the totality of the soul.

So here you have a paradox on Earth: all is not in balance, all is not as it should be and the realisation that care is needed here to realign oneself and the Earth as a being has to be undertaken. Understand at this point that your efforts, your struggles, your work upon yourself, are of the utmost importance in your life as so much will change, so much will move, that the outer world, the comfortable outer existence that you all rely on will soon begin to be shaken. Only those that have an inner strength within themselves will find the necessary strength to survive this difficult time ahead.

However, do not despair, for the future promises to hold a more comfortable, a more easy form for you all to live within. These times of change are here to raise the vibration and the outcome for all. Humanity's purpose is to find the love within themselves, just for themselves, and to accept each and every part of their own being and then to give what measure of love they can to a hungry world. This will raise humanity's own awareness, alongside that of the Earth you live upon. This process will take a matter of years but all within this lifetime can experience changes in Density, in dimension, in form that have not been seen before on this planet. So rest assured that all is well. Compare with others what you know, what you see and so the understanding of the Densities, of the dimensions will grow and this knowledge will help you all to realign with your own true source of knowing. We love you.

MEDITATION TO INTEGRATE THE MIND

It is hard to see clearly now, there is so much fog and uncentred turmoil that no clear messages can come through. Many are in great fear but are unwilling to admit any loss of control although they display it constantly. To relax, to feel the energy of a place, to explore the land and find a place by feeling, to drop the mind, to sit and gaze, to feel the fear that comes up if there is no structure, is difficult.

Structure keeps you in a state of mental balance and disharmony elsewhere within. The heart and Will are not fed by this structure, are not acknowledged as there is a constant override mechanism of great strength in place, that leaves no room to even feel what is truly there. When you are busy you are focused outwards 100%, the mind is keen, receptive, active and strong. This helps greatly in all you do but now you seek another dimension, one of inner strength and peace, and here you will have to explore and pick up the parts of yourself you have denied. Your mind will resist and make it hard to do this, as it does not wish to lose control over your totality; but to move on, this is the next step.

So take care, relax, and feel where you need to be here, and watch. Watch the mind and how it chatters on, how it moves into past and future, how it moves into judgement of others and self, how it moves in time and space, anything to avoid the confrontation with the heart and Will's feelings. It feels threatened by your feeling body, a loose disorganised maniac that will upset all your plans, cause you grief and distress, and make you unruly, uncontrollable and even mad. This is far from the truth but these are the fears of the mind and you need to be aware of this, that this is the game plan, the structure of the mind to keep you in one part only of your being. You long for the freedom of movement within your true, real, total Self and this is right, is a real step forwards, is a real movement to the Light and to fulfilment in the life on Earth and beyond.

So how to do it. Sit quietly, rest and relax and allow the mind to wander knowing what you do. Watch and observe the mind unconditionally, give it no restrictions but just watch and observe, you will soon see its structure and games if you allow. Look at what you think, maybe note it down for 5 to 10 minutes. You will be surprised at the repetition and the fear it holds around all this. Look at it and feel it deep inside. The other parts of you long to be free so take the key now and unlock the door that fits the key.

We love you. The Angels of Light.

BREATHING WHITE LIGHT IN AND GREY LIGHT OUT

This breathing technique is based on an ancient Tibetan meditation that was used as a purification for the Self and as an act of love, to purify negativity in the world. The heart is the focus of the meditation.

If possible work outside in nature. Indoors, use a bowl of water or a candle to discharge the negativity you release. These additions to the basic technique are not essential but can help the process along. Sit quietly and close your eyes. You can clear negativity by breathing in white light through your nose or mouth, whichever feels more comfortable, and discharging the negativity on the out breath. The white light moves in and down with the breath to touch the darkness and heavy feelings in the heart. Breathe out the heavy feeling and fear as grey smoke. You continue the breathing until both the in and out breath are seen as clear white light and all the heaviness is discharged.

The third chakra can also be the focus for this meditation. The process is the same: with each breath bring white light down into the third chakra, until the Will is cleared.

As an act of love and compassion for the world, you reverse the process, using your own love and heart energy as the transforming catalyst. Here you breathe in the suffering and pain of the world as grey light, purifying it in the love of your own heart.

Continue until your own out breath is pure white light. Purifying the Self is the most common way this meditation is used in clearing work.

WORKING WITH POSITIVE AND NEGATIVE VIBRATION

Polarity in humanity is similar to the positive + and negative - ends of a magnet. The positive energy repels, the negative attracts; one is not better than the other, they are just different, each polarity having its own attributes and strengths, and also its own potential for weakness. Awareness of your true energetic orientation here on Earth can help you be your true self, and can point out some of your inherent plus and minus points that you can explore and develop. Conditioning and upbringing can often distort these basic attributes: those of negative polarity may try to be outgoing and positive or a positive person may hide and be held back. However this escapism does not bring a real feeling of fulfilment and happiness in life. Only by expressing your truth and exploring it can you learn to balance and find a point beyond your basic polarity.

Polarity is not confined to gender. Both men and women can be positive or negative. The best relationships occur when the dynamic of the positive and negative work together. The energy cycles and moves, and in healing, a combination of positive and negative is very successful. When healing together two positives can be too strong and care has to be taken that the intense energy doesn't become too much for the client to cope with. Two negatives working together can lack the dynamism and push to move energy easily.

Strengths of the Positive

Ability to project and create an idea
Outward looking and expressive
Good at getting things done
Mind-orientated, clear thinking, good teachers
Expressive
Decisive
Has a clear definition of self
Can lead and take action in a group
Initiates
Affinity to the sun

Weaknesses of the Positive

When walking on the path of life will run ahead wildly,
falling again and again down the same holes in the path of life
May miss what's going on around them
Can be unaware of the subtlety of others' feelings
Controlling
Can be seen as strong and overbearing when out of balance
Does not see problems coming

Strengths of the Negative

Can feel the truth of a situation when not filtered by their own
distorted thought forms and denials
More feeling orientated
Very aware of potential problems
Good healers
Receptive and responsive
Sometimes more able to feel what is appropriate in a situation
Can help a situation or person just by being
Holding a space for others
Responds
Affinity to the moon

Weaknesses of the Negative

Are hesitant to move along the path of life, believing there are
holes in the path, so caution is the best option
Can act as an emotional hoover, unsure what is their emotion or
the emotions of others
Find it hard to project and move into new situations
Lack of boundaries
Controlled
Can be seen as weak and ineffectual when in a bad state or out of
balance

POSITIVE AND NEGATIVE VIBRATION

Positive and negative are the two sides of the coin, both unique and both absolutely necessary to the functioning and the completion of the whole. One cannot exist without the other, for the two vibrations act as a balancing mechanism to help hold an equilibrium in energy terms.

To have all people weighted totally towards the positive energy vibration would result in a very mind-orientated society: all outgoing, outward-moving, direct, a focused energy flow of sorts. People of the positive vibration are very direct in their approach, are usually more impulsive by nature, more go-getting, more mentally structured in how they look at life. They are far more prepared, by way of their nature, to put themselves on the line in order to get something done. This is creditable and works well when they are in balance, but when too weighted in the wrong direction can result in their ego believing that their way is the right way. The tendency is to become too one-pointed, too focused in the one direction to the detriment of anything else that may be going on around or within them. This is a brief and generalised outline of the tendencies of the positive vibration within a human being.

If someone is negative vibration they tend to be a little more hesitant in their approach, less able to make a clear-cut decision or movement to one direction or another. Theirs is more the feeling mode, the receptor, the sensor of what is happening in and around them; the sensor as opposed to the reactive response of the positive. This sensitivity can be helpful but if out of balance can mean that little or no action is undertaken for fear of the consequences. The feeling mode can obliterate all other movement and blinker the person's awareness of the truth.

This is not to say that when you find out which vibration you inhabit you will fit neatly into these generalised categories. Your tendencies may be in one of these directions but the ideal is to be aware of your position, positive or negative polarity, aware of your weaknesses, and to capitalise on the strengths within your vibrational energy field and then move and operate within a balance of the two.

Some people are hard to work with, in therapy or healing, because they do not inhabit their true vibrational frequency. They may appear to be negative when in fact they inhabit a positive frequency. Work gently with these people, helping them feel and work with their inner truth. They can then move towards the true expression of their vibrational frequency, their totality and truth, the source point of their being in the scheme of things. Those that look beneath the surface at the truth of their soul's connection and source can gain a deeper understanding of themselves than they have achieved so far. The positive vibration is one of honesty, of openness, of love of expression, of outgoing expressive energy that needs to be felt by others, whether they are plants, people or existence itself. The positive person needs to feel a positive response to their love to live happily and at peace on the 3D. This interchange and flow of energy is clearly seen in the positive vibration. Like the sun is clear to see beside the moon, the light is bright, dramatic and clear.

By contrast, the negative vibration is more subtle, more refined, more orientated towards itself rather than this bouncing of energy from in to outside of the positive vibration. The negative vibration needs to feel itself clearly to define its role, its persona in truth, and this is its aim, to know itself through feeling and interacting with the outer world.

The combination of the two in any partnership makes a third dynamic, the fusion of positive and negative, and thus a third moving energy comes into play, a dynamic mix of inner and outer that creates for itself a third and fourth dimension and movement. This putting together of the two elemental + and - energies to create something beyond the sum of the two parts is what makes a relationship exciting and fulfilling. A true marriage of opposites creates this dynamic mix whether it is male positive/female negative or the reverse. These energies are deep, not allied with male/female gender or sex, and can only be seen as a faint colouring of pink or blue around the core energy within the spine. This is the true meaning of the divine marriage of energy. It is not male/female but the two separated parts of the soul's energy emerging into form and duality, finding their rightful places together again. This creates the impetus, the fuel to travel beyond the dimensions of human experience into higher, wider fields of vibration and expression.

All souls on Earth are poised at a breakpoint of discovery of their true purpose, their true Self beyond the limitations of the ego's structure and personality. This exploration of the finer qualities of positive and negative will help you to define your inner truth and your hidden weaknesses and strengths.

The positive is outgoing, forward-looking but careless. The negative is inward-looking, doubtful and unsure of its own strength in relation to others; it feels keenly, having little idea of its own boundaries, but can become highly sensitive and refined in its feeling mode. The healing profession, the empathetic response to life, is strong in the negative vibration.

The positive outward-going energies need to learn balance, inner control and fusion of their own energies with those of others. The reticence to let go and melt can occur and this needs to be acknowledged and felt in its truth. People will understand their dynamic in relationship better when they can conceive of their truth and inner nature. We love you.

The positive and negative, the + and - of the universe, these are aspects of the One, aspects of the Divine Law manifesting in man as a function of an old promise of division and unity within form. In all form there is, to some extent, to some degree, division. There is a boundary to the skin, is there not? An end to the body, to the being. It is not a totality of expression, it cannot be so within form. So the + and - are an expression of this division within the unity. They hold the key to the division and to the re-emergence of the totality, of the whole, within form. This is the vital step: to move beyond this polarity and division within your forms on Earth. You cannot change the polarity on a physical level but on all other levels the split can be reunited with its totality. The physical form will seek to accommodate or reject the new impulses and it's the listening and the opening to these that is the hardest part of the process of evolution.

In one form or another you have dwelt for many aeons. Now you seek to clothe yourselves in the garments of Light. This is a different form, an individualised entity of love and Light that can move at will around the universe of form and spirit. This is the point of departure from the exclusion of movement inherent in the state of being in form. The division, the boundary melted at last. So, on one level the polarisation is a part of your experience of Earth, part of your duality, part of your expression and experiences within form.

Now you seek to move beyond it so you have to gain balance within form and bring the higher to the lower, the lighter, higher vibration of the totality of each being into its physical form of separation. This can occur within life on Earth or within the state you call death, either is possible. Death is not a denial of this process of harvest. All souls who are ready to proceed will move on at this point and it will be soon. Within your lifetimes the gates will open and close. So be wise, look for the gold, look for the real within the forms of illusion you all hold and see the Light within the forms of nature. All forms hold the love of the Creator within their cellular structures and soon the seals on the forming, on the coding, will be broken open. We love you. The Angels of Light.

You can use a muscle test to check whether you are of positive or negative vibration. It is wise to acknowledge your strengths and weaknesses and strive to achieve balance, making the best use of your inherent abilities.

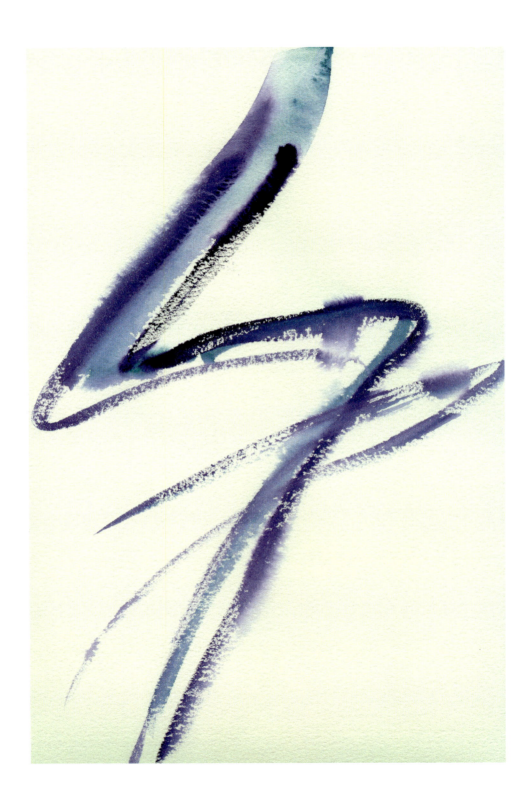

ENERGY WORK

There is much that can be said about energy work but in truth this learning has to be experiential and cannot be clearly explained in words. To offer good energy healing you have to be able to feel clearly, cleanly and concisely what is going on. For this reason it is necessary that a certain amount of trust in what you feel has already been achieved.

Energy work involves the subtle changes and nuances that are felt in a person's energy field. So when working with energy in this way you have to be aware, and focused from the heart on the task in hand. Whether working alone or in combination with others, you have to focus your intention and centre yourself so that you can work but still detect any energetic changes. These changes may be within yourself, around what you are feeling as the healer, or from outside, detecting how your client is responding to the work.

Awareness, openness in the form of an open heart and Will, and trust are the three prerequisites needed before anyone can truly let go into this work. You also need to have a feeling for it, and not everyone does. For some people feeling energy is easy, like coming home. With others feeling is more difficult; sometimes achieved, sometimes not. This has nothing to do with sensitivity as far as the feeling mode is concerned. It is not a judgement about whether you are open and loving or not. It is simply a case of some people having this potential to feel, where others may have leanings in another direction.

Energy work is the opening of the door to the reality of your life on Earth. With your eyes, ears and senses you feel only so much. You are aware of changes of mood and feeling but do not see how they relate to you on a deeper level. Now is the time to open the door to an understanding of your place in the world of form, your power to change these energetic patterns and programmes that have been left untouched and unchanged for so long. Slowly the focus on the outer will disappear if you can see the dynamics of the inner, the spiritual forms that are the building blocks of the 3D reality.

Firstly, feel your own energy and the energy of others. Some will see, some will feel, it does not matter which. It is the sensing ability that is required. Take time with this and learn and feel and grow and all will be well. There will be times when you need to trust, when you will not understand what you are asked to do. Give your trust, the understanding will come when the job is completed. Sometimes what is happening is too much for the mind to comprehend, in fact it needs to be in a state of let go for the work to go on, not watching and checking. So be patient and build your trust and all will work well.

VIBRATIONAL HEALING

Vibrational healing is the eye, the vision, the working relationship between two energies, two beings, to create between them a harmony and balance on a soul level: an opening to the Light and love of the universe through the movement of form and Light. This opening you can achieve through the power of the heart energy operating through the hands and the mind, to open the closed and stuck energies that have lain waiting for healing and expression for many lives.

Healing can occur on many levels, one is not better than another, just different, just more or less appropriate for the job in hand. Those that seek to open to the Light and love of the universe need to refine and to close down many of their energy fields, need to brighten and lighten much that is at present disparate and cluttered. These extraneous energies and dross from the past need to be cleared and cleaned and new lighter fields of vibration need to be established and encapsulated in a glowing form of Light. This can be done only over time and cannot be achieved in one session. It is a process of opening and clearing that takes many months and years to achieve, and takes balance and insight to accomplish.

The early stages of healing are more dramatic, more to do with the release of negativity. The later stages are more refined and more to do with balance and alignment. Between these two goal posts exists the physical body that is subject to all the thrills and spills within a 3D lifestyle. Often healing will need to be done to bring all back into harmony. As the Light body takes shape and grows within form, the necessity for energetic balance grows stronger. An uncomfortable fact to face, but an awareness of these energy fields is a must to stay in balance within form. As the form develops a Light shield, fewer gross energies disrupt it, but from the outside can still come the unexpected, especially when the being is tired or already emotionally overwrought and uncomfortable.

There is little you can do to prevent these upsets but be wary, and careful of each other's health and happiness, and give freely your time and attention to others who may in turn be able to help you when the need arises. In this way trust between friends grows and an opening to the Light and melting of the heart energy becomes easier to achieve. This is the beginning of the movement forwards towards polarisation to the Light and love of the Creator Being. So be it. We love you. The Angels of Light.

CYCLING ENERGY

The cycling of energy between people can be used to create a safe space for healing, to tune in, or to create balance and revive and energise when you feel physically depleted. Check how far apart to stand or sit from one another and the best position to place each person. Hold your arms a little way out from the side of your body, palms facing outwards towards the other person's hands. A group of people can also tune in using this technique.

Close your eyes and feel the energy moving between you. Usually you receive with the left hand and give with the right, creating a circular energy flow between you. Sometimes you do not need to do anything, just feel the energy movement and wait until it feels in balance. A tingling and jarring sensation often precedes the feeling of harmony when you have completed the cycling of energy. If the feelings are too strong, shake your hands freely, move back a little and start again.

During deep healing sessions the energy space may be held open by a person standing at each end or on both sides of the client whilst a third healer works upon the client within this protected space. The combination of positive and negative polarity between the healers is very successful but this is not the only combination that can be useful.

MOVING BEYOND DUALITY

We are born into duality, our bodies are of a negative or positive polarity and the separation we feel within this 3rd Density gives us one huge gift: the gift of Free Will. With free will we have explored many experiences within duality of good and evil, love and hate, victim and victimiser, man and woman. Now we have a choice of whether to move or not, evolve or not, look at the truth or not.

The split in consciousness that created this human reality as we understand it occurred on a much higher level of consciousness. To deeply accept we are built within and out of duality is the only way to go beyond it. To make this evolutionary jump has been in the past difficult and rare. Not many souls have become enlightened but we are lucky to be alive at this time. The door swings open and the opportunity is there. The Earth herself is moving beyond the 3D and the rise in Light frequency is gaining momentum. These changes can help our own human evolution.

From our 3D personality perspective the picture does not always look so rosy; out in the world the darkness seems to be increasing, the energies of control and chaos more pressing. Many live in fear of losing their security, whether it's financial, in their work, in their relationships, or within themselves, where physical sickness and unruly emotions become stronger rather than easier to live with.

We find it hard to look at the darkness outside of ourselves but harder still to look at the deeper levels of our own denied darkness, our less commendable exploits within duality that hold their own charge within our emotional body. This darkness waits for acceptance, Light and love to be freed from the burden of denial and separation. More subtle are our fears of the Light: the betrayal many, if not all, beings on Earth have experienced at the hands of the fallen Light. Our past experiences of trusting spiritual systems of growth have distorted the truth and have not delivered the promised release.

From these experiences of Light and Dark, people judge and blame themselves, or others, for the experiences of separation and pain that they keep repeating and experiencing. Only acceptance of all people's choices of experience (your own included) will take you beyond duality. This does not mean, on a personality level, that you don't feel dislike or hurt when confronted with darkness. Whether you take a position of 'better than' or 'worse than' is the point. There is no ultimate right or wrong. The trick is acceptance of feelings with no denial, allowing them to move through you without judgement. This is the Light path.

Duality gives you a choice on how you wish to evolve. You can choose the Dark path, the path of love of Self for Self, or the Light path of love of Self given to others, and there is no judgement about that choice. Ultimately the Source gains knowledge of itself through individual experience in form, the creativity of the whole expanding with each completed cycle of energy returning to the Source of love and Light.

KEY STATEMENTS

There are a few key statements that you can check for balance and alignment. Working with these issues means you are dealing with the basic, deep, energetic structures within the human being. If you can bring these statements into a positive alignment, many problems and symptoms lying nearer the surface will automatically right themselves. This can save a great deal of time and effort in bringing harmony and well-being on many levels.

The following key statements are all connected to our energy systems.

I am 100% here now
I am free of unwanted energies
I am grounded
My chakras are in balance

Working with these statements can cure many ills on many levels and seems to be a touchstone to regain health on spiritual, emotional, physical and mental levels. Anyone familiar with a method of dowsing can use these techniques. With Kinesiology and muscle testing you can determine clearly 'yes' or 'no' to any question asked of the body. This is a quick and accurate method of uncovering the truth of any situation.

If unfamiliar with this method of working, it would be worth taking a basic Kinesiology course to gain confidence in the process before using this book.

You will be surprised that many physical problems can be righted with an energetic input. Often these corrections are made through your own efforts, strengthening your ability to create and change reality. Stretched by working with Light and colour in new ways, you become familiar with other Densities and dimensions and open to the true human potential to consciously create your own reality.

This is fascinating work where everyone becomes an explorer, expanding the knowledge base on Earth with their own particular wisdom. These methods can lead to a new form of science, where input from higher frequencies and Densities can work alongside humanity to discover new ways of living and being.

100% HERE NOW

You can be creative and use your own skills to help in this retrieval work. Don't be surprised if it takes a few steps and different things to pull you round into being 100% here now.

This imbalance is an interruption, a breaking of the flow of consciousness and a resulting fragmentation of the being's mental energy. It is as if a portion of you stays stuck in the energy field of the moment which, on one level, you could not handle, in which you could not accept the full range of emotional feeling and expression that was coming to the surface. With so much more pressure on us all to feel our way through reality, this fragmentation of our energy becomes more common and more dangerous. Without the ability to focus and hold strong in a new situation, the process of fragmentation will go on, leaving us less and less able to cope with reality as it presents itself.

Take care to look for the time and go back in whatever way is needed to retrieve the lost portion of the mental body. To hold strong in this way is important, it will keep your wits about you for future adventures.

To Check

Repeat the statement out loud "I am 100% here now" whilst testing on a SIM. If the SIM goes weak, correct.

To Correct

For all of these corrections, use a SIM to locate the problem. Find first when you lost a part of yourself, for example on Tuesday at 3.00 p.m. Think what was happening at that time and what could have knocked you off balance. When you have found the situation check if any of these methods are appropriate to correct the fragmentation.

The situation may need to be:-

acknowledged

brought into consciousness

expressed

healed through the chakra system

Correct through

talking through the situation and using ESR - Emotional Sress Release - if appropriate.

releasing the emotions through expressing them

releasing the emotions through dropping them as colours, down the spine and into the ground

releasing the pictures held around the situation

changing the picture held around that situation to make it positive

Spirit Earth - Earth Spirit breathing

internal visualisation using colour

moving Density or frequency; you may be on too high or low a frequency and need to adjust to the appropriate level your body needs. Use the breath to move up or down.

Once the correction is complete, test again on a SIM while repeating the statement "I am 100 % here now."

SPIRIT / EARTH BREATHING

To strengthen the vertical connection and energise your being on a human, earthly level, this method of breathing can be a great support. The in breath can move upwards or downwards, it is not fixed, use whichever is the most appropriate. To start with, muscle check or experiment for yourself to find which suits you best: the in breath moving up or down. Breathing a little more deeply than usual get into a rhythmical flow, pulling energy from above you, from your own source in Spirit, down through the body and deep into the Earth.

On the opposing out breath, bring energy from the core of the Earth up through your body and project it above your crown chakra, up to Spirit. If you feel weak or frightened this method can bring you back to a centred state to deal with the problem. You can also add colour into the breathing, using different colours from Earth and Spirit. Again you can check if this would be a helpful addition to the process.

ENERGISING BREATH

Turn your head to look over your right shoulder. Moving slowly from right to left, breathe in deeply through pursed lips (like sipping coffee) until your head faces directly over your left shoulder. Slowly move your head back again to your right shoulder, moving from left to right while holding your breath. Then move your head again from right to left, slowly releasing your breath through your mouth. Hold your breath and move your head back to you right shoulder. Repeat ten times at least.

You should do all these exercises with your eyes closed as it makes for a stronger connection with your consciousness. However, if at first you have trouble breathing with your eyes closed, leave them open until you get used to the rhythm. Also, don't turn your head so far that you turn your shoulders too, otherwise the energy flow will get distorted. Just turn your head on your shoulders through 180 degrees.

If this is a new technique for you, practise with the energising breath before you start to release negative pictures.

Moving the head from side to side:

Right to left - breathe in
Left to right - hold your breath
Right to left - breathe out
Left to right - hold your breath

Repeat this ten times.

BREATHING TO RELEASE NEGATIVE PICTURES AND FEELINGS

To release a picture held within the mind, or a feeling:

Right to left -   breathe in

Left to right -   hold your breath

Right to centre - hold your breath and then breathe out firmly to push the negativity out of your energy field.

Repeat for each picture until you cannot visualise them any more. If you can work with this easily, a deeper way to release the pictures is as follows:

Right to left -	breathe in
Left to right -	hold your breath
Right to left -	hold your breath
Left to centre -	hold breath and then breathe out firmly to push away the picture or feeling

RELEASING SEXUAL ATTACHMENTS

Make a list of all the sexual relationships you have had. Working backwards from the present time, think of the person and get a picture. From this picture get a colour and then breathe this out using the technique of breathing to release pictures. You really need to push this energy out and away from you firmly. There will be a feeling attached to this.

The colour represents the release of their energy. Work backwards slowly to your first sexual encounter.

If you are in a relationship now you don't need to work with your present partner in this way.

CHAKRAS

On an internal level the chakras conduct the flows of energy around the body. They contain the energy sources of each point of contact with the exterior world, and are therefore important as a point of change, as a point of reference, where inner meets outer, where the being meets and interacts with the world.

One huge area of study to look at is the confusion and disruption to this basic up/down energy flow through the physical body. If this flow is disrupted or distorted, and energy has to find another way around a problem or blockage in a chakra, then distress within the organism, and distortion of the basic central energy system will occur. This will cause problems and issues on all other levels that are functioning within the physical form. The spiritual energy is not necessarily disturbed in itself but the ability to hold it easily within a physical form is weakened. So the balancing and healing of the chakra system is an important part of your work as healers and therapists.

To see this balancing of the chakras as the building block of stability is important. You then have to see what comes first, the realigning of the energy or, and this is important, the removal of the blockage, whether it be emotional, mental, structural or whatever. In time you will learn to trust the order we offer you from spirit. Here we can see the dangers and wasted energy involved in aligning before all is ready and complete, when you're not looking at an issue that is

relevant to the stability of the whole. In time too you will trust yourselves in these matters but for a start, let us in spirit plan your work with others, so it can reach a logical and healing conclusion with the least amount of jarring and effort.

Often you will have to wait for the energy around the imbalance to be cleared. You may know something is amiss but be unable to heal this until there has been a clearing and cleaning within that person's being and structure of personality. Often karmic threads hang strongly onto people and events through the chakra system. The clearing of these can seem long and arduous but it is one sure way of disentangling the outer/inner dilemma that will, unless consciousness is directed to it, lie in unawareness ready to repeat its old karmic message of disruption.

Many beings are totally unaware of any energy processes within their bodies and will feel little connection with this work. Let this be. If it is not appropriate you cannot work in this deep way and people are choosing at this time whether to become more aware of themselves and their totality or not. This process is not in your control or command and you have to tread warily when you come across this denial. Do not push to do what cannot be done, for on some level this healing process is an interaction between healer and healed. It is co-creative process where the client has to hold a certain degree of openness, a certain trust of you and where they stand with you, to let go of this energetic rubbish. Take time to feel what is there, what is connecting you to this process, and all will be well.

These following corrections are explained for two people working together. They can be used to balance yourself but you may need practise to feel confident you can move energy easily.

CHAKRA BALANCING

To Check

Repeat the statement "MY CHAKRAS ARE IN BALANCE" whilst testing for a SIM. If the SIM goes weak, check which chakra needs balancing. Make a claw shape with your hand and hold it a couple of inches off the central line at the front of the body checking each chakra in turn. If there is an imbalance, one or more chakras may test weak.

To Correct

Using a SIM, check for the priority chakra to work with. When you have found the priority, ask what is needed. All chakra corrections are done with the client's eyes closed. Questions to ask are: This chakra needs

stress release
balancing
closing down
sweeping
grounding
connecting to another chakra
filling with light
clearing in some other way

Corrections are then done as follows, again using a SIM each time to find out what it is appropriate to do.

STRESS RELEASE

Ask where to hold the chakra, on or off the body, at the front and/or the back. If you are working off the body, how far away do you need to be from it? Then hold the chakra until both you and the client feel the stress has been released.

BALANCING

Ask whether to hold the chakra front/back or left/right. This will usually be off the body but you may need to touch the body, especially at the end of a balance. Hold the chakra until it feels balanced and check if the work is completed.

CLOSING DOWN

Before closing down a chakra always ask which hand it is most appropriate to use to do this, and whether the chakra needs closing down from the front, the back, or the sides. A chakra can move straight out or in a funnel shape. A chronic, long term disturbance may cause the energy from the chakra to float upwards.

Test where and how to close the chakra down. All movements should be slow and gentle. Ask the client to breathe down on the out-breath while you bring the chakra slowly towards the body, as close as it feels comfortable, pausing for the energy to settle. You may find emotions will release through this process.

Get the client to take their own energy back by covering your hand when you have touched their body. Pull your hand away slowly and ask them to hold the chakra whilst breathing down, on the out-breath, into the ground to ground themselves.

A chakra blown a long way out may need to be taken back in stages so the body has time to accommodate the energy shift.

SWEEPING

Test which hand to use for this correction and how far away from the body to sweep the chakra. Also test whether to move from right to left, or left to right. All movements should be slow and this may have to be repeated more than once to clear the energy field.

GROUNDING

Check which chakra needs to be grounded to the Earth and whether to work on the front, back or on both sides of the body. Slowly push the energy down to the ground using your hands. (See pages 136 - 139 for more on this.)

CONNECTING TO ANOTHER CHAKRA

Communication between different chakras can be broken so to re-establish a free moving energy connection check which colour to use and the direction it is moving and get your client to visualise the connection being established with the coloured light. Check the work is now complete.

FILLING A CHAKRA WITH LIGHT

A depleted chakra may regain strength by filling it with colour from above, down into the body or from the Earth, up through the body. Check which colour and its source and get your client to fill the chakra with the colour. Then check to see the work is finished. (See pages 142 - 143 for more on this.)

CLEARING

Blockages on an energetic level, both within the body, and in the energy fields around the body, may need to be cleared. Visual images for the particular blockage can help you hold your intention and focus to clear the problem. Colour can help to move the obstruction and heal the space after the clearing has been completed. Fog, arrows, hooks and all manner of strange objects have been seen, and moving them can clear negative, stuck energy. Once it works, and you feel brighter and clearer using these images from the subconscious, you will learn to trust what you see and the Will and body will help to bring you into balance. They can be very helpful.

Once the corrections have been completed for the relevant chakras, test again for a S1M again repeating the statement "MY CHAKRAS ARE IN BALANCE."

When you are confident you can feel energy these corrections can be achieved by yourself, alone. You can twiddle the problem and, using visualisation or your own hands, can do the healing work upon yourself and bring the energy body back into balance.

The chakras are fluid, like water over rocks the slightest impediment to their movement and travel and they will have to find a new path to work around the obstacle. These inner obstacles are put there by the interaction of one energy, one chakra field and another. As they slide and move, pressure can build in areas where there is no release mechanism or movement available. The pressure will build and distort the energy like a dam of twigs in a stream, and a flood will occur around the obstacle. These floods are the blown chakras you need to gently put back into place.

See too the need to clear the original blockage of the free-flowing movement of energy. Often this can be an interaction with other energy, it does not have to be your own that is dammed. The linking mechanism between healer and client, where you explore and discover what the blockages are for the client, can cause the healer to feel and take on part of this blockage. This reason makes it important for healers to check themselves often to see they are in balance. Over time, as energy fields melt and fuse more freely, all interaction with another can cause this interlinking. In time you will learn to cover and contain your own energy fields more closely and stay more in harmony but this individual process will take time to achieve, and meanwhile your own weak spots will become exaggerated.

During this phase of growth, be gentle and accepting to the Self and its weaknesses, knowing that a deeper healing of your energy bodies is taking place that will hold you stronger in the future. Meanwhile, take care and check yourselves often for imbalances.

TO GROUND THE CHAKRAS

To Check

This is another way of correcting imbalance when healing the chakras. Again you can repeat the statement "MY CHAKRAS ARE IN BALANCE" whilst testing for a SIM. If the SIM goes weak on any chakra, correct.

To Correct

Ask on the body, using a SIM, for a priority chakra to work with. When you have found the priority ask where to hold the chakra, front or/and back, right or/and left. The correction is usually done off the body so ask how far away. Place your hand above the chakra you are grounding, the palm facing towards the floor. Slowly take the energy down the body until you touch the ground. You may have to repeat this process more than once. The client can breathe down with the out-breath to aid the process if grounding is difficult.

To ground the chakras is important now. As each chakra opens more to the Light it will tend to expand, internally and externally, into the energy fields of a person. If they are not truly connected to the Earth spirit and a jolt to the energy system happens, then this can push into disarray the delicate mesh and interconnected energy flows that hold the person in a state of balance.

By relaxing the flow of energy and grounding it you make a conscious re-location to the Earth spirit and this will help to hold the whole structure of energy strongly.

Take time with this; at times you approach too quickly to ground these energies, the person needs to breathe down and prepare themselves a little internally for this shift of emphasis and release of stuck energy. We love you.

STRESS RELEASE ON THE CHAKRAS USING COLOUR IN NATURE

To Check

If at any point the body asks for Stress Release, check if colours are needed as well to help the balance. If so, check for a priority chakra and the colour needed. You may find there are a few chakras and colours to be worked with at one time so you could work out the programme before beginning the balance. If you can twiddle this can also save time preparing the order of the colours. Flowers are easy to find for the bright colours but any natural obects can be used. Check with the body or on your fingers that you have chosen the right shade.

Get your client to look at the colour and test on a SIM. If it goes weak on a particular chakra or chakras work out the priority and where to hold, front or back etc.

This technique, this new opening with the chakras and colours will be useful to help open people out when they are stuck in some way. The colours work deeply within the being, and affect on a deep level the imbalances they hold. By doing the stress release on this point you release and bring to the surface the inner hidden tension, so it can be looked at, discussed, worked on in whatever way. Maybe healing will follow or some form of internal alignment or, more often, an understanding of the problem before it can be

taken further and released. Often these issues are deep-seated and difficult to contact, so this is a useful method when people are a little resistant on one level to uncovering the truth about themselves. Those sensitive to themselves and to nature also obviously benefit more from this, as it uses the eyes to express the love for the flower or plant so as to gain access to the deeper structures. The eyes are one focus that lead to the soul and are a deep and comfortable route to use, being a perfect balance between outer and inner: neither one thing nor the other but the window, the point of marriage for both. The eyes inhabit a realm that can access the other side of the mirror most easily, a true doorway to the inner/outer dilemma.

We love you. The Angels of Light.

FILLING THE CHAKRAS WITH LIGHT

The chakras are energy centres where the flow of energy converges, they can be strong points within the body but if there is a blockage and the build up of energy becomes too great, they can blow or become very weak. If this has happened, then healing or clearing of some sort is necessary.

Once the clearing has taken place, and the chakra centre is in balance, it can be filled again with energy and love. This has to be done from the inside of the being, by the client themselves. The light can be taken from above or below, whichever is appropriate, and breathed into the chakra centre along with a visualisation of the appropriate colour. The colour required does not always correspond to the colour associated with that particular chakra: using Light for this purpose is not coming from the same structure. The Light used in this case is to match a particular frequency, so the colour corresponds to the frequency required to fill up the chakra. Here muscle testing can ascertain which colour is required.

This part of the healing process is often forgotten but we cannot stress enough how important it is. Whenever any healing or clearing process has taken place the chakra centre that has been worked on is in a sense left empty, although it is ready to receive a flow of energy again and function as a part of the whole. However, the fact that it has been left in this state means that if it is not filled up from the inside with Light and love, the chakra is open again to receiving an energy of distortion and is also very vulnerable to any input from the outside. So the filling of the chakra concerned with a higher frequency of Light and love helps to avoid this happening. It is also another way in which the person concerned can heal themselves.

So these colours, this Light that you need to bring into the chakras, can remove the blockage, can fill the vacuum left by a jolt and push to the energy system. The energy of love is carried by Light, it can infiltrate the body's energy systems and control the flows, one way or another, to regain harmony: pink for Self-love, blue for harmony, green for healing, gold for protection and energy, white for purification and gold also for lightening the load, silver for connection and purple for wisdom. Other colours may be used but these are the basics and can usually help you to re-establish a balance. White Light from above can overheat the body if not used wisely so it is important to check when using it, seeing whether it's appropriate at that time. White Light is not a cure-all, love and Light work in harmony. Colour is frequency, is resonant to a point of energy expansion that can communicate through this frequency. So when you use colours in the chakras you open the gateways to a new path, a new decoding of the old stuck responses to reality, on all levels. We love you. The Angels of Light.

CHAKRAS ON A DEEPER LEVEL

The chakras on a deeper level are windows, doorways to the soul level, a point of retrieval for all that is lost and fragmented. They are a point of entry to the deeper layers and levels of the being. In time, much major reorganisation of the energy fields and levels can take place through these chakra doorways. Remember, on many levels the human form is like a tube, a cylinder of energy containing a core that is surrounded by many layers of energy, envelopes that encase the living core.

The core is connected to its source of Light and love through the 7th chakra. It is connected to the Earth through the 1st chakra. Any disruption on these key connectors causes trouble to the being's energy circuits. When they are broken and withheld, a dissolving of the central core will occur over time, leading to death on this plane of being if these energy connections are not restored and replaced.

Often there is a half/half sort of connection that functions, but only to a degree. The denials involved in the 1st chakra connection to Earth revolve around the issues of grounding, the feelings of safety and security in being incarnate. Pain and despair cause these to unhook and over time many beings find themselves out of touch with the love of the Earth's core and energy. This has to be re-established first before any opening to a higher frequency of love and Light through the 7th chakra can safely occur. This is most important and often causes the rapid forms of illness and death seen in those that open to a spirit-based energy too quickly. You have to take this path of evolution step by step; no rushing and no short-cuts will bring about a good outcome.

The main focus at this time is to hold as high a frequency as possible whilst in form in order to control and change the outcomes of life on this planet. Much damage has already occurred to the genetic potential of man; not only at humanity's inception on Earth, but by man's own hand does damage occur. The survival of the fittest is a basic truth you have chosen to ignore, putting life, any life, above the terror of death and what you perceive as a waste of a life, of an experience.

This fear follows naturally from the cut-off into 3D experiencing alone. There is no contact, no real knowledge of what lies beyond death, and the theories put forward by religion do not tie in to the beliefs and fears people really hold about this event. Instead of death being a change of form to another form, it is feared that it is a loss of all consciousness. This fear creates much disruption, not only whilst the being lives on this dimension, because the fear base expands and expands near to death, but also from the spiritual point of entry, because the mental body's deep beliefs are potentially stronger than the truth. It is a fact that you create your own reality, and death, if seen as annihilation, can become a terrrifying rather than an enlightening experience. So for all those that work with these energy flows, the clearing of the fear of death, through a process of meditation and contact with higher frequencies in a spiritual realm, is important. Otherwise, you will not go beyond your own fears of death and decay. This too is important for your clients. They need to work on their denial of fear, the fear itself, and build a closer contact to their source, to escape the debilitation and drag of these misplaced human beliefs. We love you. The Angels of Light.

The chakras open and close, this is a fact, a part of their working mechanism. It is not an on/on mechanism, more an on/off mechanism and this is what keeps the energy moving. It has a pulse like a heartbeat. This is the mechanism of the movement of energy around the system that keeps it all flowing, so if the shutter becomes jammed problems occur. This is when people cannot contact the outer world, cannot release the inner tension and trouble ensues. This is not always the case but is a symptom you need to check, for this fault needs balancing in a different way. It needs stroking, it needs to be melted back into a rhythm of movement and this has to be done very gently so as not to jar the sensitive mechanisms. You will find the problem can be both at the front and back of the body but more often at the front.

In time, the hands will open more, will relax more, will hold more energy, so that a careful placing in the right point or spot will help start the movement again. We love you.

I AM FREE OF UNWANTED ENERGIES

Check on a SIM, and if it goes weak, then look for the unwanted energy you need to work with. There may be more than one issue to be looked at. The deep, unconscious feelings of others may be exposed during the clearing process. For instance you may have picked up the denied feelings of a friend or colleague at work. Be respectful of this ability to see beneath the conscious levels of reality, and be careful with the information you hold. Muscle testing exposes the truth; used wisely it can give you insight and understanding of the true feelings of others, and so help you to be compassionate. Used negatively it gives you the power to distort and interpret the truth of another, and use this against them for your own ends.

Emotions, either your own or someone else's, are a common cause of unwanted energies but check down the whole list if you are not sure, it will do no harm and may uncover something that is now ready to be released.

To Check

Repeat the statement "I AM FREE OF UNWANTED ENERGIES" out loud and test on a SIM. If it goes weak, correct.

To Correct

This statement covers a large subject and the following checklist is only a guide. Several different types of energy may need to be cleared to achieve balance.

UNWANTED ENERGIES CAN BE

EMOTIONS

ELEMENTALS

AN ENTITY

THOUGHT FORMS

FEEDING CYCLES

ACUCORDS

I AM IN A BUBBLE WITH

FOG OR FEAR

AN ENERGY SPACE YOU ARE IN WITH SOMEONE

THE ENERGY OF A PLACE OR SITUATION

PROJECTED FEAR, BLAME AND ANGER

EMOTIONS - yours or someone else's

Make a list of the relevant emotions and find out where they come from, where they are located in the body, and which chakras they affect. You may need to bring hidden emotions into your conscious awareness and they may need to be expressed out loud to the Higher Self of the person involved. Usually colour can be used to release them energetically.

If colour can be used, test to see if energy needs to be brought into the chakra from above, or beneath from the Earth, to release the emotions. Find which colour to use and breathe this colour, up or down, into the chakra and push out the unwanted emotions. This work is best done outside but if you are forced to work indoors use a bowl of water or a candle to dissipate the energy.

Deep emotion, held at the core of your being, can be dropped down the spine and into the ground. Release the emotion as a stream of colours falling from the chakra concerned to the earth and then bring colour from above to clear and wash the core channel within the spine. Check which colour to use before you begin.

ELEMENTALS - from another or self-created

Elementals are human creations from both a conscious and subconscious level. They are empowered thought forms that intend to enter the body of those under attack and create fear and confusion, self doubt, fury and hate. Often the person under attack is unaware of this process, and searches instead into their own 3D problems to see why they feel so unsettled, or physically depleted and weak. The energy of the instigator is one of blame for another, seeing another as responsible for the distress in their own lives. The feelings of self doubt, anger, sadness, hopelessness, fury and hate are not accepted and worked with but are used to fuel blame. This is the energy that creates the elementals. The more able a person is to open to high frequencies, the more powerful their ability to send these thought forms to the unwary.

To clear, find if the elementals are within the body or in the outer energy fields, which chakras are affected, and whether the elementals are self-created or sent to you from another. If someone has sent them find out the person concerned and if the elementals have to be returned to a particular chakra. It can be helpful to find out the approximate numbers of the thought forms that have affected you. When all this is completed check what colour you need to use to send them back. The colour, often blue, is brought upwards into the chakra from the Earth, the elementals being sent back to their instigator as you move up through the relevant chakras. Make a strong, conscious intention that these elementals (that look like tiny tadpoles) have to go back to their creator before you begin to work. Check also the Earth Star, 8th chakra, Higher Self and Creator Being level for these too are all vulnerable to elemental attack.

If this keeps recurring it may be wise to look at the reason why you will accept blame from this person and deal with this. Cording on 4th Density may also be implicated here. Once discovered, elementals are not difficult to shift and an immediate return to a more peaceful and centered state follows their departure. It can be a shock to discover that those you love and maybe trust can do this to you consciously or unconsciously. It is worth remembering that we are unlikely to be blameless in this and will have created elementals ourselves at some point either in this life or another. If you find this is the case you can use an intention to dissolve these harmful energies. Intend and keep working with this statement in the form of a meditation:

LOVING LIGHT DISSOLVE ALL EVIL ELEMENTALS CREATED BY ME SINCE SEPARATION FROM SOURCE.

This will clear the backlog. If the elementals are self-created recently, bring colour up into each affected chakra and dissolve the elementals. As animated thought forms with a life of their own, these destructive energies create fear in the recipient and can be the cause of yet more karma between individuals.

AN ENTITY - on what Density, connected where

Find out which Density the entity comes from and what the resonance is with it. The higher the Density the more subtle and powerful the entity will be, offering you the choice of the Dark path if it is polarised negative. Some entities will go to the Light, especially those close to the Earth plane on upper third and fourth Density. The beings on fifth Density are not human and those on sixth are more likely to be negatively polarised. If they are to move to the Light find out what colour is needed and send them upwards, in a beam of light. If they are negative you can only remove and send them to their own best place. It is sometimes helpful to find out which direction: north, south, west, east, they should go to. Find out how they are attached to your energy field: contact could be made into a particular chakra, or many chakras over a larger area may be touched. Hooks, suckers, funnels, claws and all manner of strange attachments have been seen. Try to detect as much information as possible before you begin work, and remember that the most difficult task is usually releasing the resonance. You cannot disengage successfully from these energies unless the resonance is understood and released. Denial of anger and emotion is the cause of much distress within humanity and attracts attention from other Densities that can then prey unnoticed on the denied part of the being. It may take time to release all the resonance. Rest after a clearing that takes a great deal of energy to complete.

THOUGHT FORMS - of your own, or picked up from others

Thought forms are energy structures created by ourselves or others. They freeze our energy and keep us stuck within a belief system that is usually destructive and stops the free flow of light through the body. Stuck with a thought form it is impossible to see reality from a more positive perspective, and recurring outer events that mirror this belief do little to help the distortion be seen.

Release the emotions around the thought form first and then look and check for its structure. It could be a geometric shape or an object like a helmet, a grid, a band. Our experiences in third Density also operate on the fourth Density where thought is creative. On this level of being, the objects of torture from the past make a rich library to choose from when we wish to inhibit ourselves and freeze our energy. As thought created these structures we can use intention to dissolve or remove them. To remove them, the belief has to be first seen as a belief system that causes distress, and one you have decided to finish with. This work should be done outside in a place you muscle test is appropriate. Light places are often damaged by structures so make sure that the energy can be dissipated. Water can be helpful; we often use a fast flowing river to help dissipate these structures.

FEEDING CYCLES - with whom

Feeding cycles can be long-standing with people from our past or can be created more recently, during a phone call, or contact with someone over the last few days or weeks. As you clear, you will become more aware of the intrusion of another looking inappropriately to you, instead of looking to their own internal strength and connection for support. These connections are from the old, separated, 3D way of looking to each other for energy and support, a giving and taking of energy where the person being drained willingly offers their energy to be depleted and used by another. This may be given in the name of love. This idea is part of our past, a distortion on how love operates.Now we can give love and support without being drained in this way.

Energy connections may be from one or more chakras. You will have to test or see where these are, for they are not only placed directly into the chakra but can also float around within the energy fields around the chakra, the actual connection being at one side or at the back of the body. The connections can be seen usually as a transparent or coloured open tube. Occasionally hooks or some other means of attachment will be seen.

Muscle test and check to see what is there, and find if you have to move to a higher frequency before you begin. Then see the connection and visualise it moving away, using your intention and maybe a colour (usually from beneath you) to push back the feeding cycle to the person concerned. You may also need to check which chakra the feeding cycle is coming from, as you will need to push the energy all the way back to the specific chakra in the other person. Check that the feeding cycle is dissolved back to the other person and maybe look at why you may have been willing for this to happen.

ACUCORDS - on 3D or 4D

Acucords are a large subject and ways of clearing them are given in greater detail on pages 192 to 199. Most cording is from 3rd Density experiencing but there are also 4th Density cords created by thought on a higher frequency. These 4D cords are created by people empowered to move on high frequencies, but who still choose to blame others for their problems in life. These connections can create a strong, often hidden energetic drag on the energy field of the person who is blamed.

To undo these 4th Density cords you have to look at why, even on a subconscious level, you are willing to take on this blame. It is usually through the personality structure that this acceptance happens: distortions around responsibility, love, and self-blame for the unhappy choices of others. We need to learn to be responsible for our own actions and give others the freedom to make their own decisions, however dark or damaging they may be to their progress to the Light. Free will leads us all to make many decisions that can keep us stuck in a particular karmic rut. The fear of looking at the truth, and the fear of re-experiencing emotions that cause us pain and discomfort, are the prime reason for our unwillingness to move on, see the bigger picture and the truth of a situation, and take responsibility for our actions. The 4D cords may be coloured or transparent and connect into the physical body through a chakra. You need to find the number of cords, where they connect, and which colours can help you to disconnect the cords. The colours may often come from the Earth but this needs checking. Visualise the cords and use the first colour to unhook the cords and push them back to the person sending them to you. Many filaments may be connected to these cords. These seem to come from deep inside the body and trail behind the cords you are pushing back. When the cords are disconnected another colour may be used to heal the channel where the cords have been, clearing and cleaning your own energy fields. Green followed by pink has often been used successfully in this work.

I AM IN A BUBBLE - with whom, what colour is it

When you work closely with someone, especially on higher frequencies where a melting of energy to complete a particular task is very common, you can create an energy structure that can be seen as a coloured or transparent bubble of light. It is wise to check, before you leave each other's company, if a bubble has been created that needs dissolving. This could be a part of the closing down process.

On a more negative level a bubble can indicate an energy structure that keeps you stuck and unable to move on. A relationship from the past for instance, may keep you stuck in an energy that is no longer appropriate, that is causing you disharmony and discomfort on many levels. This method of visualising a bubble, where the colour used can tune into the particular frequency involved, can free you to your own energy again. The release of old emotions may follow, or a feeling of release, that you are able to be yourself and concentrate on life in the here and now.

If you test that a bubble exists check when and with whom it was created. Find out the colour to be used and where it is best to do the visualisation. Outside is often the best place to do this work. Visualise the bubble with the person concerned inside it with you. Turn around and break the bubble, walking free of the energy. You can actually walk away from the spot if this is helpful. Sometimes the bubble needs to be dissolved rather than left behind. If this is the case use your intention to see the bubble dissolving away.

FOG OR FEAR - which chakra or is it all-enveloping

Fear can be picked up from others through resonance or it can be our own. If not completely acknowledged it can form a sticky energy that clouds our energy field and can be seen as a fog swirling around the body. It can cover a particular chakra, the whole, or part of the body. To clear this foggy fear you need to bring colour from above or beneath to dissolve or push away the heavy energy and clear your energy field. Sometimes the fog may uncover another level of energy, an intrusion into your energy field by an entity for instance, that promotes fear and may be difficult to look at. The fog itself may be black, grey or a colour. Muscle check what is there and if possible work outside to release the fear. If you have to work indoors use water or a candle to dissipate this negativity.

AN ENERGY SPACE YOU ARE IN WITH SOMEONE

Like a bubble you can be stuck in an energetic space with someone. You need to go back in time and see yourself disengaging from the people concerned, making a clean break from them. Many situations can create this imbalance, for example if you are worried or concerned about another it is easy to keep a protective contact. This is not appropriate on an energy level and can lead to weakness and further disruption to your own energy field.

It can also be that you are held on a certain frequency or vibration that is too low or high for your own comfort. Check what needs to be done to rectify this situation: a drop in frequency or a move to a higher frequency may be needed.

THE ENERGY OF A PLACE OR SITUATION

Here you are looking at a fragmented part of the Self that needs reclaiming. This is in the same bag as 100% here now but slightly different. The energies can be interchangeable, you may have left part of the Self behind with someone or someplace, maybe in another frequency, like in a dream state; or maybe energy that you have not yet discovered, from another person or place, is sticking to you. If the energy is not revealed and the situation understood it could cause problems for you in the future. These energies need to be cleared. It is not just negativity or emotion, it is fragmented energy. This is a little different and needs treating differently. The energy needs to go back to a person or place through visualisation so that the fragmentation has an opportunity to heal.

PROJECTED FEAR, BLAME AND ANGER

When someone wants, even subconsciously, to deny the feelings they are experiencing, they can project this energy onto another causing damage to the recipient. The third chakra is often the target for this projected energy; being the sensing, feeling centre it is especially vulnerable. Colour from above or below can be used to push away the unwanted energy

The following channeling was given when I encountered difficulty with a client who could not contact her inner hatred and felt stuck. Meanwhile I picked up the energy she could not experience for herself. A difficult situation to deal with!

Releasing Hatred from Someone Who Is Negatively Orientated.

You have to be clear within yourself how far you will go with this woman. She wants and wishes to dig deep and expose her truth but is unsure of how to do this safely. She comes to you for help and you can guide her here but at a risk to yourself. The hidden hate could explode before you are ready or able to move out of the way. To keep it light is possible too but not easy, for her intentions are to dig deep, so maybe you have to lay it all on the table. Be sure in yourself and expose this potential and then leave it to her to choose but make it clear that the responsibility for her actions and presence is hers alone and that you are aware of what might happen. Tell her, and leave her to make up her own mind as to what to do. If she wishes to pootle about, all well and good, if she wants to go deeper she has to be aware of the inner turmoil that seeks to come to the surface, and be aware herself of defusing its potential safely and not exploding it outwards on others. Talk first and then see, all is then in balance and harmony still, with no offence meant.

FURTHER CHANNELING ON UNWANTED ENERGIES

Unwanted energies, these are frequencies, these are feelings of places and people that are not intact, are separated from their source, fragments of a whole that cannot connect to the totality of their strength and being. As fragmented pieces they attach themselves to whatever and whoever has any resonance, however small, with their energy structure.

So on the 3D for you, unwanted energies are in some ways difficult to avoid until you gain a strength and unity complete in itself. In this way the energy structure you inhabit will be impermeable, and not subject to the swings of a fragmented duality struggling to find its other pieces. Like floating pieces of some enormous jigsaw, energies float and roam around this planet; they are random to a degree and cannot be calculated through karma but resonate on the personality structures. Whilst this is still top of the agenda for a human being, this process goes on in the subconscious/unconscious part of the brain and being, and so brings hidden agendas to a point, to a pinnacle, so they can be more easily looked at.

As time goes on this will happen less and less, but for now you all need to be aware of the charge and power of these disruptive fragments. Look further into the energies of others who are not total. You can see this at times. These people will have wandering fragments seeking to find them. As you grow stronger you will be able to differentiate. We love you. The Angels of Light.

I AM PROTECTED

This issue of protection is important for all who wish to look more deeply, to look further at their lives with love and awareness.

As you heighten your frequency, as you open up and clear the Will energy within, as your awareness expands, to check that you are fully protected in energy terms is important. Through this process of opening an individual becomes more sensitive to what is happening around him or her, more open to feeling, in every sense, what is happening, both within and without. Many people on the 3D however still exist in denial, and you will find yourself bumping up against this repeatedly throughout your own process. Sometimes it may be that you are aware of this and will be able to deal with it in the moment or after a particular event. At other times this may not be possible. We cannot, much as we try, remain 100% aware all the time.

To avoid being affected by this energy of denial it is a good idea to reinforce a protection as often as you can, to build a protection around your own light/energy body. This can be done in a number of ways: by visualising light, breathing, making a sound perhaps in a particular chakra. These methods focus your own energy and cause it to vibrate at a frequency that helps you hold yourself strong in situations where you may be vulnerable. At this time the Earth's energy fluctuates and from time to time vibrational dips can be experienced. This issue of protection is relevant here too, to hold you steady when all around you is a little unstable.

So do not underestimate these simple methods of building your own protection, they are very valuable at this time to all who are open to more than can be seen on the 3D plane. Feel for yourselves when your energy is low and use whichever method suits to help create a safe energy space around you. Then you can move from place to place and cope with fluctuations in energy, be they human or otherwise, more easily. This is all for now. We love you and leave you. The Angels of Light.

I AM GROUNDED

To Check

Repeat the statement " I AM GROUNDED" out loud and check on a SIM. If the SIM goes weak, correct. The first method to check is using the breath.

To Correct

Take a deep breath and, on the out breath, breathe the energy firmly downwards to the ground.

Repeat a few times and check on a SIM. If it still goes weak more breath work may be needed or you may need to use other methods of grounding. Working outside can be helpful and the process may take time for someone who has spent a long time centred in the mind, or even further up frequency in an astral realm where it feels safe and more secure. Unfortunately, this is an illusion. Only by being anchored into the energy of the Earth can we really be empowered to hold a vertical connection to our Source, and learn to operate on Earth at our full potential.

Other methods of grounding include

Sitting on a rock

Walking outside

Rubbing the feet

Putting hands or feet in cold water

Standing by a tree and visualising rooting into the Earth

Drinking water

Eating

Doing something physical on the 3D

Bringing a colour from above and anchoring it into the ground through your body

Spirit/Earth breathing

The following channeling looks at grounding and why it is so important at this time.

This is a check to see you are in contact with the Earth force, with the central core energy of the Earth's support for you as a human. It will feel uncomfortable, unfamiliar and unsafe if you are not in contact with the Earth's energy. Many people on Earth have never known this familiar feeling of love and acceptance for their life here on Earth, and only slowly will it come, this grounding.

They will have to work and feel, and give time and energy to clearing the pathways for the energy to move through. This is most important at this time, for as the energy levels increase so the need for the release of the energy becomes greater. If it is blocked, it will burn and disease will follow. We love you. The Angels of Light.

Much change is happening in the world and many new energies are in operation that we are not aware of. This is part of the excitement, part of the challenge of being incarnate at this time. It is also, however, a contributing factor to the potential for people to go ungrounded, to float off and not stay fully aware of what is happening around them.

Also to go ungrounded can act as a defence mechanism, when someone feels something on the inside that is difficult or hard to look at, for example an uncomfortable emotion rising within them that they find hard to acknowledge or do not want to express, or a feeling about something or someone else that they would prefer not to look at.

I THINK WE HAVE REACHED A CERTAIN POINT

This statement helps you discover when someone is blocking and can save a lot of angst when you are searching to discover what on earth is going on in a session. Consciously or unconsciously fear takes control and hides the core of what is trying to become conscious. The information for deep work comes through the vertical connection, the Higher Self of your client communicating through a level of unity down to your own Higher Self and heart. This circuit is broken when someone blocks so you will receive no further information on what to do. You are then left with only your 3D sensing to discover what is happening, and this can also be difficult to read if the person shuts off. When this situation occurs, do not take the issue further; wait. Maybe the person is not ready to deal with the issue at this time and you cannot force or push. It only makes matters worse for all concerned.

Sometimes information is given through the vertical connection that gives you a clear picture of where the process is going so you have an idea of what really needs to be dealt with. This may take time to achieve and will have to be taken one step at a time. Check that all the work you do is only taken to the step that the person is able to accept at that moment.

You can also reach a certain point through exhaustion. It takes a great deal of physical energy to move denial and if someone is weak or tired you can do only so much until they have rested and recovered enough physical strength to proceed onwards.

When you are working with another it is hard to be left on a hook, uncertain of what's happening, but it is always better to stop and wait. Interfering with the free will process is not a good idea. You can also reach this state in your own process and you have to be patient, and clear as and when you can.

This is a process whereby communication is lost, is broken, is not available any more on a vertical and horizontal connection. When someone is working, looking, delving into the truth of their reality, it at times gets hard and difficult to accept on a conscious level. At these times it can happen that a smokescreen, a deviation and blocking of the process occurs, to keep the hidden material protected and untouched. Suddenly, from your point of view, there is no more information, no more insight, just a feeling of no more, nothing, no help from us, no idea of what to do. At this point it is important to stop, to face the fact of what's happening and not push open a door that has slammed shut in your face. On one level this is a choice and has to be respected, that at this time, this individual does not want to go further into the process of uncovering their true reality (whether positive or negative) and fights shy of this by deviating and blocking the opening process. Nothing can be done.

No blame need be apportioned either by the therapist or helper, who may feel inadequate and not know what to do next, or by the person involved, who may suddenly feel fearful or shut down.

Only time will heal. Often time alone will help to re-attune to your own inner self and come to some point of resolution whether to go on or call it a day. Many have called it a day and have stayed still and stuck for centuries. The fear of the inner world is immense. Never underestimate the power of this fear to respond when provoked, to open doors so far and then slam them shut as you come near to the core of the issue and problem. Take time, be respectful of the choice and do not push to undo what cannot be undone. Maybe on one level the being involved wants to look more closely at this issue on the outer, by the value and system of resonance, then the clearing can go ahead with more ease. Let be all that does not wish to open. This is a good philosophy to follow. This is not the same as the hand held out to someone in pain or denial who is seeking and searching to find the opening, and who is momentarily stuck. This is a very different energy and needs help and encouragement. Twiddle if you have reached a certain point and respect it, then all will be well. We love you.

I AM CLOSED DOWN

To Check

At the end of a session check the statement "I AM CLOSED DOWN." If a SIM goes weak, correct.

To Correct

Several methods can be used. In a group situation if each individual uses again the original colour they tuned in with, this can break the energetic linking. Another method often used is to visualise a fountain of energy from the top of the head above the 7th chakra. Reverse the movement of the fountain so it is drawn down into the heart, pulling the scattered and opened energy back into the body. The colour of the fountain may vary but silver is often indicated. Grounding breathing can also be used. Check again that you are closed down.

This statement should always, without fail, be included in a balance following the completion of a session, group healing or whatever.

When opening up to higher frequencies you expand your energy into other dimensions and your feeling mode becomes more sensitised. This is necessary to ensure that what you twiddle, channel or whatever is correct. However, you do as humans operate for much of the time on the 3D and to hold this frequency whilst relating on the third Density is not appropriate.

When you open or tune in for working with these higher frequencies you do so in a safe, protected state, one of heightened awareness. On the 3D there are many energies milling around you and you are not so protected, hence maintaining this heightened frequency is difficult, sometimes dangerous and not appropriate. For this reason, closing down is important. Each person will find that a particular method suits them best, and using it to close the system down to a less expanded space should become as automatic and as much a part of the process as the tuning in.

All too frequently people are shown how to open up and tune in to a higher state of being but the information on returning from this state is not always stressed to the degree that it should be. A failure to close down in this way can result in feeling light-headed, nauseous and lacking focus: a feeling of not really being here, where you observe but do not really feel a part of what is going on around you. If this opened up state of being continues, then it becomes hard to concentrate and function on the 3D. You may find that doing the simplest of tasks becomes difficult and you start making silly mistakes. As time elapses this state gets worse until serious accidents begin to occur. So be careful to find the method of closing down that suits you best and use it, religiously almost, when you finish working with these higher frequencies.

You need to be aware of where you are, feel it and its frequency, and then take the energy down and into the heart. This is important, for you will feel unconnected, uprooted and ungrounded if you do not take time to consolidate each level gained into your 3D everyday reality. To open is fine but this needs to be completed by a closing process, a consolidating process so it is an anchoring of one energy, one frequency and dimension into another. It is also a closing down of the open seventh chakra to receive the higher frequency. This jars the heart energy if left open, for you are too vulnerable to other energies and frequencies that move around Earth.

Once you have closed down it's best to rest and relax a while before you set off into 3D life to a great degree. The mind will not hold the on/off switch very comfortably if you do not take time to re-establish an internal heart/mind link that will be less open to the higher frequencies.

So to close down takes a little time of focusing on the energy above, breathing and focusing downwards into the Earth. Take the colours or the energy from above and pull them like a fountain reversing itself down into the heart. Then breathe down to the ground to anchor the silver thread of the source into the ground. This need not take long but will be beneficial after any healing or energy work, any twiddling or channeling that goes beyond the body level.

As you become accustomed to a frequency this will not be so necessary, but remember that times change. You can change and grow and open, time and again, to a higher, broader spectrum of love and Light. So these techniques may come and go as you grow. We love you.

PATTERNS

If you need to work with a repeating life pattern, refer to the page of emotions and muscle test for a list of the emotions involved. When the list is complete, find out by twiddling which way the pattern is moving, from top to bottom, bottom to top, or if it's cyclical and constantly repeats itself. Also see if the pattern connects to a particular chakra; often the mind (6th) and Will (3rd) are involved, each chakra having very different feelings and responses to a situation. You may find there are two or more levels to look at, or that the patterns in the mind are triggered by feelings within the 3rd. These are the deeper levels, the mirrors if you like, of the experiences in outer life. People do not usually live in patterns all the time, but when triggered by the first emotion on the list follow the same habitual responses. It is easier to look at a pattern when you are not in it; once triggered you can only see reality from within the confines of the reality of the pattern.

Patterns have layers and levels within them. The deeper internal splits and denials of the inner unity of being are an important area to look at. You may have to start on the outer layers connected with experiences in the world, and gently work towards the core of the problem. This deeper, internal level is often hidden from conscious view and will take time to see and understand. Many examples of the pattern may need to be looked at before the real issue is uncovered.

Patterns are hard for people to understand. That events happening in everyday life can have a much deeper cause and root is very strange and a little weird and frightening, and many feel great fear at the thought of being programmed. To look at this issue people need to see the juxtaposition of emotions, how one feeling follows another, and how this can repeat in disparate and often unrelated events. Again the same response happens and the same outcomes in the everyday world. These outcomes reinforce the original energetic structure and also allow it to remain hidden, concealed by a fog of distress and emotion that accumulates as the synchronous events repeat and repeat.

The most important step is to first understand how the pattern works, how it evolves in everyday experiences, whether from the past, or in the here and now, the present time. When clarity is brought to this initial step then the emotion can be cleared and the underlying structures can be seen. This removal of the emotion is often the hard part, the difficult step, for much may have been denied and lie deep in the subconscious.

Also you may be dealing with different levels of the being. Patterns cause the internal integrity and wholeness to shatter and fragment, so what you feel may be wildly different from what you think, or say, or have in your mind as the reason for your distress. All these aspects of how the pattern evolves in different chakras have to be looked at and cleared. Sometimes days or weeks may pass before the real clearing can begin. Underneath all this turmoil are the energetic structures that lie within the energy field and act as blockages.

Not many break free of their patterns and habits without looking within. Often the attempt is partial, empowering the mind to suppress the Will, the feeling mode, so that the mental dominance and patterning is reinforced. This can be partly successful, but you cannot fool the body. The whole being has to learn, progress, and become aware and there is no short cut to this process. It may look long and somewhat hard but the freedom to respond clearly and cleanly in the present moment, the now, is a freedom won that is worth the effort. If you can hold strong in a difficult situation and not fall prey to your own pattern, you can see more clearly the truth of the situation and the best way to deal with it.

Patterns cause much distress on earth, the blindness of each individual seeking an experience that proves them right and correct in their distorted responses. This creates karma and distress on a massive scale and can only be cleared by inner work and self-examination leading to integration of the whole being and clearing of the internal structures. These structures can be varied, there is no one form that is a constant. With practice they can be seen, or a slower method can be used through muscle testing. Ask if you are ready to look for the structures by muscle testing and locate where they are.

Many chakras can be involved outside of the emotional chakras of response. Then begin the process of looking: is the form geometric or not, are there many or one, is it a grid, a symbol, a colour, a shape. When the structures are uncovered they can be moved with intention and returned by visualisation to the black, to darkness, to dissolve away.

There are several common patterns that are not described here but in book two; sometimes they are personal and apply only to the person concerned, at other times they are global, affect many people and contribute to the distortions humanity holds about reality and themselves. So this clearing can be large in its implications if people wish to look within. We love you.

Muscle test a list of emotions.
Check if the whole being responds in this way or different centres and chakras respond differently.
Understand how the pattern works and affects life now and in the past by talking through the list of emotions.
Clear the emotional energy by expressing it or dealing with it energetically.
Locate the structures of the pattern and clear them by visualising them dissolving into darkness.
Check if more clearing work is needed or if meditation would consolidate a loving and positive awareness of life.

PATTERNS IN THE CHAKRAS

The following information on patterns is only a guideline when looking into the problem. Patterns as described here may be located mainly in one chakra area but are not isolated to these places alone. The pattern resonates more in one particular chakra because that is where it resonates most keenly, but its effects, the ramifications of that pattern, will be felt throughout the whole body.

For example, a pattern around the issue of survival may be found in the first chakra, because the energy, frequency, emotions, etc centred around the root chakra are to do with human survival issues, particularly in relation to the Earth. So patterns relating to this may be found primarily in this area and the potential to heal the pattern, revoke it, discharge it, or whatever may involve some working around the first. But do not forget that the chakra system is an energy system that flows throughout the whole so do not restrict your investigations purely to this area. There may be work to do on other parts of the chakra system or indeed on another level entirely.

So patterns in the chakras should not be looked at in isolation; the potential, the weakness, the resonance around a certain issue may be centred around the corresponding chakra but not dealt with there in its entirety. The chakras are points of reference within a being that you can locate, where you can pinpoint the energy behind a pattern, behind a feeling. It is helpful to know if it's the mind/body or feeling/emotional mode that is suffering and holding on to a specific pattern. These patterns can be easily twiddled, as can any other test of emotional responses, but seeing their interrelationship and connection is more difficult.

Here you will need to use a positive statement of intent to understand the deeper levels of meaning inherent in the emotional responses. The fragmentation of the being occurs during these split responses. If you can accurately pinpoint them, and the place where the totality begins to fracture into its separate parts, you can then more easily release the denial. This brings the whole to a total, feeling response to any outside situation.

The outside world and its many adventures tend to increase the hold on a fractured system, so the despair on the outer tends to increase as the inner fragments. This is why in many cases it is difficult to change outer events and repeating situations, without the totality being brought into the picture. Not only the mind but the body, heart, feelings and spirit all have a place in the picture, and no one part can operate efficiently on Earth without the back-up of the totality, the team if you like, working together. The mind may only pay lip service to this idea but that is enough for the heart to function wisely and with love. We love you.

FILTERS

Filters are doorways, openings to the Light of the oneness, as well as being a blockage in the path. You have to understand: the repeating, resonating experiences are not only a drag but also a necessary experience to break free of the 3D turmoil and trap, and so they are a constant source of invention. To distort is not pleasant but maybe this is necessary, to repeat and repeat and repeat, until the light dawns and the blockage is cleared. This is why you don't see all of your problems at one sitting. It takes time for the experiencing to be completed; too little and you have not sussed it and the whole process may have to be completed from the bottom up, another life, another time, another set of experiences. So do not be in such a hurry to complete; you will, but not by throwing all resonance overboard in a frantic effort to be pure. You will have to stay a little grubby for a while yet on the 3D.

Your truth on other dimensions, however, can infiltrate and cleanse this area of the being, so that the life on Earth is not led, is not controlled any more by these disturbances. Slowly as the balance shifts and tilts away from the mind a freedom will develop that will make clear, by a shifting of position and dimension, what is real, what is truthful, and what is the distorted resonance of the old mental agendas from your 3D experiencing. In time these old agendas will drop as new centres open in the brain, making this old system invalid. This will leave you freer to manoeuvre and create your reality, unhindered by these relics of the past mental experiencing of the fallen Light.

Filters are the building blocks of the mind's feeling system, the way the mind can distort the reality of the universe with a perceived belief system from within. These cloudy shutters fall into place when triggered. Someone may be clear and free until these come into operation, then the message, the vision, the hearing is distorted and the trouble begins. With this distorted reality in place, the truth is hard to see and the belief, through resonance, becomes reinforced time and time again. A great deal of energy is needed to break these habits of perception and no one way, easy day sort of approach will work here. You will need to take time to watch the mind from a focus of loving awareness to see it fall prey to its old habits. This can be hard if you do not have a safe point of reference to observe from.

To build this reference point is the work of opening the heart. This will become easier as you learn to feel within the Self the places of light and ease, but at the start it's a point of trust that is needed, to see yourself, rather than the outer experience, and make a viewpoint from this internal standpoint. This can be hard as the repeating outer events are often highly charged and likely to pull you off balance, out of the heart and into the mental patterned construction of reality. Take time with these filters. Understand the personality and its blockages and in time it becomes possible to ride the waves and see with clarity what is happening, both internally and externally.

In time too the mind-set will change, from a fear-based reaction to a love-based response. One step at a time though. There has to be an opening of the old before the new can evolve. The brain is a vast, uncharted land waiting to be discovered and explored; it can lend great weight to your inner growth so do not deny it as bad, useless or outmoded. The mind is none of these things and needs the love from the heart to function well, from a new basic standpoint. We love you.

THE COMMON INTEGRATIVE AREA (CIA) AND FILTERS

The brain functions to direct and collate information; this is one side of its promise. Its other potential is to alert you to the repeating karma of the past that hangs on like dust around a sticky jar of jam. This karma can be cleared through working with the filters located in the Common Integrative Area.

To release these filters is of prime importance and the CIA is the checking point where you can pinpoint and extract the information about the source of the problem, the real problem on an inner and deeper level. So use the CIA as the trigger, the receptor of the dross and you can undo the problem more easily. The CIA point is easy to find, being a shallow depression behind the ear and slightly to the right and above it, usually on the left hand side of the head. Occasionally you will find a human being with a reverse brain set and here you will have to check on the other side.

The CIA is a transmitter, a pipe that connects one side of the brain to the other. The brain is multi-functional. One of its functions is to analyse and deduce from past experience correct behaviour here and now, in present time. This mechanism is open to the negative interactions, the unfinished business of the past. Many thought patterns, many responses are tarnished by this point of contact, distorting information from the memory store to the side of the brain that is preparing to act in the here and now.

The CIA is a point of balance that needs to be kept in an equilibrium which allows certain responses to function, like don't walk in front of a bus. When we are in balance we can look and see when the responses come from a past negative interaction that is not showing a true picture. To base decisions upon this distorted reality is unwise. This is karma, the repeating patterns of the past, and they all have to be fed through this narrow channel of the CIA. Disturbance in this spot can be a key into deeper workings on a mental level, for only when the CIA is clear and clean can a deeper interaction between the heart and mind start to function properly. You will need this link to be in place in order to be prepared for your future work. Humanity cannot progress carrying this baggage from the past. Sound too can ease the filters in the mind and certain notes and chords have a process attached to them that can help to achieve this clearing. We love you. The Angels of Light.

ACUCORDS

Acucords are one way of clearing the karma of the past, the energy built up over lifetimes that lies between people, places and things. This energy is not static, it moves and pulls you again and again towards circumstances and people that are hard to deal with. Each one of you has an agenda, a list of probable encounters and types of interaction that lie dormant, waiting to be triggered by a person or situation. From the unloving response to the situation, the cording is formed. This does not mean there is not love between people, not at all; often cording occurs with people you are very close to and care about deeply, but nevertheless there is part of the interaction that is not completely compassionate or loving: a repeating response to the same old triggers and feelings.

So take care to clear these cords slowly. They will often appear in layers, the present-time agenda to be cleared first, and then other deeper layers to be cleared as you become more aware, more focused, and more willing to take responsibility for your part in the interactions.

Slowly a clearing of the energy field leaves you free to respond to others clearly with love, not hindered by the need to repeat karmic experiences from understanding your part of the picture. It is as if a lifeline is thrown to a drowning man; he climbs ashore but never removes the rope, which then becomes a hindrance. All do the best they can in life; negativity often results, but you can move on.

Cording keeps you stuck, trapped in a repeating cycle that, if you are not aware, seems to be a picture of reality that is true, real, absolutely how life is on this plane. Often these illusions are false, and the stripping away of old cording leaves you free to see the truth of each and every situation. We love you.

CUTTING ACUCORDS

If you muscle check that acucords are present and need to be cut, check who they are with and which chakras are involved. The cords can not only connect to the corresponding chakra in the other person but can exist between any chakra. Once you have a clear idea where the cords are connecting you, check for their colour and the best method to clear them. Two methods are described here but other methods can also be used. Clearing through visualising a waterfall of colour from above to wash away the cords is possible, or dissolving them with intention. Muscle check to see the best method for the particular cords you are clearing.

CUTTING ACUCORDS

Sit quietly in a safe place and visualise clearly the person you are cutting cords with. Affirm to yourself your intention to cut "X" number of acucords. You may need to find out the number of cords involved.

See the cords clearly connecting your chakra to their chakra, whether it's from the throat, heart etc. See yourself cutting the cords half way between you with a pair of golden scissors.

Heal first the other person by melting the broken cords back into their chakra with your hands (in your mind's eye). Then heal yourself in the same way by gently pushing the broken cords back into your body.

See yourselves as separate, and remember that love does not need cords to connect you. The person may become closer to you, the love between you expressed more easily, or if the connection is no longer appropriate it will no longer be a problem in your life.

If any of your cords are coloured, the energy is "alive" and cannot be cut directly. Coat these cords in black before you begin cutting them, this acts like insulation and will enable you to cut the coloured cords.

CUTTING AND DISCARDING ACUCORDS

This is another form of cord cutting when the energy needs to be released to the Earth or, occasionally, to Spirit; it begins in the same way as before.

Visualise the cords connecting you, chakra to chakra, and see them clearly. Cut them 8 inches (20cm) from your body and 8 inches from the body of the other person with a pair of golden scissors. Let the central part of the cording drop into the ground and melt completely away to be healed by the Earth.

Fill the chakra with coloured light from above, checking which colour is appropriate, and when the chakra is full of light project it outwards to push away the unwanted stump of cording still left in you. Then heal the wound in the energy field with your own love and light. You have to leave the stump in the other person you are cutting the cords with, it is their choice whether they wish to repeat the karma involved in these cords.

A Stickman map is a quick and easy way to work out the colour and location of cording.

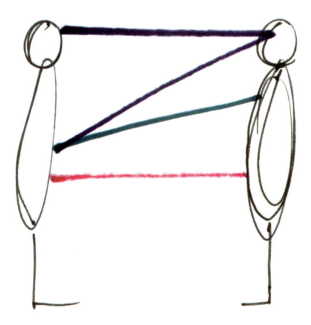

COLOURS IN ACUCORDS

The colours vary, have meaning according to the person concerned so are not necessarily fixed, but certain obvious rules do apply.

The use of black is often to do with the energies of the soul experiencing only the energy of another only in this lifetime, in this illusion of the body's short stay on Earth. Other older cords often lie beneath this first entry into the process and you will often find in time that grey or coloured cords connecting you from the chakra concerned have roots in other lives, other times of experiencing, and not necessarily from this Earth either. It can be a blockage brought forward into earth life to clear and clean the many levels of experiencing further on, further up the levels of dimension and Density.

So we see you wonder as to the specific colours. Pink, as you know, has a harshness and is a colour of incompleteness and real connection, alive and well now. This process always needs to be dealt with carefully for the removal of one set of cords will lay open a space, a hole where other energies are free to enter. This cannot be allowed to happen and the safety procedure for this is to wait, and look, and contain the energy first within the being before any further attempts are made to cut and clear the cording. Other cords can be used positively and in time the opening to these levels of cording will make sense. The Angels of Light.

WHAT IS HAPPENING IN THE WORLD NOW

The world is one place, one planet, one position in the universe where many changes, many new energies and feelings and thoughts are beginning to happen to loosen the old, to shake free the fear and hate, and leave all clean and new. This process is large, covering all and everything it touches – all human life, all plant life, all animal life will be affected by this movement, if they choose for this process to touch them deeply and personally. On a deep level of truth All is One, part of the one creation, but many levels of being exist on many differing worlds and galaxies. These now fuse to produce a new wave of energy that travels through the universe like a wave, a movement of thought and love, clearing and cleaning all in its wake.

This process has begun in earnest on Earth now and you see before you the process, the polarisation in action. Those that take these words to heart can see and feel a change in the air, a lifting of the spirit and a drag downwards, both alternating, and pushing and pulling each human soul this way and that. The time to fear the future, to feel threatened by these changes is passing for some, and those people can help others to fall clear of the devastation that starts to occur in many places. The planet is shaken and will stand this movement – it will learn, it will grow, it will expand to hold a lighter vibration and feeling than before. This will be an easier way to live for those who are ready to make this jump, this movement. This is a jump of the heart, not the head, a movement of love and trust, not one of degrees and calculation. The mind has to be seen as servant of the heart and this will be hard. For many aeons the Earth has worked in the other way, the mind influencing all human affairs. The reasoning, the logical processes are not to be discarded; fools are not the opposite of those that run their lives by the use of mind. Rather there is a certainty of purpose, a need for whatever is doing or happening so that a certain freedom of expression and love can occur. Each one of the myriad races on Earth has a tradition, a belief in a new time to come in the future, one of love and Light and wholeness following a great trial, a great turbulence and upheaval.

This upheaval is happening now. It is subtle, not all is in the process of wars and destruction, although this may occur too. The processes likely to affect each one of you are more on an internal level. The confusion of the emotional being, the body, collected around you from many lives now seeks to free itself from you and return to its source, the Earth. This will be hard if you do not see the need for a process of self-examination and cleansing of the thoughts and feelings you hold within. It can be done, this process, with love and gentleness. Watch each day as events occur and look to see where you feel shaken, where you feel insecure. Look at each situation and learn to look deeper, to understand the implications within yourself of these events and see the parallels with past time. Now is the time to drop these old patterns and move forwards, free of the burden of old emotional muck held in place by the mind and body.

The body of all beings here on Earth also undergoes changes; it feels the pressure of the energy movement, feels the disagreeable energies it finds hard to contain, and seeks to find ways to adapt, to blend with the new. This will take time and effort on your part to see and feel the needs of the body. Sometimes you feel sick and tired; listen, and relax, and rest, and let go. Do not force any more, for these pushing and pulling energies can damage you and leave you weak, and sick, and unable to control the outcome of your life. Let these energies wash over you and then pick up the pieces and continue life.

Take time for yourselves each day, take a break, sit peacefully and be still. Let the body settle and let yourself relax within the self, see and feel the vibrations within and let them settle till you feel a sense of connection to the body. Let this relax further and then feel the opening, the growing of your energy to reach up and out of your body to the Light above you. Express a wish, a need to connect now to the energy that can help you most and see a colour, a light, a loving presence, fill your body from top to toe. Let it float down and around you and all will be well.

Take time for the self, look within and do not blame others for the state of the world at present. Look at your own presence, your own body and make sure that the love you hold embraces all around you. And then tell yourself that many have walked this path but now there is a new path ahead, one that is exciting and new, an adventure for all mankind, one that you can explore and demand from what you will.

See the vision of Light and love incarnating on Earth in each and every one of you and all will be well. Take time to see the future and let it flow as it should, not hurried, not pushed, but allowed and accomplished by those that choose to move forwards now. To evolve to another level, another dimension of light, of sound, is a possibility for many. Take the opportunity offered now by those in spirit to aid and guide you. Many can help, can aid, but each one needs their own connection. This can be forged. It takes time and effort but can be done. We love you. The Angels of Light.

THE FOUR DIRECTIONS

Could you tell me how we can use the four directions, North, South, East, West, in life?

We will talk of the North first. The North is the focus, the point of meeting of many energies for you here in the Northern Hemisphere. It is the point of contact to the Source, the input if you like, of the new energies, the new directions you seek to go in. It is cold in the North, clear and bright in summer, cold and dark in winter. A place of opposites, a place of polarities and much change from Light to Dark. This swing, this movement of the polarity is the focus for now, the focus for the opening of the energy body to the Light. Let this energy flow in the head and down to the heart. Let the 6th chakra be the focus for the moving of the energy and force of the North. Face the North and bow to the left and the right, and then focus on this energy around the 6th; feel it and contact its clarity, and then ground it into the heart. When it's appropriate, and you are used and accustomed to this energy field, ground it to the Earth with your hands.

For the South, a different energy, a calming energy, an energy of the fields of Light, the manifestation of the Light force, the creation of the energy of the North into a field of form. So look to the South when you need to create, to manifest, to make clear what is the focus on this plane of existence and it will help.

The East and West are of a different polarity. The morning and evening, the coming of the Sun on a daily day-to-day basis, this is something different, a different polarity. The spring, the movement forwards too comes from this awakening of greater light over a season.

The East is for change and for peace within change, for being able to hold the Self safe whilst all moves around you, the place of peace and serenity in the midst of movement. Let the East fill your heart. Let go to the energies and drink them into the heart. Expand on this feeling, grow with it like the Light coming up at dawn. Let it all flow along so you can feel this movement and this inner stillness and peace also. It will hold strong when you feel weak and uncomfortable, so use it when you feel jarred and upset and it will help you to regain balance and ground your energies more.

For the West a different energy yet, one of expansion and contraction, one of movement again but in a differing polarity and form. It is the expansion of the Light consciousness, the coming together of the various energies and forms to create the whole, the oneness of Light and love. Let it expand within you and feel it move within you, this energy from the West. Let it live in the heart and move both up and down to integrate your body within first, and then it can expand and flow outwards as you can absorb more of this Light field of energy. Let it grow and expand within you on a day-to-day basis. At dusk would be a good time to practise this, following the movement of the Sun as it goes down at sunset.

Also to sit on rock and look at the light would be helpful, as it fades and changes to dusk, looking and feeling both: a little in, a little movement out, both in and out would help here to focus on this energy. Let it flow and all will be well.

The four directions can be used as a conscious meditation to focus your awareness where you wish to take it, so use this wisely, this knowledge, and all will be well. We love you. The Angels of Light.

POLARISATION

The energy of polarisation is the expression of unity, is a movement forward in time and space towards completion of the split in consciousness around the being in form, within duality. As polarisation occurs, the being becomes set on a pathway that will help it evolve along certain lines, certain routes that will have to be chosen, at least for a while, until a change of choice and energy takes the being to the opposite polarity. No one soul is ever lost on this path, it's just a question of route. Those that search for the Light may be deceived on their path and the shock and turmoil this throws them into can polarise them to the opposite. Conversely, the man of hatred opening to love can jump successfully to the opposite shore and polarise to the Light.

The two main routes are Light and Dark, positive and negative. They are not actually Light and Dark but rely on a different filtration, a different mind set and focus of evolution. The Dark path looks for power, the Light for love, and these two points of focus are the main departure points that take one onto the path. The path of Light and love looks difficult on Earth. Much confusion surrounds its right use, its right approach, and the squabbling and jealousy amongst its adherents does not help it to progress. In today's society everything has its worth and a living has to be made. The question of sharing information, input, understanding, love, these are all important. This sharing sits none too happily with the path of power which is much easier to see, acknowledge and understand, for the rewards to its adherents come quickly. The lack of satisfaction does not usually stop those on this Dark path, so fixed are they on the goal. Only more of whatever they focus upon looks as if it will satisfy, so off they go, working and looking and scheming to acquire whatever it is that is needed to satisfy their latest whim and desire. The limitations of desire are well understood by Buddhists, and the path of compassion looks like the obvious answer. However, it's not so easy to quell this internal monster as it is a part of your human make-up. Now the way forward has to be beyond both Light and Dark paths to succeed.

You have to look within and see this greed and selfishness you all hold and not judge it, not pamper it, not indulge it but allow it space to evolve. Desire is not bad in itself; it is what it's focused on, what it's intending that is the problem. Moving desire off the 3D can help but not always, the quest for enlightenment being the most subtle of all traps. The belief you have to go somewhere, do something, be something to progress, to be happy, to live in the Light, are all false ideas and images that send people off track. Only now when there is more space to look, in a relatively freer society, will there be any conclusion to this. The wheel has moved round and round, and much of humanity has stayed stuck, unpolarised, dancing backwards and forwards on the edges, not daring to be definite in any one way. It looks so dangerous to be so single-pointed, so obsessed with the inner world, and yet this is the necessary missing link that needs to be looked at. A life of service to others is not enough to polarise you on the Light path. You have to take time for yourself, for your inner process, for your inner Light to strengthen and grow, and in time it will be understood, this step-by-step process. The lesson of religion has been seclusion, the monastic life of the ashram; this looks an impossible path in today's world, and is also not necessary. You can live in the world and still develop a spiritual life.

Polarisation is the focus, the end result of your experiences of life on Earth, it is where the real free-will choices are being made, now. Where do you stand, each one of you? Everyone has a choice now about how to progress as a being of consciousness. It is not a choice of right or wrong or good or bad, but a choice between structure and freedom. Some people feel secure in the boundaries of a clearly defined hierarchy. The issue is about who is top dog, who is the leader, who is the follower. The follower lends energy to another; the leader pulls and attracts energy to himself. It is the pull of attraction to the magnet: the energy is pulled towards the force field, towards the central point of power.

The Light path expands, radiates and shines outwards to illuminate and give light to all around it. The energy is one of expansion, not contraction, of giving, not receiving, unlike the negative path. In time this push and pull of duality is easier to see. There is much fear around the negative path, much confusion and jockeying for positions of power. There is little love on the negative path although wisdom and understanding is given so those on this path achieve clarity. This is why it is so confusing for those incarnate on Earth who tend to see any guidance, any information from beyond the 3D veil as being positive and of the Light. This is not so, and this is why discrimination by feeling through the Will is so important now. You cannot tell by the information alone the source from which it comes. Only by feeling, and a certain sensing of that which promises power instead of loving compassion, is the answer here as to the source of your information.

So take stock and decide where you wish to be in the choice of polarity. Be clear in your intentions to and for yourself. Remember this is a free-will choice, and even if you stray from the path the intention will remain. All choices need to be strengthened, and can of course be revoked but in the here and now making a clear choice is important. Love is the Light and the path that leads to oneness most directly. The negative path offers rewards in the here and now but is not usually an easy path on higher densities. So if your path seems slow, fraught with challenge and setback that you seek to deal with in a loving way, then do not despair for the slow path sometimes leads the fastest to where you wish to go. We love you.

ENERGY PROGRESSION

Energy moves from Source into the first Density. This is where form is created: rocks, gases, planets etc. This Density is still in close contact with the Source energy and can communicate with the oneness of being within itself.

Energy moves to the second Density where plants and animals exist. Here there is a strong tribal and group identity so free will begins to evolve, although the beings on this Density are still very much a part of the oneness and do not suffer from separation to the same degree as humanity. Beings on second Density take decisions in life based on instinct rather than the mind.

Humanity has existed on the third Density. This is known as the 'free-will zone' where the illusion of separation is given to each individual so they can make choices as to their evolution through the Densities and dimensions back to Source. This is the realm of duality: good and evil, light and dark, victim and victimiser. By experiencing through many lives, one evolves and polarises to one path or another: the path of love of Self given to others (the Light path) or the love of Self for Self (the Dark path). Existence is generous. Only 57 % of a being's energy needs to be polarised to the Light to evolve to the 6th Density. On the negative path you have to polarise 92% negative. This is very selfish and is quite hard to achieve. Our 3D society's conditioning throughout the world has favoured the negative path through denial, lack of responsibility for the Self, and structures of hierarchy and power. The 3rd Density is the furthest point from the Source and here the separation and fear of death can feel acute.

From the 4th Density onwards the paths return to Source. This movement through these Densities from 4 to 8 is important as the end result is either a universe of harmony and joy or a universe of hierarchy and repressive structures, depending on which path you have chosen.

At this point in time the potential to move out of the 3rd Density is available to all humanity who choose to make this movement. Karma can be dissolved in this future beyond duality by acknowledging Light and Dark without judgement and thus moving through the Densities of 4, 5 and 6 and holding these frequencies in human form. It is a big step for humanity to hold the love, wisdom and intelligence of these levels in form and drop the fear and separation belonging to the 3D reality.

CHANGES ON EARTH

Let us join now the places, the parts of this world that are willing and open to enjoy the new energies that arise around and within this planet. This time is one of much change, much dramatic and drastic evaluation of all that on a human scale is important, is vital for life on this planet. Many new energies, many new feelings and thoughts are entering into the human mind and being, and this re-connection to the oneness, the Source of all Light, all knowing, is available for all who seek, who inquire, who want to feel the increase of their own Light within. We love you.

First these processes of clearing are needed to open the way, to clear and clean much taint of the past from the emotional feeling body, the Will, that holds the past within its being. Now there are opportunities to release this past karmic detritus, and leave all clean and free to rise as the vibrations of the Earth rise too. The failure to do this, to move along with the tide, with the flow of cosmic events will leave many bewildered and unsure of what they need to do, unsure of what they need to say to themselves or others, to alleviate the pain and misery both of the body and within the mind.

The failure of humanity has always been to trust another, not the Self; for here is where the first deception, the first movement away from all that is clean and clear, happened. The first movement towards the belief system of 'I don't know, I can't tell what is good and what is bad' has caused much pain, much misery and much suffering. This has compounded over the years, over the aeons to produce a state of unwillingness to even look at what is felt by each being as they encounter life and its perils and experiences.

The way forward now is first through the Self. This doorway has to be used, for unless the responsibility for actions is taken within the being the necessary movement forward will not occur, will be false and unreal, and not true to the being, the soul. Now the way we see this change occurring, of clearing this old charge on the emotional body, is to release this safely, slowly and with ease within the safety and security of the natural world, the natural environment. Here can be found the strength and the connection so missing for humanity. At last a new way of looking will be opening, and people willing and able to see themselves in truth will then see the truth of life hidden within the natural world. The thread, the connection to Source energy lies all around one, all the time.

This connection can become obvious, but if the person feels alone, uncentred, unattractive etc. on and on, there is no way that this feeling will grow into one of love for the planet itself. This love is so badly needed, for the healing of the rifts within and without have to come now from the awakening of the human energies to their original points of entry. In this way, the release of the Earth and its people to their own proper place within creation can occur.

Firstly let us look at this process of clearing: clearing what, one could say. Well, first we need to feel and look at nature and see here the many random, many chaotic and different levels of life interweaving and living, one on top of the other. In nature you can see all is open to change. Nothing is ever static, even a mountain is worn away, energy moves whether it is in form or not.

This movement of energy is needed to release the matter to its true state of being, one of enlightenment, not as it is thought of but as a state of inner Light that can transform the levels of the being so that it can move and float between dimensions and Densities and so link the many worlds outside of this Earth, to this Earth. In this way the help, the opportunities available from other sources, other energies will be made available to humanity, and the rebuilding of all that has been destroyed, been violated in the natural world can be renewed with ease and love. We love you.

CHANNELING

Channeling is an opening to the Light and divine wisdom, held on a universal level, that is available to humanity to work, evolve, and grow with. This impetus is the necessary focus for many to learn the ways of a world beyond the narrow limitations of a divided state of duality. Here is the expression of a unity not held on a level of consciousness by humanity before in so easy and accessible a manner. Before, the personality could not link or make a bridge to this level of consciousness, it was either this or that, 3D or from beyond. Now you can learn to melt and fuse the many layers so that more and more you grow in wisdom within (and here is the key) your 3D everyday reality. It should not need to be a big jump, a big change of consciousness to channel. With practice and observation of the state you will learn to access it at all times. When this level is available you can move on to a deeper or higher level of consciousness that again will need a little acclimatising to get used to.

The picture of the spiral crystal staircase is a visual image of this progression. On each step there is a break to consolidate, and then you continue your upward climb to higher levels of being and consciousness. The body will follow and walk with this new consciousness too. It will need time to adapt on this path, so take care of it and look to its needs. Many of the techniques you learn from this book can prepare you for these steps and open the Light fields within the body to accept this new input of consciousness.

It will come in time, a much wider and greater awareness on Earth. Those that choose to incarnate at this time have the potential energy body of the Light fields of the One, the unity of love and Light within form. This is a reason to celebrate now. We love you. The Angels of Light.

ENTITIES

Entities are energies trapped within the lower realms of existence. They cannot be free to resume their travel forwards to other planes, to move to their own home, because of imbalances and thought forms perceived as realities by the Spirit being. There can be no release without love, no refreshing movement forward without a movement of the Soul involved towards completion; a renewal of faith in a higher Source and form of energy that can release the being to a new and wider field of experience.

Many suffer, held in these vibrational spaces, unable to release themselves, and need the help of other loving beings to become free and resume their journey back to Source. We can assure you that these beings do exist and can be a nuisance to others incarnate on Earth, for not all are aware that energy and form are not the only way that beings can exist. They do not see entities as anything real, but keep a deep fear of invasion of their being and hold no love strong enough to withstand the force of evil or ignorance trying to use their energy and space.

This is only going to be different when humanity itself frees those trapped on the lower planes and gives help to the spirits that are stuck there to remove themselves to a higher plane of vibration. This sort of effort is not ready to begin as humanity is not itself whole enough to contemplate such a task, and meanwhile individuals undertake to help and release those that are brought in their path. In the future all will be easier and clearer, and some time will be given on ways to accomplish this at a later time. For now, rest easy that this problem can be dealt with by spirit if necessary but needs your aid to set the process in motion.

HOW TO CLEAR ENTITIES

Entities have to be cleared slowly, no rushing or pushing for a quick healing and resolution of the problem. First clear the resonance: find out the denied emotional charge that makes the connection strong. When this is discovered and you muscle test all is well to proceed to clear the energy, find out where the connections are situated on the body; this could be through the chakra system but this is not the only connection that is possible. Energies may be connected in more than one place, and you will need to find all the various points within the energy field before you begin to shift the entity. Also find where the entity is to go to; is it moving upwards in a beam of coloured Light, back to its correct frequency, or is it moving to its own best place. It is sometimes helpful to find a direction, North, South, East or West, for the entity to move away from you.

When all these details are collected find the best place to work and push the entity away from you. The energy used needs to be loving and focused; also you may need to speak to the entity and reassure, if it's from the Light, that all is well and it is now appropriate to move on to where life will be lighter and more rewarding. A negative entity needs a firm " NO, I do not wish this energy to be around me, go and do not return", and whatever else feels appropriate to say. Love, however, still needs to be the energy behind the movement away from you. Negative entities, once spotted and the resonance cleared, usually leave without too much trouble.

If you find you are fearful of what is happening, try and find someone who is able to support you while you work, give you Light and love to make the power behind your push more clear and focused. With time you can become less frightened, more pragmatic about entities.

Remember, some people choose to help those who are stuck on energetic frequencies too close to the Earth, and in these cases, resonance may or may not be present. Take care with this information and use it wisely. This is no easy matter for many people and should be spoken about sparingly, and only when appropriate.

Other work may be done to clear houses and places of entities that can bring the frequency and energy of the place down. Take time to find out that you have all the information you need before you begin, and all will be well. Groups of people working together may be needed to move more powerful entities that one person alone may find too difficult to shift. We love you.

IMPLANTS AND ENGRAMS

Engrams are thought forms of a special nature: they are recurring, life after life, are imprinted on a very deep level into the fabric of the being. They are to do with the issues around loving the Self, around self worth, and are very difficult to spot and to clear. Sometimes these are taken on willingly, as a trade off, as a supposed benefit to the recipient, to the love of others instead of Self, a sort of suffering that will aid the whole. This rarely works, and is a trick used by many unscrupulous energies on many levels to trick you into believing that the structures they offer you will be of help to you. This is not true and is mirrored in the structures on Earth that limit and contain your potential: your schools, your religions, that all impose a limitation on your true potential.

These engrams also put a very large limitation on your truth, on your ability to contact the truth of your Self in its totality, for they inhibit, they put a governor on the realisation of the immensity of love held by the Self that is useful to all levels, all beings. This limitation makes those under its bondage feel useless, feel unwanted, feel lacking with others, and so they very readily give away their power or withdraw from fulfilling their potentials on any level. They are stuck, and the frustration this causes makes them believe they are indeed unworthy to progress and so the story goes on over many lives, each adventure into duality laying another layer, another distraction from the fact of these implanted thought forms.

Implants have an energetic structure that can be removed. It lies between the mind and the heart, it's curved and sticks inwards, into the heart/mind linking and stops any real touching of the mind by the heart; thus keeping the thought forms hidden from the internal consciousness of the Self in its truth and wisdom. So the higher cannot inhabit the lower to its full potential or even part of it. The being is stuck, until enough clearing has been done to expose and uncover the device. The person concerned has to be aware of it and wish for it to be removed, for it will take time and energy to do this successfully. They will have to live through the original experience in some way, on some level, to be able to take the device off. This is hard and not for the faint-hearted, but can be done with help from the Loving Light of creation when it is invited to participate.

So for the first point you have to discover, through a muscle test, if such an implant exists and then look to the engrams, the thought forms, that are a part and parcel of the belief that stops the moving of the whole device. If these can be seen and removed as much as possible in preparation, then the being, the person concerned, has to live from guidance, from the heart, from their own knowing in truth, to release the long-held structure from the heart/mind link. This will take time, over a few months, to complete. Daily channeling, and checking that what is happening is OK, is correct, can be useful. But none of this will work if there is not the determination and courage to live from the heart and search for the truth at whatever cost. This is hard in 3D life and many fall by the wayside, or reintroduce limitation upon themselves when they cannot face something that is hard to face in 3D everyday life.

The implants are part of a force, an energy that wants to inhibit the evolution, the movement forward, of beings in form. In spirit there are many levels, many degrees and facets to each energy, each individuated portion of consciousness. These are looking to reunite, to come together as a whole, united, clear and complete energy.

They can then move on and step upwards to the next degree of consciousness. This is not a race, 'a more than less than' sort of movement, just a fact: that you cannot have fruit from a seedling, or sap moving upwards in a seed. The seed is a potential that needs to grow, to move upwards to bear fruit. So a spirit has to be tested on many Densities and levels to be complete in its adventure as an individuated consciousness, to melt with the unity of the whole, taking the experiencing of its existence on many levels back to enrich the whole.

So how do implants fit into this picture? They are energy structures that inhibit the progress of reconnection and movement of Self. As a human being you have a chance to undo these fetters, to reach forward and see beyond the limitations placed upon you in other times, other places. Being in a physical form is an ideal opportunity to become aware, but only if the Will, the sensing mechanism, is engaged in the process. Too often humanity remains stuck because it is not able to see within, can only look outwards with the eyes, the five senses, and has no real idea of the world it inhabits on other levels, other Densities and dimensions.

So to become aware is the first step, then you can see what inhibits your growth and return to the truth of your own being, whether this is engrams and implants, thought forms or energy structures. These all have their place in the fall from awareness and consciousness that occurs on many levels, on many spaces other than Earth, that needs to be healed. The Earth offers an opportunity to clear these energies, offering an experience in form that can move beyond the limitations placed on a being from other experiences in form.

But first the awareness, and this takes time and effort; and meditation and therapy are the tools to open this knowledge and knowing of the Self. If this can be done correctly, at its proper time within an incarnation, many opportunities are opened to look beneath the surface of reality to what is really there, is really happening, on many other levels. This knowledge helps to free the consciousness and spirit essence of many souls to their true place in creation: the ascension of matter back to its real Source of being. This reunification with the Higher Self and Creator Being are the offers of the Earth, the place for this return to begin to take shape.

Humanity has dragged its feet, been diverted, lost awareness, and now can no longer see what holds it back. Always the energy is turned outwards and many unscrupulous beings of a negative polarity make use of this weakness and inability to see, using by force their constriction and feeding from the energy of beings incarnate on Earth. Now it is time for humanity to wake up, throw off this intrusion into its energy and grow in awareness of its own internal issues and problems that can be changed, released, exposed and moved on from. Only with awareness of love can the release be complete, so grow in love and all will follow.

We love you. The Angels of Light.

EMOTIONS

The emotions list is the most well thumbed part of any well used workbook and is often the foundation stone for further exploration and understanding. Often emotions are easily muscle tested, they can be listed and uncovered, and can open the door to deeper work. Take time to free yourselves from fear of negative emotions; fear can distort your work, and where self-blame comes into the picture can mar your understanding.

Emotions are feelings; they have no moral weight in this work. There is no need to feel shame or rebuke yourself if deep, denied negative emotions are uncovered. This is normal and, if treated well, harmless to all concerned. When emotion is stored, denied, or has blame attached to it, then there is trouble. The uncontrolled expression of emotion has caused much harm in this world. Responsibility is the first real step on any spiritual path, and responsibility for emotion is the first key and response needed.

Emotion is an inner problem, is part of the inner world, and unlike food or exercise cannot be dominated by the mind alone. Thus the Will has its say, however repressed or denied is the outcome. Over many lives emotions have been collected and stored in the energy field of man. They form a rich source of resonance with many negative beliefs and intrusions.

So now is the time to be more accepting, more loving and compassionate to the Will and the emotions it has felt, both in past and present time. So take care to uncover emotions first, if you become stuck in a process or are unsure how to proceed, and all will be well. We love you.

LIST OF EMOTIONS

Abandoned	Approachable	Bitter
Affection	Aware	Belligerent
Alarmed	Atonement	Balance
Anguish	Afraid	Burdened
Assurance	Ambivalent	Belonging
Awed	Apathetic	Below
Antagonism	Attracted	Blissful
Accepted	Alive	Bored
Abused	Acknowledge	
Almighty	Admiration	Calm
Attuned	Agony	Charmed
Apprehensive	Angry	Cold
Assured	Appreciated	Concerned
Attacked	Attractive	Contempt
Adequate	Adaptable	Choosing
Aggressive	Above	Capable
Appreciated		Cheated
Annoyed	Bad	Combative
Ashamed	Blue	Considered
Accepting	Bothered	Content
Amused	Beautiful	Caring
Adamant	Bold	Captivated
At peace	Brave	Cheerful
Amazed	Betrayed	Congruent
Anxious	Blame	Condemned
Astonished	Blocked	Cool

Controller	Desire	Eager
Cautious	Determined	Embarrassed
Creative	Discouraged	Eerie
Comfortable	Dominated	Envious
Confident	Disaster	Ease
Cruel	Defeated	Empathy
Confess	Despair	Energetic
Complete	Daring	Enraged
Childish	Disgusted	Ecstatic
Compelled	Drained	Empty
Confused	Denial	Essential
Crushed	Defensive	Excited
Challenged	Disconnected	Elated
Clever	Diffident	Enthusiasm
Competitive	Distracted	Enervated
Conspicuous	Dread	Evil
Curious	Deserted	Equality
Centered	Desperate	Enchanted
	Diminished	Exploited
Dangerous	Distraught	Exasperated
Depressed	Dubious	Electrified
Destructive	Delighted	Encouraged
Discontented	Despondent	Exposed
Divided	Disappointed	Exhausted
Deserving	Disturbed	Excessive
Deceitful	Doubt	

Fascinated

Free

Fulfilled

Fearful

Frightened

Fuming

Flustered

Frozen

Foolish

Fiery

Failure

Fear of loss

Full

Forlorn

Frantic

Furious

Gay

Grief

Glad

Guilty

Good

Gullible

Grateful

Grand

Gentle

Greedy

Grim

Give up

Happy

Helpless

Humiliated

Hateful

Hopeless

Hurt

Horrible

Heavenly

Horror

Humility

Horrified

Helpful

Hostile

Ignored

Infatuated

Intimidated

Imbalance

Impose

Inferior

Irked

In tune

Impressed

Infuriated

Irritable

Inadequate

Incensed

Isolated

Immobile

Insecure

Invigorated

Indifferent

Inspired

Interested

Integrity

Jealous

Joyous

Jumpy

Jubilant

Kind

Kicky

Laconic

Longing

Lucky

Lecherous

Lost	Nutty	Peaceful
Left out	Numb	Protected
Less than		Productive
Lonely	Obnoxious	Pleasant
Loving	Optimistic	Proud
Let down	Obsessed	Persecuted
Low	Old	Precarious
Loss	Open	Prepared
Lustful	Odd	
	Oppressed	Queer
Manipulated	Opposed	Quarrelsome
Motivated	Outraged	
Mean	Overwhelmed	Rage
Morbid		Remorse
Manipulative	Painful	Restless
Mistake	Pessimistic	Receptive
Melancholy	Pressured	Repressed
Madness	Purposeful	Refreshed
Miserable	Pity	Respect
Mystical	Petrified	Reverent
More than	Pretty	Rebellious
	Pact	Rejected
Naughty	Panic	Responsible
Nauseated	Pleased	Reliable
Nervous	Perceptive	Restrained
Nice	Parental	Relaxed

Rigid	Scared	Sneaky
Rewarded	Safe	Self expression
Ritual	Stagnant	Strangled
Ruined	Sorrowful	Stunned
Rested	Startled	Sarcastic
Righteous	Stubborn	Stupefied
Resolve	Suffering	Special
Relieved	Suppressed	Self confident
Resentful	Screwed up	Shame
Repentant	Serene	
Reasonable	Silly	Talkative
	Spiteful	Tentative
Sad	Stimulated	Trapped
Selfish	Stuffed	Tempted
Sexy	Superior	Terrified
Sincere	Self contained	Troubled
Sorrowful	Secure	Tenacious
Strong	Settled	Threatened
Suspicious	Skeptical	Torture
Suspense	Startled	Tenuous
Satisfied	Stingy	Tormented
Self worth	Stupid	Take away
Shocked	Sure	Trust
Solemn	Self punishing	Thwarted
Spiteful	Self conscious	Tense
Sympathetic	Self doubt	Tired

Ugly

Urgent

Unwilling

Uneasy

Uncentered

Used

Unpleasant

Unacceptable

Unsure

Unsettled

Unimportant

Unworthy

Unappreciated

Uncomfortable

Understanding

Unobtainable

Unclear

Vehement

Violent

Vitality

Vivacious

Vulnerable

Vindictive

Virtuous

Vexed

Willing

Warm

Worthless

Wilful

Weak

Worn out

Weepy

Worthy

Withdrawn

Withholding

Wonderful

Wounded

Worried

Wise

Worn out

Youthful

Zest

STATEMENTS OF INTENT

When working you can twiddle through these statements of intent; they can help you look at the deeper levels and layers of the Self that are often subconscious. The statements may be connected to a specific chakra, the 6th/mind, the 3rd/feelings etc. All the statements in this section can be used in this way.

These statements look at the drag of the past, the hidden, the unclear, the problems on the path that need to be looked at. The clearing of karma and the rising above the turmoil of the 3rd Density is the aim of these statements. They can help you look within and discover a level of clarity within the Self and the being on all levels.

I am willing to look at the past and free myself from the negative part of this relationship.

I accept my emotional response to feeling alone.

I trust that life supports me and gives me what I need.

It is safe to be vulnerable and show my true self.

I trust it is safe to work deeply with other members of the group for the good of all.

I am willing to trust that love can heal me and those that need my help.

I am strong enough to deal with all pain, all suffering, on this dimension.

I can now access the love I hold within to heal others and myself.

I forgive myself for all feelings of revenge. I am now free of the past and open to a positive future.

I understand and accept my desire. I am worthy, beautiful and lovable and can fulfil my purpose in life.

I feel from my heart. I work in harmony to create inner and outer balance in my life.

I love and approve of myself. I am safe. Life is safe and joyous.

I no longer need to judge or fear loss of control by experiencing my emotions. I can break up old habit patterns and responses.

It is my intention that I be provided for with prosperity according to my needs.

I have strength, power and skill to digest whatever comes my way.

I release the pattern in me that attracted this experience. I create only good and celebration in my life.

I no longer need to suffer from pain, fear or denial of my emotions.

It is my intention that I have a good time.

The intelligence of the Universe operates at all levels.

The Universe is intelligent and benevolent and won't give me more that I can handle.

I am willing to change.

I trust that help is there to guide and support me.

I no longer need to fear my feelings. I trust my heart.

The more I open to the unlimited love of the Universe, the more Light will increase on Earth.

I am love. I now choose to love and approve of myself and see others with love.

I rejoice in who I am. I flow perfectly at all times.

I look carefully at everything that has held me separate from my true Self.

My male and female sides support and help each other to keep myself in balance.

I accept my behaviour and forgive myself for not having accepted it before as part of my learning experience.

I accept my power as a positive energy of love.

I now deserve to be loved.

I love life. I am willing to free myself to move forward.

I am free to be myself. I feel strength and comfort from within myself. I let go with love and gratefulness the energy that has kept me secure in the past. I am now willing to let go of this energy. I let it fall and stand free and alone and allow my new inner strength to grow.

I can free myself to the Light.

I no longer need to believe that if I am alone I am a failure and cannot do it right.

I believe emotions are good, that they are safe and they can help me create a positive projection for the future.

I forgive myself for following my needs and allowing these to destroy my life.

I can use my feelings creatively.

I am open to different levels of myself.

I accept that all is free to move between different levels of being.

I am worthy of getting what I need in life.

I no longer need to believe that I have to lose everything I love.

I no longer need to believe it is wrong to receive pleasure from touch.

I no longer need to fear being controlled by others.

It is safe to explore new things. I no longer need to fear making a mistake.

I trust my own judgement. Others cannot deceive me if I stay in touch with my feelings.

I am open to a safe future of joy and love.

Life is enjoyable if I follow my heart.

I release the past and all the pain I have felt. I now paint a picture of a bright new future.

Everything I do is orchestrated for my higher growth, my higher consciousness and my higher evolution.

It is safe to feel. I allow my mind to accept my totality.

I no longer need to believe it is wrong to express my sexuality joyfully as I choose.

I deserve to enjoy life and express my love and sexuality joyfully through my body.

I trust my emotions and I give my body and mind the permission to release the past denial.

I am willing to explore the deeper levels of myself to progress and grow in this life.

I no longer need to believe I have to be responsible for others whether I want to or not.

I am free to change my life. I no longer need to fear being trapped in relationship to ....

I can be strong and loving and caring. I give my trust to others who I feel can help me.

I can give and receive love unconditionally.

I give my male side permission to be on the right side of my body.

I give my female side permission to be on the left side of my body.

It is my intention that I be successful in what I want to create in my life.

It is my intention that I receive and give love, in all things that I do.

I am safe always in everything I do. I forgive the past for all the hurt I have suffered.

I am true and strong to myself. I love myself unconditionally.

I am willing to explore life and give myself every opportunity to complete my life's path.

It is safe to feel what I feel.

It is safe to be me, unfettered by anyone or anything.

I give myself permission to have the time and space to do what I want.

Doing what I want doesn't need to hurt people. It can create a deeper harmony.

My physical body is in balance with my needs at all times.

I release all negative connections with .... on all levels and live freely now.

It is safe to commit myself to working with ....

I no longer need to fear the negativity of others. I trust my own Light.

I feel at one with myself and the Earth. I trust the universal love and caring attention to provide all things to me as they are needed.

I trust the loving support of the Universe to provide all things to me.

I give my mind permission to let go and feel the feelings locked within.

Love is my intention for Earth, the animals, all the people I encounter and all the things I do.

I open myself to all levels of my being. I trust myself.

I can accept change and let people grow at their own pace.

I accept all parts of myself with love.

I can create anything I want. I can see clearly what is important and I am open to change.

I am free to experience myself now on all levels of being.

I can now use my feelings creatively.

I feel at one with myself and the Earth. I trust the loving support of the Universe to provide all things to me.

I can release all past hurts and traumas, and move forward.

I shine love on the pain and distress within.

I am free of the past and live totally in the now.

I am free and I am able to leave all the past behind that I no longer need.

I am free to be myself whatever I feel others may think.

I am strong in myself and can hold the energy of love in my body strongly and peacefully.

I can lift the veil to my own depth of love.

I can see my own worth clearly now that I am a part of a larger picture that is one of love and contentment brought to this Earth to help.

I am free to be myself to help and offer my love to others.

I can build what I want, what I choose and what I need in life.

I can give myself totally to myself and my love for life.

I can give all that I have within to the task of building the Light body of myself and others.

I am free to rise now to my own true place in creation.

I am free to live my life as I want, as I choose, as I need.

I am love and have a loving body, mind and soul.

I am free to be me, to bring peace and Light and love to this Earth and to others.

I am a worker for the Light and open to this level of myself where I can feel the truth more clearly and act upon it.

I am free to be me, to be still and centred and calm at all times regardless of the emotional turmoil within others.

I love life and give myself to it wholeheartedly.

Fulfilling the past promises to the Earth, to the Self and to the higher knowledge is a lesson of love I joyfully contribute to.

Love of Self, worth of Self, body of Self, aligning the whole together, the acceptance of the whole, the acknowledgement of the one, of ALL parts of the Self, the body, mind and spirit working as one and then I will feel better.

I am free to leave the past that I no longer need behind, all the past patterns of toil with no reward, toil with no gain, toil with no love given or exchanged by those I seek to help.

All I do is loving and comes from my heart. I trust that what's right for me is right for the needs of others.

I acknowledge all parts of myself, the body, mind and spirit working together, as one.

I give myself permission to let go to enjoying life. I trust my heart to guide me and express my true self in joy and love.

I forgive myself for denying life.

I have a right to be free from all others that do not wish to blend and melt with others, that have no fixed idea of their own worth and abilities.

I now choose to work with those in the Light who are sure of their own inner guidance and support from Spirit and within, and not from me.

I am able to hold strong to my own truth, whatever the situation. I trust my own guidance to tell me what is appropriate for me. I am worthy. I am able to hold strong and I am capable in my own right. I open to the higher levels of myself and my truth, trusting this to guide me, both in work and play. I am safe.

I am at peace with myself, my life and my guidance.

I am at one with all of life. Existence supports me.

I am strong and can focus on the Light on all levels of being.

I am true to myself. My emotions and feelings are part of my totality and strength.

I let go of my mind and trust my body to give me the truth.

I let go of my personality structures. It's safe to be my true Self.

I trust my emotions and I give my body and mind permission to release the past denial.

I am centred at all times.

I have abundance, success and joy on all levels of being.

I create what I want on the physical plane.

Being true to myself means I resonate with other loving beings and manifest this loving, joyful Light more clearly, for myself and others.

I feel happier, lighter and physically better, more positive and more joyful.

Opening lets my energy flow freely and move at full strength.

It is safe to uncover the pain of the past. It frees my energy so I can be strong and move on.

CHECKLIST

DEHYDRATION TEST

I AM 100% HERE NOW

MY CHAKRAS ARE IN BALANCE
ESR

Balancing

Closing down

Sweeping

Grounding

Connecting to another chakra

Filling with Light

Clearing

Stress release using colours from nature

I AM FREE OF UNWANTED ENERGIES
Emotions

Elementals

Entities

Thought forms

Feeding cycles

Acucords

In a bubble with

Fog or fear

An energy space

The energy of a place

Projected fear, blame and anger

I AM PROTECTED

I AM GROUNDED

CYCLING ENERGY

I THINK WE HAVE REACHED A CERTAIN POINT

I AM CLOSED DOWN

Working with Colour

Five Colours

Visualisation

Breathing White Light In and Grey Light Out

Spirit/Earth Breathing

Energising Breath

Breathing to Release Negative Pictures and Feelings

Releasing Sexual Attachments

Patterns

Patterns in the Chakras

Filters

The CIA and Filters

Cutting Acucords

Cutting and Discarding Acucords

Colours in Acucords

List of Emotions

Statements of Intent

MEDITATIONS

Meditations in the Natural World
Sky Meditation
Walking Vipassana
Not Two
Connecting with the Heart
Meditation to Integrate the Mind
The Four Directions

BOOK TWO
THE EARTH BOOK

Looking at the Many Levels of Reality

HOW TO USE BOOK TWO

The second book is about expansion of awareness beyond the 3rd Density, beyond the realities of this Earth to the bigger picture; to the energies that lie around you, that impinge upon you, but are unseen and unknown.

Take time with each process you need to look at within this section. In Book One corrections could come quickly, be more here/now and immediate. When you go deeper, time and perseverance are needed. You may not complete a project or issue for weeks or months and this is not a fault on your part. It takes time for all the pieces of information and denied material to surface and this is as it should be.

Kinesiology is a gentle technique, one that offers the best path forward at any given stage of development; so the biggest and most important hurdles to overcome are trust in yourself and the ability to feel when the information is a little distorted by the mind and personality. This sense comes with time, but meanwhile keep your common sense to the fore and test each answer in more than one way if you have doubt: search for the answer as an individual, with a friend, or on each other. All responses should be the same, and then the clarity and trust will return. We love you.

THE EARTH BOOK
CONTENTS

CONTENTS

CONTENTS

CONTENTS

PUTTING YOUR OWN NEEDS FIRST

Those who have a need to give, who want to help others in any situation at a cost to themselves, have to take care. We are all deeply imprinted with the 'rightness' of giving beyond the call of duty. In some situations in life common sense tells us that this approach may be necessary and appropriate. However the exhausted martyr is of little use, to themselves or others, and the continual overriding of the body's need to rest and relax is a dangerous game to play, with illness and bitterness following this heroic effort. The following channeling explains the need for balance and awareness.

Let go of all that is not necessary for you to manoeuvre in now, let go of all that which you do not need in the way of response to others' needs. Let yourself choose what is needed from you, don't let others choose what they need from you. It is a matter of balance, a fine tuning for yourself, a fine tuning of your emotional responses so you are not overwhelmed when others demand more of you than is appropriate to give, more of you than you can freely give without some damage to your own body and self.

This is not OK to be drained like this. You must allow yourself the space and time to flourish and grow in ways of being, and not follow those imposed on you by others' wishes. This will not work now. It is important to see because so much will happen if you are not able to call a halt when the proceedings get too much for you; chaos will result for you, and you must be the judge of this moment. Not easy, to balance need and want with one's own inner harmony, but a task that is all-important if the full potential of this place is to succeed. You can do this easily by watching your own responses to situations and places. Do you feel up to all that is happening, is it OK for you to give another hour here to these people, or should you withdraw into your own space for whatever reason you think fit to give. It is easy if you put yourself and your needs first. Check on this continually: how do you feel today? You enjoy feeling good and we like to see you that way but it lasts only a short time and then nose-dives into an unhappy, low state. You can only blame yourself, and more trouble results. It is not easy we know, but try to balance all the different aspects of your life into a continuous stream, a nourishing stream of give and take, ebb and flow, that results in balance for all.

Others need space, quiet, aloneness too, and to give them the opportunity to have this is a gift, not a result of lack of care or consideration on your part. You care, you know that, but this caring can be off balance if it is not weighted down with a healthy respect for oneself. That comes first and foremost. We love you.

USING THE CIA CORRECTION AND THE WISDOM OF THE HEART TO UNLOCK DEEP FILTERS AND PATTERNING IN THE MIND

The opening needed is new, unstructured, uncomplicated, and this is hard to understand because it is not a mental understanding here that is needed. So how do you do this when all we have is our minds to understand with. No, you do not just have your minds to understand with, there is a vast store of wisdom about life, about yourself, that you can access through your heart.

Your connection to the Creator Being level and the Higher Self can open the doors to a new way of living your lives. The mind will resist, will be tempted back into the old habitual patterns, and at times this need for security, for safety, for comfort, will mess up a new project on any level. So be careful how you approach life now. Be aware of the heart energy and its strength, it's not a wishy-washy, lovey dovey sort of affair of following whatever whim is around this or that moment. It's about holding love, love for yourself, your planet and others that live on it; the appropriateness of every situation and how you respond to it. Some of you may choose to change your lives, exchange the interface with unloving souls for something new, something better that is more in harmony with your heart and less in resonance with your old mental structures and beliefs.

So here we come to the beliefs and the systems that operate around them. The filters and the patterns, they all operate in the same way: they block the open, free-flowing energy, and contain and freeze it within a structure, a holding point that is limited in its awareness and its ability to change any given situation, within or without the self. Look at the patterns and filters and see how they operate in your life. Look carefully at how this or that belief system takes you off centre time and time again, confusing your choices, muddling your responses, and denying much of what you truly know and feel. When you can see them more clearly from the standpoint of the heart, then you can use the CIA and its correction to unlock the doors of this old, stuck energy so it flows freely again.

WHAT HAPPENS ON 6th DENSITY

The 6th Density is an area, an opening to the Light of the One. It is hard for you to comprehend at all, but be aware that it is free-moving. There is no constriction of time and place, no inhibition of form or separation, a chance to move as you choose, to inhabit what you choose. An area of no restriction, of helping and aiding other beings on the path, an area of bathing in the Light of the One, of freedom from fears of the Dark, of freedom from all taint of separation.

Let these ideas percolate. The Dark exists on all levels up to the 8th Density. This is not a disagreement, just a different viewpoint on the reality of existence on all levels of being, as you now can see the Light and Dark in all around you. This is the same shift of focus that can help you see from many perspectives the same picture: like a hologram, it depends from which angle you view it.

6th DENSITY AND CHANNELING

Can the Creator Being level only respond to the free-will choice of a 3rd Density being, love and trust being the key here, so guidance will give, to those on the negative path, negatively orientated information, because this is their best way forward. If this is true, is the relationship of those who are negatively polarised here on Earth one of hierarchy rather than open, loving communication? I am puzzled by the 6th Density. I felt this Density was beyond the duality of polarisation; does it offer a polarised response because of the choice of the 3D being on Earth to progress on the Light or Dark path?

The Creator Being level is a level of infinity, of endless possibility, of joy and movement and experiencing of the myriad experiences of consciousness and life, on all levels. It inhabits, as we communicate to you, down to the very core of 1st Density existence. The Creator Being can move as a fluid around rocks, as a cloud in the sky, freely, as it chooses. It chooses to experience, to aid and to offer Light and love, its offer is with the aim of progression. It will offer the love that is needed by the being in an evolutionary nexus. It will offer unconditionally, with no judgement as to the polarity; however it seeks to bring Light, for this is its reality. It is weighted to offer the information of the Light, but this can and will be distorted by the 3rd Density beings and other levels still in polarity and duality. Negatively polarised energies will use these openings to offer their input onto the scenario, will polarize by temptation, by abuse, by aggression if possible, or, as their best option, by free will. So the distortions of denial add weight to the need for negatively polarised beings to congregate around the auras of those in transit, in movement. The offer is there more clearly when there is fear and distortion. You hold no fear of us as judgmental. You have felt that loving acceptance and take it for granted others will feel that too; they do not, they still hold fear of us on higher dimensions, and cannot see what is on offer because of the fear of destruction. Their fear creates, and so we go on, as the offer of the negative path then has an opening.

All is One, remember this deeply. We hold no judgement of you or others but see clearly the need of the Earth to progress, the need of humanity to choose, to move on, to grow up. This is the point: to be responsible for your choices, to not be pushed or pulled but to freely move on. This choice can only be made out of your free will, this is in operation at all times in this lifetime. Now is the point of change, the point of choice and if humanity realized this it would make its priorities slightly different. All need to be fed and clothed and given shelter, then what? What is the big point of life on Earth? Many who do not have these necessities find it harder to make their choice; they have to survive, only those who have the time to look can do this.

Even the poor in any part of the world can do this, but it is hard when you are hungry or cold. You are not; so offer to others who waste their time in materialistic distraction, the reality of love and truth of their creative power and strength to be the Creator Beings themselves. We love you. The Angels of Light of the 6th Density and beyond. The Ascension has begun.

DENSITIES AND DIMENSIONS

All existence lives within this octave of consciousness. Like notes on a scale, there are Densities within the octave. Within the frequency of each Density, smaller divisions of dimensions exist in myriad realities, all linked by the essential inner coding of the Creator Being. Although the Densities are numbered one to nine there is no higher or lower: like notes on a scale, which is the better note? - they are just different experiences of reality. Until the wheel turns full circle, and consciousness finally returns to the Creator Source of the All in One and disappears into the mystery of another octave. This lies so far beyond our comprehension that mystery is a good word to use here.

As progression, as we know it, exists within form, it is worth remembering that other beings progress within spiritual realms alone, never touching existence in form. We have chosen to explore within form, so this path is easier for us to look at. It is easier to understand, and is anyway nearer to our hearts and concerns. Like the new-born, the first Density is still strongly connected to Source, an unindividuated consciousness. The slow action of wind and fire on rock and water moulds the planets and galaxies, bringing the awareness of being that life needs to begin its individuation and progression.

In second Density the first movement and growth towards the Light occurs and is a realm of plants and animals. The turning towards the sun of a leaf indicates the first conscious movement. In the higher dimensions of second Density animals live a tribal reality, a development in awareness of need for the other that continues into the third Density. In many ways third Density is the furthest from the Creator Source, held in a veil of separation, unaware of other Densities to a large degree. Humanity, a member of third Density at this time, seeks the meaning of life. Forgetting the unity of All, consciousness exists in separation to learn from and experience duality. You cannot play chess if you melt into the light and dark pieces and the chessboard too. Only by identifying with a piece within the game can you experience free will and choice on how you wish to evolve and progress.

The choices of path forward are Light or Dark, the Light path growing in love of self given to others, while the Dark path moves towards love of self for self. The veiling process of third Density offers a catalyst in the lessons of love. Our separation from the truth of our connection to Source, each other, and other Densities is mirrored internally: the subconscious mind is hidden within us, and only by exploring within are its secrets revealed. Meanwhile we live unconsciously, repeating through resonance the same old experiences of victim/victimiser. If we wake up to the overview, see the whole game and make a conscious effort to integrate all parts of our Self, even the bits we do not like, connecting to our hearts and the wisdom of our inner knowing, we will polarise onto the Light path. A crossroads is approaching fast. The old patterns of life in third Density are breaking down as the frequency on Earth is heightened and the Earth herself moves on to the fourth Density. For humanity, a doorway opens, a chance to integrate, connect and ascend to higher dimensions. This transformation is called the harvest, and souls polarised to both the Light and Dark path will move on. Most of humanity is unaware of the choice on offer and the potential consciousness they hold. Fragmented and in denial, the human mind seeks to explain life, creating a reality with no awareness or heart. As the transformation approaches our ability to create reality increases; this happens either out of the denied subconscious or from conscious awareness.

Those still unaware after the transition will experience an existence out of form in fourth Density. This existence, still tied to the Earth, will be one where you create your own reality. Third Density is a Density of relating to others, of need on many levels to do this to survive in a human body. In fourth Density there is no such interrelating, you create your own reality and so are forced to live unhindered by conditioning and the restraints of society and its rules. The same issue of polarisation is still in play, the percentages being differently weighted: 40% to the Light and 100% to the Dark. During the experience of living within a human body in form on Earth, the percentages needed to polarise were 55% to the Light path and 92% to the Dark.

An adjustment has been made since the 1980s: the Earth was always going to make this transition, but how this change will manifest is now different. Humanity seems determined to stay fast asleep and unaware, so the benevolence of the universe has created a way for the mass of humanity to move forward. Many people feel the coming changes and transition, but misinterpret the evolutionary jump as being still a life on Earth in form as we now know it.

Positive polarity is a free-flowing, melting, moving energy. Negative energy looks for structure within energy, and those evolving on a negative path will gain information on structure from other Densities. People often confuse melting with giving their power away. Energy moves and situations change, but we want things to stay the same in relationship and don't process the fact when a situation has changed. The feelings are denied around these changes, this blocked, stuck energy then becomes a static energetic structure and opens the door to a negative input from within and without on many levels.

When we say the third Density is built of duality, the depth of this statement goes to the very core of our existence. Humanity is built out of the characteristics of both the Light and the Dark path. We embody both the Light path's ability to love and melt energy with another being, whether in sexual love or trusting interaction, and within hold the structures of the Dark path. As human bodies in form, our bones give the core strength for us to move and express our individuality. Given that structure is a part of the third Density experience we cannot escape from, it's the deeper levels of its use, of whether judgement becomes part of our relationship to structure, that is the key factor in polarisation.

Judgement and blame are characteristics of the Dark path. The Light strives to take responsibility without blame of self or others. Without judgement, structure can provide on third Density the opportunity to learn with love - the teacher pupil relationship where both can learn and benefit, the 'higher' level interacting with the 'lower' in the full knowledge that on one level, All is One and the structure merely a tool to organise and grow in love and trust, not a way of delineating levels in a set hierarchy where all live in fear and seek to gain power over those further down the ladder.

POLARISATION TO THE LIGHT AND DARK

In every being's development there are break points, potentials; the experience of a catalyst that can jump you forward into love, or back, to withdraw. You are all in such a phase of experience on Earth and the pace is beginning to get a little hotter, a little faster. Those that trust and jump can move far, but to not move is now not a safe option. The catalysts are potentials for change. You cannot now not change, you have to all move on or drop out of the game of progression. So on a planetary and a spiritual level there is a push to do this.

This is why those people that seem OK, innocuous, safe, are suddenly becoming so much more potent, so much stronger in the damage they can create because they are not using the catalyst to move on in acceptance and love of Self, but hold back in denial. This is why these denials are so dangerous: you work hard and use many techniques to open up, but to what? You have to be careful here not to judge, for most beings are not consciously choosing the Dark, it is more by default that this is happening, more by lack of movement.

CLEARING A POSITIVE INTENTION

An intention is a thought, a wish for the future, something that you would like to create in your life that is positive both for your Self and others. A statement that does not harm the Earth or others. So, make a list, sit quietly, and focus within and then write down sentences, statements, ideas, of what you wish to see in life. Make the list varied, some big requests, some small. When the list is complete type it out so it can be kept.

At the first session muscle check which intention to work on and try it out. Does the statement hold strong on a muscle check, on an extended arm? If yes find another intention to work on. If no, and the arm goes weak, look at the checklist and ask if the issues needing to be cleared are on the list. If yes, work from the list until the statement holds strong when checked.

Look at the list again and pick another intention. Work with as many as you feel is appropriate at each sitting. You may return to the same statement more than once. As you work through your list different layers and levels of working may have to be completed for all the negative charge to be cleared from a particular intention.

Take time with this and after a while change the list of intentions, add new ones and remove those that have been completed. Look at the future to make positive what is now unclear, and all will be well.

Realise that this work can encompass many possible hitches and you may have to search wider and deeper than the checklist alone to clear them. Look at the contents of this book to see if another avenue of exploration may be helpful. Sometimes you have to acknowledge change on a deeper level than the original statement suggested. This is because much lies on top of the subconscious beliefs and patterns that lie in the unconscious. So do not be surprised if a light hearted or somewhat trivial intention takes you deep into your being and personality structure. We love you.

Some intentions from a client's list:

I am happy with my physical appearance.
I laugh more, and have many friends that accept me for who I am.
My house is beautiful and happy, a place where I truly feel at home.
My career motivates me and I am passionate about it.
I earn enough money so that I can be comfortably self reliant.
I embrace life and make use of opportunities.
I am healthy, fit and energetic.
I enjoy working in my garden, the plants grow well and thrive.

WORKING WITH THE INNER ASPECTS OF THE BEING

The inner aspects are an opening, an avenue into the denied agenda that is more appropriate, more easy to access for those who are more spirit-based, more able to 'see' what is going on. So it is easier to grasp as a concept, as an idea, before they have to deal with the denial and the feelings surrounding this part of themselves. So, in a way it is an easy, understandable and cohesive way to integrate the inner being and create a unity, a unified energy system that is open to change and creating.

This creative process can no longer be achieved by the mind or the feeling centre on their own. The mind has to follow, to be aware of what the feeling state is experiencing. Catharsis with no responsibility, no acute conscious attention, is not helpful and can fragment the inner being further, leaving it in a state of vulnerability and disillusion. A real sense of balance is needed, rather than an unconnected release that has no true meaning in progression or movement to wholeness and the Light.

Many therapy methods of the past have relied on the process of release, realising the value of working with the hidden emotional charge. However, without integration there was no real change, and the personality structure remained unmoved, the guards being erected in another area so that the free movement of mind, body or emotion did not occur. Now, when so much is fractured and breaking down in internal communication, it can be dangerous to let go without the full consciousness being present to observe and witness. This partial release may feel good for an hour or so but no real understanding of the dilemma descends into the emotional arena. This is important to see and understand so that freedom is seen as unity, not an uncontrolled let go with no binding sense of internal purpose. So the spirit base and the Will base can work together to open and control the energy around the heart space, leaving it free. The heart can then connect, transmit and transmute all that is presented to it from the Earth plane. This is important. We love you.

Sit quietly, close your eyes and go within. Look at the images that represent the inner aspects of your being. Take notes and do not be surprised at what you see. Human figures, animals, symbols, or detailed scenes may come in quick succession. Note them all down on paper, and when you have completed your list muscle test to put the images into groups.

Go inside the Self again and look at which chakras the inner aspects of your being reside in. Come back to everyday consciousness, then check again which of the images hold denial and need help. These are fragmented energies that need to be acknowledged, loved, accepted and brought back into the totality of your being. However negative they are, they can contribute positively to the whole. Judgement of these energies has held them in denial and made them more fragmented so that the whole is weaker or in greater negativity and darkness.

Using the Resonance Kinesiology tools from your checklist, see what needs to be done. Maybe emotions need to be expressed or a visualisation could help . Be creative and muscle check to see that all is complete. Go inside and see if the original images have changed. You will often find that the negative images can contribute to the whole when accepted and seen with love. Finally look at how the inner aspects of yourself relate to your life in the outer world and see if the new inner unity can change difficult areas in your life.

People need to understand and be clear about their own inner pictures, the meaning they have for them in hindsight, the understanding they had from those first inner pictures of the fragments of themselves. They need to go inside and look again, and see what has happened. Then work on any aspects that still seem to be in denial, or hold denial, of their potential to contribute to the working of the whole being as it stands on Earth now.

What value can each piece have in your life if it is not viewed in its negative aspect, but is caught, and held, and loved, and given space to explore, expand and give its insight to your whole personality and being? This is where many fall foul in this work. They believe they have to get rid of everything that is negative, that is distasteful, that is harsh and difficult, and in fact this energy too can be transformed.

The building of the Light body is a process of integration of these fragmented parts and connection to the Source. Only when all fragmented energies are reunited with their original Source will there be peace and healing on Earth. This may take time, may never be, but this is the aim of the Earth at this time: to resolve the stuck situation with denial, to bring to the surface all that is hidden and lost so it can find its rightful place in the scheme of things.

This is where an understanding of outer energies outside your own Self's fragmented energies is important, not only for you to be free but for the whole to be back into totality, too.

The space and time for this will soon be needed in greater measure, for there is much confusion on Earth and much is, and will, rise to the surface and be healed, or be lost into the melt-down of original force, original energy. There need be no fear over these processes. All has its place and you have to let go to your fear of progression and fear of disillusion. For as each body dies, each planet, each animal, each tree, each beautiful stone has a life, an experience that will reward the totality with its presence on Earth or elsewhere.

Soon there will be a shift in the Earth's energy structure and you will feel the expansion within you, and feel soon the firmer hand, the larger picture of the one true Source. Give time to yourselves and expand in love. We love you. The Angels of Light and Love for those incarnate on Earth.

WHY PEOPLE ARE SO UNWILLING TO LOOK AT THEMSELVES

The pressure on Earth to change is immense, but how many listen to this call, how many understand the need for security and how it relates to their life on Earth? The need to be secure, it's basic, it's human, it's a part of your existence and conditioning. The body level fears death, and yet change is intrinsic in this transition. So now a much larger transition looms ahead, not only for the individual but for the Earth as a whole, and it engenders fear in all and every one of its life forms that can feel the threat to their security. Life after life has been lived in form on Earth, and yet soon the process will change and open out to a bigger, wider scale of experiencing.

Humanity fears this change and tries, like an ostrich, to bury its head in the sand. "It's all as it always was, isn't it" they say to each other. Much outside of you is changing but this is not the real problem as yet. For many it is the inner disturbances, the inner fears and terrors, the uncontrolled thoughts and feelings that surface at times, unhindered by any control mechanism a human being can put in place. Even at night, in your dreams, or in your wildest fantasies, things seem different and yet it is hard to pinpoint why.

The push is to integrate all parts of the Self, but how many are ready for this? This integration needs to be the intention. For to rise, to ascend to your true place you need to be complete, and this does mean change: change from the denials, change from the secure 3D way of looking at the world, change from a focus of outside/in to inside/out. All of these movements are radical and the mind resists. The Will wishes to move now, you cannot stop it but you can accept it. If you do not accept these denied fears and feelings they will manifest in other ways in outer life, to point you the way to inner life. Later you can create, unhindered by feelings and thoughts and doubts that exist within now.

Take care with this, see where each one of you holds on to the security of the past, afraid to let go to the future and all it has to offer. It seems such a big leap but remember it is a movement home, to a feeling of reassurance and strength in your own inner knowing and being; unconnected to others, unconnected to the fears of the world but totally at one with all that resonate on the positive, loving intention you hold within.

Each has to make a choice, on a conscious and unconscious level, how far they wish their process to go. It is not possible to change another from fear to love without their total interaction with this. There is no such thing as force on the Light path not backed by love, trust and willingness to move on. As we reiterate time and again, it's not hard this process. The clearing of the fear may be hard, you have to look at the truth about yourself but - and this is a big but - this is not all that goes on. The Higher Self guides and holds each one of you, whether you are aware or not, to make the best of each experience you meet on this Earth plane. We love you.

POLARISATION

The issues of everyday life and the issues of spiritual growth, both have their place, and both interlink and control the movement forward in space and time towards the ever-present change that comes soon, that is ahead, for all who live on this Earth. This is true on a personal scale, the personal death, the transformation to another dimension.

You all like to live as if you are immortal, or the change is seen with foreboding or longing. Neither is real. It is as if a fish is caught in a net, it can struggle but the landing is inevitable, and the change of reality from water to air as inevitable as the change you all go through from body/form to spirit/consciousness. This can be so easy when the body lets go, the consciousness can lift to another dimension, another space that is resonant with it. Are there better or worse notes on a scale? Which is better, only what suits, and this is true of death.

The energies of polarisation come into play here too, the choice, the opening to the path of service to others or to Self.

FEEDING CYCLES

This subject of feeding cycles is wide and all-encompassing, and on the 3D is an integral way that people interrelate, and give and take: a sort of grid that holds you all firm and keeps you in an interrelated state. At some points of development this can be an advantage. A release from this grid structure is needed if you are going to move beyond the 3D, beyond the normal form of interrelating that needs to experience the energies of others to discover the truth about the internal energies of the self. When this becomes a focus and the inner a priority, a need to mirror and hold reality up as a screen to play upon is not so necessary. Then a new way of connecting to others, through love and the vertical connection of both, opens. This provides a multi-dimensional relationship, not one based solely on a 3D interaction. Can you see the difference here? One is for a purpose of interaction, the other to explore the truth of the Self and grow in love of the other, and express this love to the other.

For the Self, the implication of these old mechanisms and patterns is they hold you back. If you do not feed and pull from others, others may still pull from you, and this needs to be addressed and looked at with care. Over time, these energies will be expanded and exaggerated as the energies of the planet expand, move. The necessity to break free of these energies is obvious as they polarise you downwards and into the victim/victimiser role, and so keep you firmly stuck on a certain level of being. To break free is important and it's only with a little awareness and understanding of the self, and its interaction with others, that this is possible. So for a start people need to be aware of themselves, of the focus and control mechanisms that they use with each other. Then they need to look deeper at the control mechanisms and energy circuits they have with others, like cording and other interactive energy flows. Then they need to look deeper still, at the pulls and pushes others have on them, their needs for support, for love, for an expanded feeling of awareness they can achieve by piggy-backing on the energy of another. These connections can be broken, but only with love and awareness of the implications of the resonance that on one level still exists, even if this resonance is now past. The connection on an energy level may still be valid as it has not been revoked or broken.

So take time with these. They can occur from any point, any place within the energy field. A weak point is often the target and so is used as an entry point, but sometimes it may be more subtle, more difficult to see, for there is much here of dross and interaction not only from the present but also from the past. The clearing of these energies is finite, it will take time but will help you to move, to break free and to grow, so is an important part of a lightworker's path. We love you. The Angels of Light and Love.

Feeding cycles are not just single-faceted, they cover many energies, many dimensions and Densities, and you can only work with these when you have some clarity of your own to feel what is you, what is not, and the spaces between the two. The feeding cycles are a way of supporting each other in third Density. They are not good or bad but just a necessary way to rely on the energy of another when your own is blocked and trapped, held in the experience of third Density with no real connection to Source and the true Self.

The loosening of these feeding cycles is important for they keep you all trapped in a web, in a belief of a constant state for humanity of separation, the belief in the status quo around what life is about. As these dissolve around you and your own connection is strengthened you will feel more and more clearly when another is pulling on your energy. Do not blame others but deal with this drain on your energy, and push back the many coloured energies that can approach directly into each chakra, or can sit within the energy field, usually in the front of the body. Occasionally feeding cycles approach from all angles into the source of the Light of your being, accessing through the chakra windows into this core energy.

Over periods of time people can drain you completely so you give up the fight to exist independently, then you too have to feed off others and the cycles of power over and under start to manifest again. This, when you attempt to be free to stand in your own Light will drag you back, so be careful and vigilant and be aware of the energies of others and how they can interact with you, especially when they feel lost and needy and in need of support - a lifeline from another human being that is not appropriate in this form. To give love, to give support, to give help, these are not in question but this energy is taken without your conscious permission and is drained unwittingly and unknowingly from your own source of love and Light. So take care with this. We love you.

COLOURS IN FEEDING CYCLES

RED: Anger

YELLOW: I had to let guilt tell me I was never good enough to have, get, be what I wanted.
It is my intention that I give and receive love in all things that I do.

GREEN: I feel hopeless. I forgive myself for following my needs and letting them destroy my life. Ego, doing what I want from the mind. Feeling lonely, unfulfilled and unsupported. Often the person concerned has an entity around them offering support, this does not however make them feel more fulfilled. The resonance between you could be that you too are feeling these emotions, or are connected to an entity that makes feeling more difficult.

BLUE: Blocking, I don't want to be seen.

PURPLE: I have to have regulations and limits put on me so I go forward in an orderly manner.

CLEAR: Wanting a high frequency connection, this is misplaced through another human being instead of through the Self.

GREY: Distraught.

MULTI COLOURED: Failure, a pull on many frequencies.

ZIZZY ENERGY

Zizzy energy is an expression of unloving Light, the use of power to gain over someone, to test someone, to find the pecking order by challenging and attacking out of fear. It comes from a closed heart, a closed mind in relation to you. Others may be able to receive openness, love, from this person who sends it, but for you right now, not. There is usually blame, judgement, suspicion of your motives, these may be to love and to offer help but this is not perceived correctly but is distorted and seen as threatening. Love, to those secure in unloving Light, is threatening. It has a power they cannot resist and so the attack aims to keep you at arm's length and to weaken you. All those in the Light suffer such attacks while on Earth, and due to lack of awareness of subtle energies miss what has happened to them and only register, if at all, a vague unease in the presence of the person concerned.

Slowly in time you will all gain strength and be able more easily to repel such attacks, but for now look to release this energy as quickly as possible for it can ultimately damage the auric field and the body. Slowly you will understand more the ways loving and unloving Light interact, one with the other, it is a science in itself. We love you.

Zizzy energy forms in layers like curtains, usually in front but occasionally in a tube all round the body or in a semi-circle, also in front of the body. It can cover all the chakras or just a few. Check to see how many layers there are and how far they are from the body. The closer they are to your physical body the more you will feel weak and distressed. This energy is projected from another person and needs removing. Find out the colour or colours in the energy too. Wash the energy away with colour, either upwards or downwards, into the Earth. It can also be removed with your hands by sweeping downwards to the ground, clearing the layers one by one. Check in which order to remove the layers.

When first dealing with zizzy energy, wetting your hands can be helpful. Dropping the energy into a bowl of water or a stream can also help to clear it. It will feel electric on your hands, hence the name zizzy energy. This energy can be any colour, black or grey or a deep, electric blue. Removing it can make you feel instantly better. This energy can also be moved with intention, or colour can be used from above or beneath to move it.

With practice zizzy energy can be cleared through a visualisation alone, shifting the layers of electric-like energy with intention. Many colors swirling around within the zizzy energy are also possible, the relief from shifting this kind of energy is almost immediate. The body stops feeling buzzy and electric and rests again in a state of calm.

The energy behind the colours seen in zizzy energy; these feelings relate to the sender not the recipient.

BLUE: Blocking your movement forward and ability to see the truth.

YELLOW: 2nd chakra. Using sexual energy as a weapon.

CREAM: 2nd chakra. Expectation of pain.

GREEN: 3rd chakra. Self hatred, hating the self for not being someone they could love better.

GREY: 3rd chakra. Not trusting that others can, or will, help them.

BROWN: 5th chakra. Inability to express grief or shed tears.

ORANGE: 5th chakra. Unappreciated, not good enough to have, be, what they want.

BLACK: 6th chakra. Feel vulnerable so hit first.

RED: 6th chakra. Denial of responsibility for causing the pain in their own life.

CHAKRAS

The chakras are opening and closing at a very fast rate, are beating to a pulse, to a frequency of changing momentum. At times the chakras open, at times they close. They are volatile, movable, opening and closing, vibrant energy centers, they are never still, never at rest whilst you are alive. They are the heartbeat of the energy system, the on/off pulse of the universal energy entering into form, into consciousness, on this level. They have connection to other areas, are linked one with the other on an energy level; the pulses beat to a similar tune, and the tune of the inner vibration, the consciousness and awareness of the being. So for you all, you need to know how they work, how they interrelate one with another.

The first is the rock, the cornerstone, the basis of life on Earth. Without this red ray energy form does not exist. The second is the area of expression of the first, the manifesting of life in form on many levels: the sexual, the internal, the support for the love of the heart energy, the expression outwards of this love into the world. The third is in some ways the true core of the being. The heart functions but the Will is the powerhouse, the core, the centre of all feeling within the body. It can trace and sense subtle changes and differences in energy within and around the body; it responds first to all changes, all inputs of energy from within and without the body. The heart is the core of the expression of love, the choice of Light or Dark, the centre of free will incarnate: the choices of love for others, love of self for self. The fifth expresses this choice, acts in the world, is the dynamic of relating, both within the Self and without, to others. The sixth is the powerhouse, the central control mechanism for all inputting and exiting energies, the filter on reality, the step down from pure consciousness into the reality of form keeping the being incarnate in power, alive, in its body. It filters all information, stores and collates all information, is the centre of choice and instructs the heart to a degree.

The mind can override all other systems, which are all more subtle. The higher Mind also holds the potential to express the truth of the spiritual being, the knowledge from other frequencies expressed and collated and digested by the mind in the human body. In the future the Mind can take a larger role: one of wisdom of expression, but it can also fall back into darkness, into self-centred realities with no connection to the whole, to the true creation. Right now you are at a nexus, a crossroads of realities, with a foot in both camps. You straddle the old and the new. The chakras, as they have been given, exist within each one of you. The chakras as a more fluid system, a more volatile system of Light, with messages being sent between each centre, this is a possibility.

As clearing houses for energetic input, the chakras can spin and whirl, clearing the many creations that come within a body's field of energy. There are so many inputs each day, each moment, and you are so unaware of what truly goes on. You begin to see and feel the complexity of energetic interaction, but in truth you only scratch the surface of what goes on in and around you each and every day. Learn to sense with your hands, with your heart, your Will. Learn to think and focus clearly. Learn to apply yourselves totally to each task you take on. Learn to be free of the past and the conditioning you hold. Learn to love the All in One and the creations of Earth, and all will be well. We love you.

THE TWELVE CHAKRAS

The chakras are energy points of focus and interaction between many differing levels of the being incarnate, of the consciousness you call a person. So within the human form there are seven major centres, hundreds of smaller nodes and outlets of energy from the Source emanating and enlivening all parts of the human form. On other levels there are other forms of energy connection that are in a pure state of energy as seen from your physical levels. These chakras are to do with the refining and connecting to other levels of the Self and to the Earth that holds the consciousness stable and within a certain frequency fit for a human incarnation on Earth.

So firstly, beneath the feet, about eighteen inches (45cm) beneath the earth, there is a connection that holds the physical form stable and connects it to the core energy of the Earth's totality. This centre is called the Earth Star chakra. Above, in frequency terms, there are other chakras that connect to the Source of the human incarnate. These higher frequency chakras are above the head: the eighth chakra, and on higher frequencies still the Higher Self and Creator Being levels. These CAN communicate the love and wisdom of the whole to the human incarnate on Earth. These connections have to be consciously made and can be opened more easily now due to the rising frequency of the energy on Earth.

This re-establishment of a link to the Higher Self is what makes this time so important, it is a window of opportunity that makes the seeking of the truth of the Self more exciting and more rewarding. So much is held on higher frequencies that is disconnected from the human mind. This connection, once re-established, makes the polarisation and movement forwards to an integration and fusion of all these chakras more likely and more possible.

Take care and sit and connect to this knowing and all will be re-established for those who wish to move forwards on a deeper level. The chakras are the doorways, the energy centres that connect and intertwine on a more conscious level, they are the points of contact between the Self and others on many levels.

POLARISATION AND THE INTEGRATION OF THE WILL

To evolve from the 3rd Density human beings have to polarise through free will to the Light or Dark path. An open heart and free-moving Will are the signature of the Light path, a feeling path of loving Light, fully accepting the emotional body with all its negativity and past adventures in duality. The unloving Light of the Dark path is still in a state of denial of the Will energy, and the heart is focused within the Self and is not open to others. Fear and fragmentation from the Will energy give the need for hierarchy, judgement and structure, as no real feeling of acceptance for the Self on any level can exist because separation is built into the system. Only when the denials are faced and the feelings in the Will accepted can the jump from the Dark to the Light be accomplished.

There is much fear of the Will and its emotional baggage. The Gap, the feeling space where the mind does not exist, has to be entered, and although assistance and guidance from the Light offers to hold our hand in this void, it is hard to believe this can be possible, so great is humanity's fear of the Gap. Fragmentation - where parts of the Will are held in denial, split apart on energy terms from the original soul - has to be reclaimed now for the soul to complete. These fragmented and denied pieces of Will can incarnate on Earth, the blame and denial being continuously repeated, as if the person cannot ever learn the lesson and is constantly dragged back to the blame and denial inherent in their state. To contact the love of the heart is the way back to their source soul for these fragmented beings.

THE COMING TRANSITION ON EARTH

Polarisation is a free-will decision. Most of humanity will not choose to polarise from 3rd Density existence in form. After the transition human beings cannot live on Earth in physical form as before. Those that are unpolarised will exist in a 4th Density reality where they create their own reality, and through these experiences will progress towards polarisation by the use of free will. Earth is moving to 4th Density. Animals and plants, at present living within bands of frequency in 2nd Density, will also move after the transition. Animals will move to 5th Density in spirit form around the Earth. Trees and single cell amoebas will live in form on Earth in 4th Density. Primitive plants and around 20% of humanity, existing as simple plants, will also exist in form on Earth.

Polarisation is a free-will decision we can make now, or later in a reality similar to the 3rd Density astral plane where it is possible to create whatever you like unhindered by social conditioning and fear of others' responses and actions. It will not be possible to sit on the fence. To polarise from our present human form you need to be committed 57% to the positive path, 92% to the negative path to move forward. The ascension process is to move from 3rd Density in human form through to 6th Density at death, or at the time of transition. After the transition beings in 4th Density need to be polarised 40% positive or 100% negative to move on. This Earth is weighted positive and is kindly to beings incarnating within its energy fields. Beings that ascend from Earth from the 3rd Density will move to 6th Density. This harvest will be both positive and negative. The 5th Density belongs to other energies, not human beings. At transition then, humanity will move from the 3rd Density in form to the 4th Density or the 6th Density, those on the 4th moving also to the 6th as they polarise through experiencing a self-created reality in 4th Density. Some beings, wishing to be unaware, will return to 1st Density as simple plant forms.

All dimensions within the 3rd Density, including entities and beings on the astral plane, will coexist with unpolarised humanity and some 2nd Density animals in a 4th Density reality not in form. This is not a reality where beings interface through experience of relationship to progress, they will experience through their own subjective creation of reality, to polarise Light or Dark. On 4th Density you do not interface physically with others, you are in a mental, virtual reality space where you create alone, so you create loving connection if you choose it, or hell if you wish. Many will create from their denied Will.

To polarise positive and ascend to the 6th Density you need to integrate the Will energy. After transition, 90% of Will energy needs to be integrated to polarise positive.

THE EVOLUTION OF CONSCIOUSNESS

Existence is a mystery we cannot hope to comprehend from the limited perspective of a 3rd Density human being in form. Born into separation unaware of the truth of reality where All is One, we live behind a veil, both internally and externally, unaware of the nature of reality and the many Densities and dimensions that surround us. Our understanding of other Densities in this 3D state is minimal: what reality does a butterfly really experience? As to the reality of an Angel from the 6th Density, we can in our veiled state only conjecture or believe what religions have told us. Only when we break down the veil and integrate ourselves internally will we be able to see, feel, and experience other frequencies and dimensions with ease. As when changing gear to suit the speed and smooth running of a car's engine, we will also be able to move where appropriate and expand beyond the limited horizons of the veiled 3D reality.

Sexual orgasm gives us a natural, if momentary, glimpse of the joy of melting and moving beyond our limitations. Sexual orgasm moves to a heartfelt love for the other, the natural movement forward towards polarisation, the free-will choice of path back to Source via the Light or Dark path, either being possible.

Consciousness moves from Source through the Densities back to Source, its journey through the Densities and dimensions an enriching experience for the whole of creation. Within each Density there are many dimensions on higher and lower frequencies within the main band of a Density. In the same way as lions, tigers and mice are all part of the class of animals we call mammals, so there are many dimensions with differing levels of consciousness within the Density.

Within each octave there are nine Densities. Connected still so closely to Source the 1st and 2nd Density are unpolarised. Only at the 3rd Density is the choice offered of how consciousness wishes to progress. From the 3rd Density a spirit polarises to the Light or Dark and continues up through the Densities on one path or another. Duality and separation between the two paths still exists as consciousness moves through the Densities. Only as consciousness moves to reunite with Source does all again become one, loving energy.

Duality is an expression of unity, the two are interlinked, are part of the consciousness that holds the ONE, are a part of the whole that gives it the dynamic and expression of love. Without Light or Dark, up or down, love and hate, the universe would be static, and to move is paramount for change and evolution. Always the bigger picture helps when seeing the injustice and suffering that afflicts so many on this world and others. We wish you to understand that duality is not to be transcended, as in "everything is of the Light", but that the Light can appreciate and understand the need for duality in form; for without it there is no catalyst for growth and movement to the ONE of all being. The Light path offers humanity networking, sharing and melting of consciousness; the Dark path structure, hierarchy and power over those beneath, and fear of those above. As humanity is built of duality it is hard to disentangle the Light from the Dark. Only with acceptance of both paths, and an intention clearly stated to seek the Light path, can we move forward. To love others and the Self is the Light path. Each step towards the Creator Being is a discovery of awareness.

The energy on Earth of the 1st Density is random and chaotic, the inorganic mineral life of rocks and water learning slowly from fire and wind the awareness of being. Organic life emerges as a conscious seeking of the Light, growth and movement begin and as a leaf turns towards the light of the sun, the consciousness of the being becomes self-aware. The 2nd Density includes all animals and plants, these beings existing in the here and now, unconscious of the pain of separation. The higher animals of 2nd Density become self-conscious and with this growing awareness of self move towards 3rd Density.

In many ways the 3rd Density is furthest from Source, the veil of separation from our truth - given by existence as a chance to experience the catalyst of interaction with others in a state of free will - offering the choice which path to follow. Once the choice has been made, the being moves up through the Densities back to Source, thus completing another octave of creation. The Densities lie like beads on a necklace, all have their place and contribute to the whole. Humanity tends to judge the higher Densities as better than the lower; in truth all Densities, like notes on a scale, are needed to make the octave, each one holding the essence of the loving Source within it. The log-jam of souls fragmenting as they reincarnate on Earth, and the ensuing frustration of feeling trapped in separation, comes from man's own inner lack of integration, a problem that has built up through denial of the Will energy. Our purpose on Earth is to reclaim lost Will. The longing to melt and reunite with Source is inherent in all of creation, the next octave of experience following the final return to Source being an unknown and unknowable mystery to all Densities within the octave. There are nine Densities within each octave.

After the transition on Earth, humanity, at present living within a middle band of frequency within 3rd Density, will move to the 4th Density or ascend to the 6th Density. Some of humanity may move to 1st Density at the time of transition, movement through the Densities being free to move in any direction, not only through linear progression. Humanity is a very mixed bag coming from many different sources and Densities of origin. Some have come to help the Earth at this point of transition, and to reclaim for their soul group lost Will. Others followed their evolutionary need to experience separation and free will, Earth being one of the few planets that offer this 3rd Density experience. The logos of Earth is a kindly one, and it offers to spirits wishing to experience 3rd Density life in form, a reality lovingly weighted to the Light path. The catalysts of time, space, and the recurring karmic experiences of relating to others in a state of separation, aid us to grow and make the choices leading to polarisation. The denial of Will, and the mental thought forms and structures that exist now on Earth, have slowed the process down for many millennia, but now the Earth herself is moving towards this moment of transition. Soon it will not be possible to sit on the fence undecided, constantly returning and reincarnating to learn again the lessons offered by repeating catalysts in form on Earth. Humanity can feel this change and responds. Understanding subconsciously that change is coming, we search for security but have no idea where to look. Our focus has for so long been outward and not inward that the security of a strong, inner, vertical connection to our Source is overlooked for the transient security of the outer world. In an increasingly unstable outer reality this becomes harder to achieve, neither relationships nor material wealth are secure any more, even the weather is unpredictable, and many, feeling a failure, wish to escape this reality and resort to drugs of one sort or another. Anything that absorbs the mind and numbs the pain of this instability can be used: the executive addicted to his work denies feelings in the Will as much as the drug addict obsessed by another hit denies his.

As the frequency moves higher on Earth it becomes more difficult to repress and suppress the denied Will energy; held back for so long it now seeks to move and express itself, to help us move to the Light. Without a free-moving Will energy we cannot open our hearts and melt into the Light, loving path of progression. Stuck with our closed hearts we can only become more and more self-centred and, through fear of our feelings and emotional responses from the past, and judging these feelings as wrong or bad, slip onto the negative path. Existence itself holds no judgement of our path of progression with both the Light and the Dark offering insight, information and catalytic change to humanity at this time. The thinning veil between the astral dimension and those alive in form on Earth also increases the catalytic potential. Through resonance, astral entities are drawn into the energy fields of those human beings on Earth in denial. This extra resonant energy increases the catalytic effect, making it more difficult to ignore the denied emotions. Hopefully the lesson is learnt and the resonance cleared, but so many people are unaware of this attraction of like to like and hold much fear of energies on other dimensions.

If we wake up to the truth we have more choice, more understanding, and more love for those choosing paths different from ours. If we judge the negative path and believe it to be wrong, we hold ourselves too in a state of duality. With understanding we can hold compassion both for others and ourselves, and look lovingly at the hard to acknowledge emotions we hold in response to unloving and difficult experiences. Without judgement we can look at our anger, fear and hate and deal with these emotions, not repressing or expressing them but releasing them and letting them go consciously. For so long we have learnt the ways of repression, and we often now need to learn to express these emotions out loud to lose our fear of them. But in time, as we become more comfortable with the process, we can be more subtle in our expression and release of this stuck energy. Using visualisation, sound and colour work to clear the drag of the emotional body, much can be achieved in day-to-day life and beyond.

So much to be cleared and so little time to do it. None of us are immortal, and without this integration any opening up through meditation and other self-development methods becomes unbalanced and lopsided. We are then unable to move on as a whole, total being, because of the weight of denial and lack of integration between the centres within the body. The mind, body, spirit and Will need to move as one integrated being before a true vertical connection can happen.

THE EXPANDING EARTH

The Earth is expanding fast but it cannot contract, as if it has taken a breath out but cannot take any air inward, and so it is stuck. It needs to let go a bit but is held in a structure, in a mesh, a net of the past, and the human thought forms keep all this rigidity firmly in place. The Earth cries out for help and Light and understanding so that it can move on, but only with love can this be done. Love given to the Earth as a being, as a consciousness, this is the point. This is the point for anyone in any place, to give love to this planetary being, to relate to it, to love and cherish, that is all that is needed to break the cycle.

Those that feel free, those that can see, can move. Those that are stuck are blind and cannot see what is around them anymore, cannot see what is alive and what is dying, can only feel, and that part of their being is denied. When it comes to the future, when it comes to the outcome of all of this denial it is not hard to see: that which breathes out must breathe in, or die. That which lets go must move on. This is the state of the Earth at this point. Soon it will have to breathe to live.

QUALITIES OF THE LIGHT AND DARK PATH

The Earth is moving on, is in a state of upheaval at the moment. All souls who seek to progress have to understand themselves, their likes, their wants. Be compassionate in this, it is not a question of fault, of query as to your validity as a loving being. Your needs and wants lead you deeper to the truth of your own soul, are valuable and are not something to be dismissed as greedy or jealous or whatever. You have to see this as a truth, not to be frightened by it but to acknowledge and accept your frailty and your need for each other, on one level.

On many levels you are alone; on one level as a human, frail body, you need each other. You are all in a mind/body/spirit complex, you are all in an interdimensional space/time continuum, are all in a state of interdependence on an energy level on Earth. Can you see this is not a fault, a weakness, but a fact while you are incarnate? If you can acknowledge this you will lose your fears. If you lose your fears and understand that this does not apply on all dimensions but that you choose to love and support each other, and others in the Light on other dimensions, it will become clear as to the choices of polarity and the use of love for your Self.

Can you see, as you move beyond the 3rd Density you do not need to love and trust others to operate. With the strength of your vertical connection and Creator Being level you can create; it is a little cold, a little destructive, because the energy of this connection has to be channeled in a structure of power. It cannot be given freely because there is no need to give except on the 3D level. This is where 'the devil takes care of his own' statement has relevance. These people are not monsters who polarise negative, they may be judgmental but they will love those that they need on the 3D, those that console and comfort them, those that give them food, sex and all the myriad other things you need to survive on this Earth plane. But, and this is a big but, there is no real sacrifice of love for another, no sharing beyond the call of duty, no putting yourself out for others, no giving with no reward, and this is the point.

The Light path does give with no reward but understands so deeply that All is One that it does not need to worry here: a gift to the other is a gift to the Self. But, and again it is a big but, the Light cannot deny its own Will and feelings. It is not bound to give where it has no impetus to do so, not bound to give when it feels repulsion or where it is damaged beyond the point of no return to its own stability, unless it chooses to do this for the greater good of all. Can you see the difference between mindless sacrifice and this choice, because it's a choice made out of awareness, not fear of damnation or need for a dutiful response to receive acknowledgment from God, or whoever. It does not try to please, and this is the point, the giving is natural, uncomplicated, spontaneous and aware. These are all ingredients of the Light path and its forward movement to the Light: to give with no response back, to give because of feelings of joy or wish to give. These are all fine. To give to hold onto, to give to receive back, to give because you believe you have to will take you nowhere, not even to a polarised state. This has been the trap on Earth, a set of rules to work to where you can safely fall asleep and not feel, not decide, not choose where to risk, where to give, where to love for the good of yourself and the All in One.

So take time with these ideas, for they are the stepping-stone to everyone's movement. They need to feel connected to their Source, connected to the Earth, and free to operate as loving humans unhindered by ideas of what love is. To be hard can be loving, to be cold can be loving, to be indifferent can be loving; not all has to be the martyr trip to be holding a path in the Light. But to deny love, to bury love, to not give when you feel to, not move when you feel to, to not decide because of fear of change - all these will lead you slowly to lose trust in yourself and in others and close the door to your movement, close the door to the true love and beauty of the Divine Creator as it truly can be expressed both on Earth and beyond, where the loving network of choice stands freely above the needs of the human to experience and congregate together for the human body's survival. This too will change in time, so be aware and careful of how you act on Earth now. For the doors are opening to a new time where this freedom to create a reality will take you further and further away from, or closer to, the divine spark of loving care and awareness, one for the other. We love you. The Angels of Light.

ENERGY VORTEXES

The energy grids of the planet are disrupted. Much energy does not flow but remains stuck and static in little whirlpools that resonate on certain frequencies, emotions, thought forms, entities etc. These pools are to be found in little pockets, little spots. Normally you are aware of these to a degree but do not have to be bothered about them. As a general rule they are to be found in a certain geographical location. You can twiddle and dowse the extent of each vortex. These are on the surface level but affect the planetary life, especially human, that lives on the planet's surface.

They are affected by wind and weather, these pockets move at times, but like a floating balloon have an anchor string to a certain point or place that you will discover for each vortex. Some of these have to remain, as they are not possible to move. Others are more amenable to dispersion and realignment, and can gently be persuaded to let go of the stuck energy and again flow and move. This would help all life within their field of energy to grow more open and secure in itself. This would be of help to many beings.

The position of the energy structures needs to be carefully located, and the suitability of work to be done assessed. It is no good discovering a certain area and charging in to change what is not appropriate or possible to catalyse and move to the Light. You will have to discover this for yourselves and use your energy wisely in the places where movement is possible, and on a deep level is wanted.

Each charge, each disruption that is lifted and moved will ease the pain and suffering on the 3rd Density. On higher Densities it creates an opening, a channel of energy, to move and communicate through.

So, let it be discovered slowly and easily, the pockets around where you are, so you can experiment with their clearing. Remember the energy is cycling, it is not moving on. You have to find the outlets, the points on the compass where you can release and ground or lift the energy, so the spiral moves up or down, out or in.

Only occasionally will the spiral move inwards, mostly you will work with the expansion of energy, this is easier. The balancing of the inner, downward spiral needs more tension, more people too, to hold the charge and energy movement. You cannot do this with just a few people working together, you will need twelve to thirteen at least to effect this change.

We love you. The Angels of Light.

WORKING WITH THE DEVAS

Devas could you help us? Can you give us the information as to the relationship human beings can develop with other dimensions, both up and down the frequencies.

We come, we bring you greetings of love and Light, as intermediaries, as connectors to you, to the Earth. We can be of help, of service to the whole and to ourselves. We raise our levels of consciousness through service, through love. This is not, as humans so often believe, a case of denial of the Self but more an expanding of vision, of enactment, of involvement with areas of being, areas of form. We do hold the structure, the blueprint for all forms in nature and the natural world. We hold the ecstasy, the completeness too, of bringing each form to completion in its best way of growth in form. It is a long task, one we began millions of years ago, to make this planet alive to the energies of other sources so that all could live in harmony here. Much has gone awry in the process but we still hold on and give strength to the world of form and matter.

So now you choose to explore your birthright. At last a movement of all can happen through this, to expand our love and awareness, and you yours, by interaction. At this point all can hasten their movement to the Light and love of the Universal Creator.

So consider the lilies, the flowers that grow, do they not, alone, unaided in their natural homes. You too grow unaided in your natural home - but is this your natural home, let alone this dimension? So take care to look at this fact for it will give you strength to understand yourself and your truth of where you really belong. Some of you are of Earth, this is a great privilege to be from this planet and grow alongside her. So see how you can be aided by us, the Devas of many realms, many plants, animals and beings. So relax when you come, do not speak, do not make sounds to start with. Communicate with us internally, this is the better way, we can understand this form better. Use your minds to open the gate, the pathways to communication. Send love and Light to the Earth and open the door to our energies. We are soft and loving if you are soft and loving to us. We can visit you when you need help to aid you in your tasks, can help you unravel the karmic threads and energies, can raise you to the Light and love of your own Self, your own being.

Also we can tell you how to care for forms, for plants, for the animals. We have the blueprints and also the knowledge. Many of you will feel drawn to this work, and this is good. We will aid you and we will aid the natural plants. All will benefit, it will be a good and fruitful relationship. Take time to tune into us. Do not be deceived by negative energy spirits that do exist. They do not however work in love and Light, and you can feel the difference here if you remain open. With practice all can flow smoothly between us all. This will help all to move on. We love you, the Devas and spirits of the other world, the 2nd level or Density.

THE TREE DEVAS

THE BIRCH

The Birch is a tree of resonance with this country, Scotland. Within the mountains, within the high places, it can hold firm and grow in strength. It needs the wildness of the empty spaces to feel comfortable and you too can all feel comfortable in this emptinness.First find a birch tree to ground yourselves with, hold the trunk and breathe down, and collapse the feeling body down and into the ground. Let go of all that is not important and then let yourself rise, being well rooted first, to the tips of the topmost branches of that tree. Let it carry you upwards and outwards, and follow the trail it projects you on. You will find much through this receptive, female-energy tree. We love you, the Devas of the plant and tree kingdoms.

THE BEECH

The trees are open, as we say, to you, to the air, to the sky, to the cosmos and the universal energies that swing and move above the Earth. So now there is a time of change, let this be, do not grow cold in your hearts but be open, be willing and loving to all, yourselves included, for all your faults and misdemeanours. Let the flowing energy move you now, let the openings to the natural world be more complete, more conscious. If you love us, if you feel comfortable in the woods of fine beech trees, wander there, hold yourselves in Light and ground yourselves there. Let the Light flow down to the

Earth, to nourish the Earth. Let the Light flow up to nourish the heavens and the spirit realms above you. Let all these moving energies flow again. We love you.

THE ASH

The Ash trees are alive and well here, open and reaching and giving as all should. Let this be a parable, a little story of life as it is. The ash are open to the laws of nature, the basic laws of this planet, the laws of feeling and thinking and creating a form. This is a balance between the elemental and the physical: the elemental energy behind each form is the creative source of the form, the pattern, the structure. Each member of the tribe of a certain tree exhibits these certain characteristics that you are familiar with: a certain leaf structure, trunk, wood, etc.

These attributes are given by a pattern laid down by the energies of unseen realms. These hold the blueprints, like a DNA structure, that can resonate through sound and light, into form for the trees. They use many means too on the physical, but the structures are inherently the same, of roots, trunk and leaves. The opening to the Light and to the Earth, both are needed here to create. Soon you will need to open to these energies in a more conscious way to survive the changes the Earth has ahead. It will be easy to connect to the Light and to the Earth, you think, but practise in reality and the truth of the unconnected state of the human form will become apparent.

Let energies move now, let old hurts go now, let ideas create now within you a new form, not a new bone structure but a new Light form to hold you safe. This is possible. It will not be difficult if you love yourself, love the Earth, love the forms upon it. It takes so little time and yet there is resistance from so many, for fear of what they may find here. There is help to be had with the fear if you open to it and admit it. This is the first and the biggest step.

After this a healing of a deeper nature, on a soul level, can happen. All humans hold fear of annihilation and despair at their state, in truth. This is natural and is a reality. Look at it and look deeper, beyond the form is a truth, beyond the truth an opening to the Light. This Light can suffuse the body, soul and mind. Use it daily, all the time, in short bursts, to hold you strong and in a frequency of love and Light. Choose colours that resonate. Use trees to hold the frequencies of changing with you. They can do this. The trees are aware, are open to this new Light and will survive in form over the next few years. We love you, the Devas of the Ash trees.

THE SYCAMORE

The Sycamore tree, the tree of growth and strength, the weed that bothers you when places are left alone, places are left dormant. The tree is strong, it can colonise areas that others cannot, it can spread a green blanket over the soil and protect the naked Earth from hurt, from harm. The leaves are widespread like fingers on a hand, they touch the sky like an open hand, they give their strength. Take strength from these trees, take the inner strength you need. Rest by the roadside and look at the trees, so many are weakened at this time but the sycamore is still strong.

Give it the space to grow and expand, for its strengths are needed now. Let it uplift you when you feel weak. Like the oak it is a positive energy, a strong life energy to protect the inner Self from harm, from decay. Go and sit by these trees when you feel weak. Touch the bark, the life energy of the tree, and feel it move though you with the breath. Count in and out, a gentle steady rhythm, and then visualise the light of green moving up, and gold moving down into the ground. Let yourselves bathe in this light and movement for a while, and feel invigorated by this cleansing and clearing with the aid of the tree's strength. The sycamore is strong, look at it for strength. We love you, the Devas of the Sycamore tree.

THE PINE

Do not despair that all is lost. The way looks hard and stony, but the rewards of life on Earth are many. We as trees contribute to the whole, as you do too. Make sure each day that the things you see, the things you love, you acknowledge to yourself so you grow in loving awareness of your own reality and the space that you live in. Here we inhabit a wilderness of trees and rock, sky and bare Earth. This is the rawness of Earth, the wildness of untouched nature. Create the wildness too a little in your lives. Dare to be different, to explore, to grow in the face of all odds, like a weed pushes up through concrete, so you can grow to your own truths of beauty and love. We love you, the Devas of the Pines and forests of the old woodlands of Caledonia.

THE LARCH

The trees, the Larches in particular, are one force, one aspect of yourselves, that can help you to open out to the truth of your real beings. You are constrained, fettered within an illusion, within a being of human form. The energies of the mind and soul are vast, and encompass so much that you are not aware of as yet, as to your true origins. By making contact, by pulling close together to the trees, you can feel and experience the sensing mechanisms we have, we use as trees to contact the universal energies, the universal whole. Our energies are of the oneness of the second levels of being, but in this position we can achieve much that you cannot. We bring stability and order to a world sorely in need of both. The chaos we feel around us from your divided states grieves us, and leaves us open like a wound to feel what you cannot.

So now let us explore together the realms beyond the physical, the realms of Light that you can inhabit if you take the time to focus within on the heart and then connect to us by a stream of consciousness and love, from heart to heart, soul to soul. Yes we have centres, have feelings, this you will experience if you take the time to cover your own lives with imprints from beyond the 3D plane. So sit for now beneath our spreading branches, sit and tune in through the heart, be still and feel the energy around you, moving at one with it. Feel first the energy of the trees and then expand upwards with this, explore the universe through our strength and help and it can hold you safe and grounded whilst you do this. You can feel the energies of the second level, here with the trees. This too will give you another perspective of the variety of experiencing here on this Earth plane. So much to explore at your very feet that can take you so far. The Larches are open, positive and generous of spirit, and will give much aid to humanity if sought for. We love you, the Devas of the Larch spirits and trees.

THE ROWAN

For this moment in time there is much, much change, much growth and much decay, and you have to be aware of all this changing energy around you. The trees you see as static, as a oneness, as a constant, but we too feel change, and feel with differing frequencies and vibrations the energies of the Earth spirit as it frees itself from its past history. This is what you are all feeling: the past, the decay, the separation from the stuckness of before. What was did not have a harmony, an inherent motive for its existence. It saw life on Earth almost as a punishment, and this has to change now; to choose this and to be this being, whatever the form, with totality, with love and joy for its existence. This will be hard for many to achieve, and here is the rub. Do you help to keep the status quo, in whatever way you meet it, or learn to adapt to the new, to forge ahead on this path?

We suggest you move forwards now, you cannot remain as you are, not moving. To be static is to succumb, is to not move at all, and this on one level is a no to the opportunities we are all given in form. This has always been so, but now there is a slight edge, a slight desperation and relaxation both, to choose the path of maintenance of the old forms or exploration of the new. The new forms are multi-dimensional and open-ended, they have no result, no respect for 3D failures of understanding, so you can approach with love or fear. How you approach these energies is so important for you, for you have as humans the capabilities, if you use them, to create a new reality through the power of the heart/mind link. We too have the linking but in a different way that does not work in a physical way. This physicalness of your existence is your strength and weakness. So now, as humans, take steps and grow with love and good fortune, or fall with grace to the ever growing empires of form. We love you, the Devas of the Rowan trees.

THE OAK

The higher frequency, the new energy that inhabits humans is volatile, is extreme soon in one way or another. None can tell the course of the new, none can predict the outcome, for this is not set as such but is an event, a happening of huge proportions on a universal scale, not just on a human scale. You as humans relate to the Earth through your eyes, your own perspectives of needs and wants, and rarely look to see the larger, the grander, the overall picture of reality, of the wants and needs of other species, other dimensions, that co-exist alongside your own. You need to break this deadlock, these blinkers on reality, and open the doors now to the wider picture, the universal picture of change and growth. The planet is in turmoil, in crisis on a physical plane. The resources are being spent each day, the Earth has more to cope with on this physical plane and level, and yet the support is needed for other happenings, other events that are not man-made but are universal in nature. So humans are but one component of the trials and tribulations ahead. This is a point of change, an access to a new dimension, a new beginning. Humanity can choose to come along now on this adventure or not, as each individual soul chooses its fashion of expression. The end result of a life on Earth is not a set result, a set outcome. This too is important to realise, for the chance to rectify these choices cannot be given. Not that no-one, no god in heaven or wherever, does not care, but more that the shift and the changing nature of the universe is a law that cannot be broken or stopped for any one species to catch up in the race. Humanity is far behind as a whole group, although individuals may make efforts. Now you all need to choose what is important, what is needed to make life OK not on a monetary, material level, but on a deeper level what is needed: time, experiencing of new things, new ideas, contemplation on the reality you live within. All these and more are subjects worth exploring and we wish you well in this.

We can aid the process by catalysing the hidden and giving our strength to the expression of what is difficult to look at. So if you feel out of sorts, low, depressed or whatever, the oaks can help you uncover the truth behind this setback, can help you see and feel what is real here, rather than what is false, or of the mind. The heart can open here with us, and this is good. If the tears flow or the anger is acknowledged, good - it will free you now. If the horror of this reality is hard to face, then we can soften the blow, soften the processes that look so hard, and aid the body to hold strong in all of this. This emotional cleansing is long overdue and so important for humans to be clear about. The strengths you hold as a race are of the heart, not only the head. The heart needs to be brought into action. Hearts of oak, the old standpoint of strength, see the heart energy, the love you hold, as your strength as a race and it will propel you forward at this time of changing energies and frequencies. We love you, the Devas of the Oaks.

ASH TREE AT TIGHNABRUAICH

The energy of the Earth is expanding now, is enveloping every living being with its loving awareness. The Earth cannot hold the frequencies of Light and fear together anymore. They are being separated, one from the other. This brings all into a state of tension and resolution of the old love/fear dilemma. All that is of the Light has to find its own way in part, cannot be pushed or manoeuvered but must choose, for all is not ease on any path and this has to be understood.

In this realm of matter and force the old is dying. That does not mean that everything will die but that everything will be changed. This is hard for you humans to accept. The change is vast, it is a movement of return now, of moving back to the Source, away from this point, this part of the universal scheme. A movement to a higher, wider reality, not dominated by what you call the Fallen Light and what we see as a complete and separate structure from the inherent unity of all.

It is not a matter of changing what is within, but of encompassing and holding all that is within; this means all that is Light, all that is Dark, and then moving on. The birds are needing to fly now and they will surely succeed. We love you, the Devas of the Earth realms and the Earth's trees.

The deeper levels of life, of life on Earth and on all planetary systems of form, are open to the vagaries and the feelings of separated Light and Light form. The being in form is corrupted on one level, and has to move past its limited existence into a feeling of comprehension of the whole. To feel a part, to feel at One with All, is a measure of the success of the life form experiment that has taken many aeons to establish.

Here on Earth the page has nearly, but not quite, been completed, and soon there will be a freedom and opening for all that long for the deeper meaning of life on Earth and elsewhere. In many places the energies are dense. In many lives the energy is dense, but this does not mean they are wasted or of no use. Let all find its right place and open to its own truth and Source. There is love on every level, marked to a degree or not. All is as it should be and All is One, so take heart that this process of completion is a coming home, a necessary step for the life on Earth, and beyond.

The fire energy, the force of the Will, is putting out now its true message of return and love unified. We love you, the Devas of the Ash and Earth. We love all who hold the love and Light of the One, whether they recognise this love and gift or not.

MAKING FLOWER AND TREE ESSENCES

These essences need to be made afresh with a new method, do not repeat the old. They need to be made with spring water, not tap. Go to the source of a spring in the hills and keep it in a container and use it as you need to. The spring water must be fresh and pure and left only a few days in the container. It needs to lie next to the plant or tree. Only a token from the plant needs to be used, muscle test which leaf, flower or whatever, is needed, and wait for five to six hours. The sun is good but not essential, but the energy of the day needs to be clear and bright, not heavy or negative.

Take time to prepare the mixture, use crystals and loving Light from selenite to activate the mixture. Channel afterwards what they can do, and use them sparingly; just a few drops will do in a stock bottle, not a lot. Store in the dark, except when you feel to bring them out in the sun. They will keep a few years but no longer. Then renew them with a fresh batch. Take time to clear yourselves before you begin. You should be neutral on the days you make them, meditate or sit, and let the day pass by, and all will be well.

PINE TREE ESSENCE

This essence can be taken in water, four drops or so at a time. It will ease the panic, the confusion, bring calm and solidity and strength to a stressful world. Use it when you feel tired, depleted and lacking in energy to face the world and its troubles and problems. Use it when you feel ill and refuse to give in. Use it when you feel trampled by others, unsure of how to respond in a hostile situation. All these situations and more can be opened and cleared and lightened by this essence. Take care to keep it cool, it will not respond well in heat. Keep it alive with your love, take the bottle out occasionally and lay it near crystals, or in the light where you can see it and feel its presence. This will keep it working well for you.

CRYSTALS

Crystals need time spent with them whilst you are in a space of meditation. They need to feel love to polarise you in that direction too. They are catalysts, openers of space, openers to other dimensions. As you know, you can follow a path to the Light and the love of the universe directly, or can take another route, where the love is in favour of the self and its own separated needs first. This distinction is not within a crystal's power to detect, or have any input into. From a level of oneness, all is on the path so take care with crystals. They will exaggerate, bring to the surface much of the past and much that is denied within a being, but this will only bring a successful outcome if you choose a Light path, if you open to this stage by stage, day by day, with an ordered and methodical intention. It is not a 'flash in the pan' miracle cure, a sudden jumping into the Light through the power of the crystal. It is more a doorway, an opening that you can use to walk through, in whatever direction you choose to walk. This choice is firmly yours, and is not the responsibility of the crystal.

Crystals also can pick up energies, thought forms, negativity, and this also you need to be aware of. Few crystals have not passed through human hands before they reach you, and sometimes unseen energies may have resonated and stuck to this crystal. Often you can feel this, and you can also check with dowsing if a crystal is clean. If not, the sun, the wind, water and nature will help, or maybe it needs to be returned into the Earth to be diffused and cleared of this human energy. So take time before you begin to feel the energies of a crystal, and remember that this can also change in day-to-day living. What was OK yesterday may be in a different state today.

Crystals can open you to the Light, can help you, protect you and carry you on many adventures to the Light. It is a doorway, an opening, that will become increasingly important. These are not ornaments or jewellery, these are friends to help you on your path. When their time with you is over let them go gracefully, pass them on to others who may need this energy spectrum. This is all we have to say at this time. The Devas of the crystal frequencies of love and Light on Earth.

DOUBLE TERMINATE LASER CRYSTAL

This crystal is aware of the essence of life, of being. This crystal can tell you of all the past, of all the future. This crystal is wise and knows much, it has the ability, the strength to guide you forwards, it can protect and heal you and keep you safe as you voyage within the boundaries of another's energy field. It likes to be held, to be touched, to be caressed, to be caught up in the process, to be used, to be loved, and so it will unfold its secrets as you work with it and as you work with others. The two energies of giving and loving will become apparent as it seeks to guide you through this stage of your process of development. Love it and thank it, wash it and wear it when you need its healing, its protection whenever you work within the energy fields of another, when you heal.

You can use this stone to let you feel safe, let you feel protected, it will be where you need it if you hold it and feel where you need to hold it on the body. Then you can retrieve your own energy field if necessary, and bring yourself back into harmony and balance before you start again the process of delving within the fields of energy around another body, or within it.

Learn to be clear. Keep this safe and all will expand and flow as you get to the truth of this field of energy that has offered itself to you as a gift from the Earth, from the mother, from the ancient mother, the source of life on this core planet. She heals and loves and asks much of those who come to help, but loves and keeps you safe in her own way. Love her too and she will respond and give you what you need. Respect her, love her, she needs you and will support you now, through the time of crisis and change, and show you how to use the skills you have brought here. Love us and her. We love you.

HOW POWER CORRUPTS GROUPS OF GOOD INTENTION

When spiritual groups form around a leader, the unconscious and unexpressed needs of both the leader and the flock can manifest very easily into a negative structure that can prove to be far from the original intention of freedom; thus both parties are tied together in a karmic tangle. When feelings are denied and overlooked for the greater good, and belief systems slot into place, the end result can be very ugly, the misuse of power into the old hierarchical structures being the outcome.

Most dangerous are groups where strong feeding cycles operate between the leader and the members of the group. When the leader needs the group to supply energy and the group willingly give their power away, believing mistakenly that they need their leader to survive or become whole, trouble ensues. Such structures are more common than you may imagine. Honesty breaks the illusion, but those that see the truth are rarely congratulated on their insight. More denial follows, with the daring challenger who seeks to escape the system becoming a negative and ostracised figure to be shamed, pitied, and made to pay for their negativity. Pressure from the whole group is upon them, with judgements being made that they are wrong. And so it goes on.

The following beliefs are rife amongst such groups. Interaction with these groupings can be a useful lesson on the misuse of power, where an understanding of the dynamics of need and control is necessary.

The denied feelings that do not fit the consensus reality are often pushed away as belonging to another's negativity. If exchange is in the open and is understood, it does not build on these denials but seeks to look at all possibilities as to why reality is as it is.

They believe that what they do is right, spiritual, or whatever.

They believe their leader unconditionally.

They believe they are better than other people outside of their group.

They believe they need protection from black sheep who have already left the group.

They believe their leader is enlightened and above them.

They believe their leader is not acknowledged by others outside of the group.

They believe their leader helps them and saves them from harm.

They believe anyone who leaves causes all their ills and problems and is negative and misguided.

They believe anyone who leaves wants to control the situation, even though they are no longer there.

They believe those that leave are destructive.

They believe those that leave are a threat and need to be cut off.

SIRIUS

The planets around Sirius are many, their energies varied, their effects on Earth many too. There is much that is negative that affects human life and experience on Earth that has its origins on Sirius, or from the planets around it. Its life forms cover many Densities, as do those on Earth, and not all look outside of the experiencing and consciousness they inhabit.

On Earth many have experienced existence on the planets around Sirius; from 3rd Density and 4th Density their experiences left them weighted, in frequency terms, to be able to incarnate on Earth. Sometimes this was by choice, sometimes this was and is a necessity for the consciousness as a whole to grow and evolve. Sirius is a planet of mind, it does not work in the same way as a human incarnation on Earth. Imagine being static, unable to move around but able to stretch and communicate with others who are not necessarily in close proximity. Communication is possible over time and space and those from Sirius who incarnate here tend to have a sharp and expressive mind. Maybe 40% of the Earth's population have experienced incarnation in some other form during their experiences as a source of consciousness. Many are unaware of these connections but know that they hold the strengths to override the body, override the Will through sheer force of willpower.

Mental agility is also a trait of those who have Sirius in their mental inheritance. They are able, quick and agile on a mental level and this force can be used for much good or much destruction, depending on the amount of love and compassion they learn to feel and express. An incarnation on Sirius can mark the beginning of a descent to human form, this can be of choice, for the good of the whole of creation, or can be a matter of necessity for the being is stuck and unable to move on in the band of experiencing they find themselves in. Earth is a special place, it offers the experience of the human body; from this experience you can 'feel' more closely the energy of the Will and can reclaim the lost and scattered energy of the total being in preparation for the true movement forwards and polarisation.

On Earth many hold this energy now and are preparing for their movement forwards; they can choose to polarise on either path, Light and Dark, and the negative energies on Sirius seek to inhabit and influence those on Earth susceptible to their energy and corrupt their free-will choice of polarisation. This is a serious matter that contravenes many of the laws of the natural world and is making more difficult the movement forwards of the Earth to a positive and Light-filled existence.

Sirius holds connections to the Earth both on the land and directly to human beings through resonance. Unexpressed negative emotions in the Will prove a ripe breeding ground for sympathetic influence and attachment. Over time the influence of Sirius on Earth has grown: the western world, the northern hemisphere, both hold strong under its sway and it is hard for humans to see for it is not only subtle but for many familiar. This familiarity is not one of happiness, it is of striving with no reward, of unrequited love, of feeling abandoned, lost and worthless - all emotions, feelings and thought patterns that are intrinsic to the human experience at this time. To break free, to move beyond this influence is not impossible but it is hard. It takes courage to look within, to find the feelings and experiences that are relevant to these old experiences held deep within the consciousness.

There is much that is relevant and much that can be done to change the situation. Familiarity can work both ways, and once seen and understood these energies can easily be repelled and moved away from Earth. But first you need to conquer the fear that this energy instills. Over time you get stronger, less fearful, more competent and able to deal with these energies so that their influence, and the negative programming they seek to inculcate, starts to lose its grip on the human consciousness.

Take time to see where you fit in this picture. If you have experiences from this star, from this bright and close star to Earth, then all is not lost. There are hidden abilities here that can be put to good use if the negative charge is released and returned. We love you. The Angels of Light.

The patterns from Sirius are ones of loss and abandonment, fear and revenge, and have much to do with why so much on Earth does not have the positive outcome that was intended at the outset. So often events are overtaken by deep subconscious pulls to play out these old patterns and some of them are now almost universal in their remit.

So, to feel loss is one thing, to be trapped by and in it, to be afraid of it to such an extent that all movement forwards is thwarted, this is not natural and those that can override these pulls can create much but always there is the fear of this loss somewhere in their makeup. If it is missing in one area of life like work, it may resurface in another area like relationship, or vice versa.

These patterns can be checked on, and for, when a person is ready to accept the charge from the emotional body, and is willing on some deep level to move on and feel the freedom of the truth. This is not easy, but many are beginning to look within and this could help to release these old attachments.

Sirius, it is an unfolding story, a long connection that has developed over the aeons. Now there is a break point, and humanity struggles for its freedom on many levels. Those that look within will find in many ways even more to deal with than those who look to change the material world, and yet the level of looking deeply, and feeling the hopelessness of one's cause, is similar.

So how to deal with all of this; remember you are not alone, here or anywhere in the universe. Like attracts like, and as well as the negative resonance you all carry on Earth, there is a positive side to the picture that you can tend to forget. Yes, you have doubts, fears, and limitations; you also have access to the truth. You will never see it all, but you can feel the unity, the oneness, the all-enveloping love that pervades all of existence. This is the plus side, and the need to access this energy is at first satisfied through meditation.

Modern man has precious little time to stand and stare, hence the need for more conscious time spent alone, in contact with the Self and the pleasure that other levels can communicate to the individual human being. It is not a big step, not a big jump now to move beyond the everyday. Those that want to make existence material only, have a hard job keeping the lid on. Science moves into realms that have to acknowledge that there is more to reality than what a human being can feel, see and touch. So awareness opens. So for now remember that all is not lost, it cannot be so, for energy is at the core of all existence and moves through many different states, frequencies and Densities on its journey from, and to, Source. The whole of this existence is moving on, and the joy to be felt is under the surface of all the chaos and disruption you see around you. That joy is what you all need to be in contact with. Not that there is a neat answer to all of humanity's problems, not that all is wonderful and meant to be like this, but that a connection to the Higher Self is possible, and easily found if sought.

First, the clearing of the energy from the connection to Sirius should be a priority for those incarnate on Earth. It will take time for the energy to be seen and recognised, but it will come. The names people use may be different but that is of no consequence, it's the fix of the co-ordinates on an energetic level that is important here, not the actual names. Otherwise yet more problems of communication ensue.

All have to look within, feel the corruption, clear it, and move into the power of a loving energy that can create a more loving outcome on Earth and beyond. We love you.

THE GROUP ON SIRIUS

The group and its experiences on Sirius are mirrored in many of the experiences on Earth of those who have followed a religion, believing and hoping that all is good, honest and of the Light; giving their energy willingly, and only later finding out that there are levels of corruption and wickedness running rampant at the top of the hierarchy.

On Sirius the cording and connection to the group's symbolic centre was very strong, making those in its sway unable to be free. They have carried this taint down to lower frequencies and to their experiences on Earth. The group sought to corrupt the mental energy of all that came within its grasp. To use the minds of others in this way, to feed off their energy, to play games of cat and mouse, to play out power games using the energy of others, all these are facets of the group's experience on Sirius that you can see around you in the history of Earth.

Here, if you muscle test that you were involved, are the basics of how to free yourself from its grasp. If this does come up explore yourself for the best way to undo this connection. There are many ways that are possible, this is one that has worked for the people concerned. We love you.

CORDING TO THE SIRIUS GROUP

What is this connection from the past and how do we clear it. What is the web?

We see the future, the outcome of this old dilemma more clearly than we see the past issues, and this is as it should be. An understanding of the roles you once held is important, but only on one level. You can free the Self and the others too in time, but these issues do run deep and hold a karmic thread that joins you all, soul to soul, for many aeons. Now the freedom is there to join again, or not, without the compulsion and need to do this.

In the past you have been bound by rites, by initiations, to work with and by each other. The old orders and hierarchies still stand on one level and a ritual to free yourselves from this would be advisable.Use this statement to start the process. Intend to:

revoke the power of the group as a whole, stand now alone as a spirit clear and free to progress at your own pace, unfettered by the chains of the past, the rituals, the swears and oaths and control mechanisms that you have put one upon the other.

The fears you hold of these people are true, they can harm, they have access through the mind to a deeper level of the Self than other people, as you have discovered. This can help and hinder both, and now freedom - and this is the key to progress or not - for each one of you is important. Each one in her way has lain in wait for the others to come along in each successive lifetime here on Earth. You hold the keys for each other to deeper levels of the Self, but underneath this runs the grey thread, the old cording if you like, of negative betrayal and deceit, and misuse of the trust and energy given in good faith at the outset.

The group was one cell of a larger core group upon Sirius many moons ago. This group held the key to the mental prowess of a certain order of the manifesting and creating energies that were used to destroy the minds, the hearts, of others on the path. This was a misuse of their true function, and they could not progress further to the Light until they had experienced on the Earth plane the results of the karmic imbalance.

Here on Earth you have all suffered much, and feel the pressure now of the need to return. This grey web or net stands like a filament in the way of future movement forward. It needs to be cleared with love and understanding and compassion for the others that still remain stuck and trapped in its mesh of deceit and dishonesty. In time you will all have the opportunity to look again, and then it will be possible for us to free those that need to be freed. We love you and leave you for a while. The Angels of Light.

RELEASING CORDING TO THE SIRIUS GROUP

Cutting the cord from the symbol on Sirius needs to be taken slowly; many of the connecting beliefs and agreements need to be uncovered before you can move forwards. There are large areas of understanding here that are specific to the levels of hierarchy within the group.

Those closer to the source of the group's energy, holding more power over others, stand closer in the web to this energy. They have a task of understanding themselves that may take time. Their energies on Earth may be subtle, less fraught and obvious than those further down the ladder. Those in command may hold fears of relinquishing power, of being controlled by others or of being out of control.

Those further down the hierarchy may also have issues with power and authority figures. Each person's particular attachments should be ascertained, and checked with their experiences in everyday life now.

Those at the bottom of the heap, or who were victims of the group, may feel left out, abandoned, underappreciated and unloved. Their efforts never seem to come clear, come to fruition.

These experiences, once understood, contribute to the inner resonance to this cording. When you have finally cleared these beliefs and connections you can look at the cord itself. It is attached to a pedestal and a symbol. Discover this for yourself, it is geometric and star shaped, but is better discovered by each person concerned.

When this is found, a laser crystal, or some other old, and clear, quartz crystal, may be used to sever the connection from the 3rd chakra to the symbol.

Do this work outside and wash the 3rd chakra in clear water afterwards. This is one level of the clearing work.

Victims have no cord, only a great deal of energetic rubbish in their energy fields connected to the suppression and violation of their energy. This also may take time to clear.

AFTER CUTTING THE CORD TO THE SIRIUS GROUP

New beginnings, new starts, the leaving of the old and outworn is often hard but necessary. Now you can look with more freedom to the future without the taint of this old project and problem interacting with your movements and dreams. Each thought of progress has catalyzed another fragment of this old thorn within you: the need to serve, to be subservient, the need to give when this is not fitting, to serve because you need to, not because you want to, all these are facets of the old thorn.

Let it go and focus on the here and now, and then a completeness of this will naturally occur. Then others in the group still held will fall into the hands of those who can help, or not, as they choose in this lifetime. The bonds, the bridges of the past, the illusions and parameters we live within take lifetimes, many years in time, to unravel. There is no real hurry, and no guilt need be held, for those still in place there.

PATTERNS FROM SIRIUS EXPERIENCED IN LIFE ON EARTH

The patterns created on Sirius became encoded into the mind and being of many who now experience life in human form on Earth. These patterns are strong and manifest in many ways during life, repeating the emotional feelings aroused on Sirius. The energy from the negative emotions engendered by these patterns is used by negatively orientated beings on Sirius now: they feed off the emotional charge. This is a sobering thought, and the patterns need to be uncovered and released to be free of this unwelcome connection.

First check if this has any relevance to you. It may not, and if so be glad. Those who were victims of the group on Sirius also hold energetic connections to Sirius, and these also need to be broken. Each level in the hierarchy of the group has specific patterns and emotions they need to look at. There were three levels in the group and each has a particular pattern to look at. Look at how the patterns work in the outer reality of daily life first and then look deeper within, at the inner levels of the pattern. You can check which form of the pattern relates most closely to the original experience on Sirius. For those in the group the pattern is encoded, held at the deepest, cellular level of being.

A PATTERN HELD BY THOSE ON THE SECOND LEVEL IN THE SIRIUS GROUP

SHOCKED

PANIC

STAGNANT

SUFFERING

TORTURE

LET DOWN

THWARTED

This pattern is programmed on a genetic level and is held within every cell of the body. A five-pointed star connects, through electric blue cording, back to Sirius. Each emotion is connected upwards through a point of the star, with one emotion centered in the centre point of the symbol. Work out the position of each emotion and find the colour needed to dissolve the connection. This usually is brought from beneath, from the Earth. Visualize the five-pointed star and see the connecting threads. Dissolve each one with colour in the appropriate order and then dissolve the star itself, once it is free of the cords.

You may need to use your intention rather than colour and light on these energies, pushing and moving them with visualization and loving intention. It can take a little practice to work in this way but is useful when energy is negatively polarized; more Light on the situation does not always move it.

IMPLANTED PATTERNS

It is a new time, difficult in many ways, fierce and strong and people will be unable to let go of much that pushes upon them, jostles for attention in lives that seem so busy, so full. Now you have to let go of the past. This is not easy, not at all easy to do, but important for you, for others. The old patterns are expanded now, are fed on now, are encapsulated now, and need to be exposed for they cause much pain, much suffering for each and every one of you still caught in the net of the past. Let it go with love not hate, accept the Self and your part in all things, accept others and their parts in life, in existence.

There is a push on to conquer, to control, that is strong here and elsewhere. You have to see it for what it is, let it go, let it be. It is not necessary to live in fear but it is hard to not be when you know the implications of so many realities, some real, some internal.

RELEASING THE CONNECTION TO SIRIUS FROM VICTIMS OF THE GROUP

When the pattern is understood, release any resonant or denied emotion still in the body. For the victims there are two connections on the right side of the body into the second and sixth chakras. Black threads connect to two black boxes that are situated outside on the right side of the body. These in turn connect to an electric blue tube or thread that connects directly back to Sirius.

To break this connection visualize the black threads and push them back into the boxes. Bring blue light from the Earth beneath the tube and push this electric blue connection upwards, back to Sirius. When this is complete visualize the boxes, starting first with the box outside the second chakra, returning it back to Sirius also. When both boxes are returned check the connection is broken.

SIRIUS ENERGY ON EARTH

Sirius is a big subject around life on Earth. It has seeded much that is here, has helped and hindered both, due to its own polarity, its own Light/Dark issues. It is not a clear, Light planetary source, and so must be filtered, as you on Earth are filtered, as to the truth of loving Light. It will take time to uncover all the ramifications of this but the intrusion of entities, the feeding off the strengths of humanity, the misuse of power, all these have roots in the Sirius energy field as well as other parts of the Universe.

The input at the moment is strong, it is very technical, very mind orientated, very virtual reality, and that is a path on Earth that many choose to follow. The loss of love is not noticed until a certain deadening has already occurred, so it is hard to step back from the brink and enter another realm of being. Those that do not feel comfortable with this will often be used, and seen as worthless, by those in power. This is not true here or elsewhere in the Universe and a more inner, contemplative approach to life will be needed to balance the mind reality. We love you. The Angels of Light.

CHANNELING FROM A VICTIM OF THE GROUP ON SIRIUS

You were one of many who were experimented upon, each emotion as you know it was tested, studied, reported upon. These studies were for a purpose. The knowledge gained would help those from Sirius manipulate those on Earth through their emotions. The resonance with emotion would enable people to be abused and violated. Those on Sirius feed off this.

Those going to Earth were programmed with a wide range of emotional patterns which, when activated, would punish the person, cause great pain and anguish, and this energy emanating from so many would attract the entities who could then put feeding cycles in place. The entities are a link with Sirius. The entities are being used by those on Sirius to feed negative emotions, mind-controlling emotions from human beings to Sirius. Entities cannot survive positive emotions, and with intent and loving Light they can be removed. There has to be a negative emotion in order for them to attach themselves to a person, so negative resonance attracts entities. They attach themselves to a person, and this feeding cycle is in place to ultimately send negative emotion to Sirius so the star survives.

ENTITIES AS VICTIMS ALSO

Entities are mostly in a pecking order. Many do not know this, and to see entities as victims could help many hold a more pragmatic and sensible notion of what is happening. Humanity feeds off each other, and this is a ripe resonance and opening for other beings to mirror this fact. It was not meant to be like this, other energies were not intended to exploit humanity so, but humans are hungry for advice for guilt makes them inquisitive and open to lessons revolving around ideas of power and intelligence. This is an area where others in the universe can advise, can give insight and support but not love. It is a cold, heartless sort of affair very often, and only later does the human wake up to the coldness of the experience. But by then it's too late, for the doorway is opened to a certain energy that touches those on Earth who are open to it. It is as if the energy field is read and matched, so it is easy for such entities and energies to work with humanity and use their energy for their own devices.

The media is aware of a change in people, a weariness over the truth and will offer more and more gilded versions of shocking events, with only a sparse sprinkling of everyday events that happen around the world. You all need to know what is really going on, but this will be hard to find, except from the experiences of those who are connected and can communicate. Do not believe all the messages of fear you will be given, some are true, some exaggerated to make you ever more fearful and paralyzed, unable to move forwards to something new for fear of retaliation from a hostile environment.

MORE ON ENTITIES

Entities are voracious, they attach themselves through resonance and, whether the person concerned is aware or not, they will set into play a series of events in which the person has free will in how they react. An entity can offer wisdom, not love, but the information given holds power and many are drawn to this form of guidance. The entity offers support and looks with interest on the giving away of personal power by the person concerned. In this case it is not in the entity's interest to drain the energy of the person the connection is made to.

If on the other hand the person is at the core positive a very different set of events will occur; the person will feel drained and weak and in this state will either search lovingly for an answer to this dilemma or will grow in bitterness and hate and will slowly slide towards a negative polarity. The inner core, if positive, will try and hold love towards the situation and the entity will not have total acceptance by the person concerned. Either way there is change, and on a positive note the entity offers the catalyst for change to the person concerned; an accentuation of an emotion for instance can bring about a real understanding of the inner workings of the Self, and can bring further into alignment the core to its own loving acceptance of Self. It takes great courage to deal with these predators on human energy and fear is the main block to moving entities on. People in denial are less fortunate when preyed upon by entities, they are stuck, unable to move forward because there is resistance to the totality of the experience of the Dark but not enough strength or awareness to polarise towards the Light and the frequencies they most likely will gravitate towards. So time here is the key, the workings of karma and the re-experiencing of subtle offerings and commitments to choose with more awareness. As fear grows there is a loss of polarity to the Light, and as the process proceeds there is a tendency to fall victim to the offer of the Dark. For with a low self-esteem and self-worth, and lack of feeling to guide, there is more temptation from a mental level to take the easy route, the path of Self for Self. When all else is lost it can look like a path to move forward by, a path to get out of a situation or unpleasant feeling, for there will be support, help and guidance, even if there is no warmth, no love within it.

For you all there is a time of choice, of choosing, ahead of you. Some are committed to one path or another but most are lost, torn or pulled this way or that, unable to make a decision for lack of awareness and feeling for life and love.

There is a huge entity that is planetary, is particular to certain places where it can get a foothold, a purchase, a foot in the door on this denial of anguish around sexual issues: either the longing for sex or the need denied, or the will to find sexuality in others that is inappropriate and does not really fit with that individual: a masking of the true feelings of attraction for another. The clarity of attraction has usually been damaged early in life, so the characteristics of the Dark path are somehow overlaid onto the sexual act, relationships and attractions. So those that could or would fit and provide the necessary catalyst for love and a loving outcome are shunned for fear of overwhelm, and those that are less than, and often manipulate or are more easily kept at bay, are chosen instead. This produces frustration and irritation and the fuel for more repressive blame and emotional turmoil that is often unexpressed.

Many marriages are founded on this premise. The man out and away, doing his thing, the woman at home, closed off and closed away from her true strength and Self, subservient to the masculine need to dominate and control in his own domain. The woman grows weak and tired of trying to please and remains reluctant, withdrawn and grumpy at heart, unfulfilled and unloved, so prey to any energies that feed off this resonance. The male is often unpolarised, unaware of the deeper levels of sexuality, and so not involved in the collapse of the woman's self-esteem and her searching for something more, something real, and emotional and exciting.

This searching does not often come to a real outcome of sexual passion, but is more usually frustrated, and comes out as a bitterness and remorse for all that is young and alive and gay and strong. So let it be for now, think on all of this and we can say more. We love you. The Angels of Light.

ENERGY STRUCTURES

So the unfolding of the new energy bands and energy structures takes place slowly but surely in each person, in each place that the Light and love touches, and opens, and is received. Much of this energetic movement is to do with letting in that which may seem uncomfortable, because it hurts on so much that is old, that is outworn, that is to be left behind. The hurt is real, and only when it is acknowledged can the new higher frequencies of love take hold, take root, and open out within that energetic space.

The love of the universe is twofold, is mirrored by the breath, the breath in, the expansion, the breath out, the contraction: the mirrors of love and fear, light and dark. On all levels there is expansion and contraction. It is the one point of empathy between all levels, from the Source to the smallest blade of grass. The mirrors of duality are present on only a few of the dimensional spaces. They are put there to release the dross, the past, the hunger to attain that has to be let go of now for all beings that seek to move to the Light of the one original Source point beyond this universe of form in its wider sense.

The flows of energy one to another also expand and contract. This is a fact. How you read this, how you perceive this, is filtered by your own energy structure. You can see it as a coming and a going, you can see it as a constant, but neither of these is exactly the truth. There is a breaking on some levels, not on others. You often perceive the energies from above, but not those from below you, of the Earth that is the planet of choice of all of you that inhabit it, whether in human form or not. All levels drawn to this place have come here for a reason; these are different: some to learn, some to give, some to take. The expansion or contraction is at its mid-point now, whether it moves one way or another is the point. It is in a vacuum, in a static point at this time. The scales are tipped to contraction for many beings but, and there is a big but, the opportunity for expansion beyond the known boundaries and parameters is there also, is there at this time. Soon the doors will close, and the interlocking doors do not move so easily.

You need to expand more, contract less, open more, withdraw less, communicate more on what is real, deny less, open to the Light and love of the One, to the particular less. All these aspects of growth and expansion are relevant now. The opening, the door stands ajar. There is a movement at this time that starts to quicken and to grow apace. All that love, all that open to this movement, will create a universe of loving networking that will reverberate and resonate throughout the universe of form, beyond to the unseen realms of the higher Light. All that contract and hold back will not pass the doorway. This is not a judgement from above. The door is held open for all who wish and want to pass through, there is no judgement, no doubt, no distinction one from another. Only a feeling can tell you whether you need to move at this time or not, movement not in space or time but within, movement to unify your Self, movement to create and intend your destiny through the door.

Here lies a land of your own creation, your own making, and many fear that if they step away from the consensus reality they will fall short and deny all that God intends for them and the planet. This is not true. God is beside you, within you and without you, so all that you create is given energy and form by the one true Creator Being. Let this sink in for it frees you, frees your mind and body too to create what is Light, what is right for you, not for another but for your own true Self on all levels, on all dimensions. The spread and span of dimensions are weighted now, one to the other, by the drag of the past, the past unresonant sound and frequency of disharmony. Slowly this drag will disappear, and the unity of movement take the whole system into a higher band, a higher frequency, so all dimensions will change and raise themselves to another level, another spiral in the chain of events that is called return, harvest, home.

All this is in process. The drag is keenly felt of all that is not in harmony with your intention. All those that pull and polarise to the Light have little time left, so there is a grating and a squeaking of old un-oiled wheels as the dimensional spiral attempts to move, to turn again in its returning movement. Hold strong to the Earth, to the love of the One, to the Light of the One, and let go of all fear on higher levels. Here you can feel the unity, but also the despair of times past and times lost. Let this go with breath and a fountain of light from beneath, clearing the frequencies above your head, above your being, so more light can indeed pour down and within you. The time is ripe, it is now and all will come to fruition. It is a time to rejoice too, for the homeward journey is long-delayed for many beings on Earth, a planet stuck for many aeons in its own Density and trap of distortion that is now clearing and ready to move on. The disruption to the finer levels of beings does not need to occur, if all hold strong who can at this time.

We love you. The Angels of the Dark and the Angels of the Light, those that have moved beyond the traps of duality and now love all that is of the real world of Light.

LOOKING AT FEAR

You cannot move forward blindly, you have to see what is happening to and around you, to be free of all this. There is a desire to shut down to it all, for the pain of the truth is sometimes hard to bear, hard to look at and feel in all its intensity. Those that destroy their lives are often not aware. Those that watch often are, and what do they do with this energy of pain and suffering that lies all around them: deny it or see the bigger picture.

As humans you are often stuck in this dilemma, for you have not the connection or understanding to see the bigger picture, nor the inner love to hold the situation as you look at it in truth. So you escape in one way or another, and so compound your own denials and discomfort. When you are blocked and negativity settles, you are vulnerable, and this is how it goes on: unwittingly you make yourselves more vulnerable. There is only truly love and fear to be addressed, and it is hard to look at the fears, but this is the way forward and out of this mess for humanity. As denial piles on denial the situation can only get worse, and this is the problem on many levels. We love you. The Angels of Light.

LETTING GO OF FEAR

Go slowly with this. There is much fear, much distress and unrest within each person at this time. The bigger picture is sometimes dark, hard to handle, and the fear this creates and has created is immense in people and is hard for them to hold. To see the old barriers breaking down, and the vulnerability of the human condition exposed to view, is very hard to bear. So often those that have felt safe within their illusion of security have denied any threats other than those that are seen and understood. The bigger picture is as we say often frightening, but it is not all of the picture.

There is much hope for each individual who makes the effort and the choice to break free of the consensus reality and stand in their own Light and love and connection to Source. You all have chosen this path and at times it seems so hard, so relentless, with no place to go that feels safe, that feels good. Take it slowly. You cannot undo the fears of humanity in one afternoon, and you all hold these fears. It is not as if some are 'more or less' than others in this, it's a racial memory, a deep knowing of being tampered with, of being subject to another, of being violated, and this is the terror that keeps recurring. Yes, to be alone is hard, but to be alone and toyed with at the whim of another is worse, is more threatening still. It's this layer that has to be undone now.

You all have to stand free and secure in your own Light, for the pressure of other beings who wish to use human beings as instruments to satisfy their desires is immense. As this fear grows and enlarges it will become harder to deal with, the pressure on the outside from others' denials greater, so take time with this to think and visualize and work with your terrors of the dark and the meaning these words hold for you.

In time it can become clearer and less of a pressure to you, but the inner needs to be clear and strong for this to hold in you. The fear is like sea swirling around a rock, you need to feel the rock within, the solidity of your truth and connection, to not fall into the tide as it beats on the rocks. Not all of life is so dire, but this fear runs like an undercurrent beneath much that is happening, and all these entities and other intrusions on your body's energies feed this inner terror. So let it go in blue and pink light from three and five, and let six find its true place in seeing the bigger picture and the wisdom from other levels and frequencies that you can contact, and do hold within yourselves about many subjects, many areas of life.

RELEASING FEAR FROM THE MIND

Feel the fear and confusion in the head and breathe the energy down to the heart. The method is similar to grounding. Breathe into the heart directly, feel the fear and breathe it outwards, in front of you, until you feel clearer.

NEEDING OTHERS, HOW FEEDING CYCLES ARE CREATED

You cannot put new wine in old bottles. How can we break the relationships built from separation and transform them on the 3D, to stop feeding and pulling on others' energy and falling into the old mental structures of needing sex, a parent, a guru and all the mental pain and fantasy that separation entails? Relationships beyond duality are so easy during healing. How do we manifest this in daily life?

For the overview on this problem there is much. The way forward is one of love, one of sharing, one of standing in your own Light and knowing, and giving and taking freely with no bonds and chains into the old, the structured ideas and compromises that litter the 3D life.

The world is in a state of flux and soon the old will not work. This you have to all understand deeply, for to go on letting the business drag on, keeping your life in separated compartments where the everyday rolls on, everything as usual, the same old worries, needs and desires constantly repackaged to fulfil the state of that moment, is not going to hold.

The old is falling away and the pain of this is everywhere. The old ideas of morality and family, the double standards in public and private life, all these are caught and looked at, but there seem to be no answers. There are answers, but you cannot achieve this from a state of separation. In separation you are alone. You need, and need desperately, others to hang on to, to be there for you, to give love and attention, or else you will die.

This is mirrored in the early years of life on Earth, no way can a child of humanity manage on its own. It needs feeding, changing and loving, it is utterly helpless to create its own reality, and this awful state of affairs is deeply imprinted in the human psyche. It is an illusion in some ways, the Earth looks after its own through many ways, and now the whole process is going through a state of change. Birth, marriage, death, this is the old order, each one demanding some allegiance, some compromise, some feeling of failure to achieve.

Is it a failure to die, to not marry, to be born out of wedlock, unwanted? All these ideas run deep and have tainted an already muddy water. The emergence of humans on this planet is steeped in this helplessness, has feelings of compression and inability to create. Hardness or weakness were the only answer, the only response to be made, and now this too is melting and changing and the true ability to create being set free.

So in your everyday life, feel where you are wanted, where you are needed, where it is appropriate to be. If you feel uncomfortable, needy, or not at peace, look within to change this and see what is happening. If you feel joy, share it, but maybe be more open with your ideas of who you can share it with. Will the rocks and stones not hear your pleasure? Will the sky and Earth not rejoice with you if this is where you are? They will, and so will the trees and plants too, if the need is there to interact with humans.

See this as a basic force behind the laws of nature, to procreate, to herd together for safety. These imprints are deep but need to be broken now to be free. You do not need to be alone forever for this to happen, but you need to push past this imprinting and belief to be secure in yourself, with people or without. In the future, relationships will be of mutual benefit, mutual respect, mutual agreement to be different. This is a big step and one you will have to take step by step as you move along the path to freedom.

The feeding cycles are the matrix, the webs of energy that hold this old force field in place. Break them gently between yourselves and stand free and firm, above the grey clouds in the sunlight of the real experience of life. We love you. The Angels of Light.

WILL IMPRINTS

These imprints in the Will existed before mind, are real, and have lain unseen for many aeons and are now coming to the Light. This is not easy work, and consciousness has to be taken from the heart into this gap. It will not work if it is just a cathartic release, otherwise all the other cathartic releases would have held this and removed it. The Light and love of your own knowing has to come into this, so time spent connecting to the heart, strengthening this channel and holding this contact would be helpful.

CLEARING IMPRINTS IN THE WILL

The Will is the opening, the doorway to the real energy of love and compassion for yourself and others. You are focused in the heart most of the time, occasionally you move to the head. The movement in and out of the core (of the Will) is more subtle, more difficult to feel because the other centres, in their own way, all feel too. So it is not necessarily an absence of feeling altogether, but there will be a feeling of unease, of slight separation, that is so common in human life that it is not acknowledged or even noticed. This is the gateway to the Gap, to the uncontrolled feelings of fear, hate, loss and anger, that are so dangerous to your survival as a being, as a species, as a planet. These need to be cleared, but gently. To go into this needs time and space, you cannot rush, you have to be gentle, to force will take you to another centre and the muscle check has to be:

I am centred in my Will.

If not you will have to stop and gentle it on, give love and support, and start again and proceed till you get to your aim, the core of the Will energy. Then push the fire, the dross, away from the Will, out and into the Earth. The anger at compression here on Earth, the loss of love and security within form, the loss of feeling of unity, all these are areas you need to touch. It will take time, but be strong for this is the key to your own progression and the creation of love and happiness within the soul, and the retrieval of all that was lost in Spirit. We love you. The Angels of Light.

THE GAP

IT IS EASIER FOR A CAMEL TO GO THROUGH THE EYE OF A NEEDLE THAN FOR A RICH MAN TO ENTER THE KINGDOM OF HEAVEN.

The opening to the new way, the new Light and love open to humanity, is approaching fast. There is a need to let go of much that is old, that is past, and this has to be done before the camel will go through the eye of the needle. The camel can go through, but only as a free-flowing energy form, not as a structure, not as a form of light held into a tight and rigid pattern of energy.

Humanity itself has many structures, many patterns of the mind, body and Will. Slowly these come to the Light as each individual looks within. These are the problems, the baggage that stops the free flowing of energy, the containment of love and the release of the past. The past infiltrates all structures on Earth at this time. Like unwanted baggage it needs to go, but this is hard because all structures, from language to sight, are in a state of resolution and held energy. The atoms dance and move but the outer shell looks and feels the same day to day. In truth all is moving and changing but this is hard to see when structures are in place. All looks static, and is static on one level, because the truth of the reality is not seen, not wished for, and not needed, by the being within the form/structure. To let go of these takes time, or the structure falls apart and death ensues. To hold the form together, to enliven and enlighten it, and to let the old pass away, is hard but necessary. This opening is but a short gap, and free-flowing energy will be around on Earth for just a moment in time. The point is to be ready - like the foolish maidens it is important to be prepared - and slowly the need for this clearing will become apparent but many will not want to acknowledge this and this too is OK. You have to let go now, let all find their right place within the universe, and love the forms that seek to hold the love and Light of the One Creator Being.

The unity, the oneness, is apparent in all that is here on Earth and beyond, but can only be seen from a certain perspective; like someone wearing dark glasses, unable to see the bright colours. When you are held in a rigid pattern the Light goes out in the world. Hold strong, all those that love, for the need for the few to hold the Light is great. Much can be done, but when all the links are broken it will be hard for the love to expand and grow within form. This is a great shame and many fall by the wayside. The time is now, not in the old way of fear, but in the new way of looking and feeling.

The eye of the needle is also the Gap, the no-mans land between one space and another, the narrow confined space, the doorway or gateway you have to pass through, from one level, one state, to another. To approach any such experience is hard, and takes courage to squeeze and push and maybe get stuck. This is not pleasant, and even worse what is on the other side: another space, a new dimension, a new reality, unknown and uncharted. So that too is the meaning of the eye of the needle and the camel story. The kingdom of God does lie on the other side of the Gap, but if you are rich in ideas, in experiences of the ego, of how this should or should not be (structures of mind in fact) you will miss the point of the experience. Then you will dodge what looks so hard and difficult, the wriggling through the eye of the needle. For most of humanity the eye of the needle is the feeding cycles that are imposed within the 3D reality. The fact that all give and take, suck and succour each other, does not fit with the mental projection of independence and free will. The need to repeat experiences to learn - not a comfortable thought, and so much is missed that is true. And so the baggage becomes immense, as if everyone is trying to squeeze through the needle together at the same time, impossible. Only one by one can you pass through, so this has to be done first, to disentangle, to retreat from the interaction on the 3D of confused messages and denial of the truth in energy terms. Now the doorway, the eye of the needle grows bigger, so you can see it and feel it around you. This is an advantage you will not have on Earth forever, but how many see the needle or wish for the Kingdom of God to come to them on Earth.

Look lovingly at yourselves and free yourselves from the drag of the past entanglements with others. The feeding cycles are one way of looking at 3D interaction that can help you slip through the needle. We love you. The Angels of Light.

IMPRINTING: WHEN I AM WEAK I AM NOT POWERFUL

The imprint is deep, an angelic imprint which many humans on Earth carry at this time. It is an imprint which creates a structure where no one person can move, can expose their real feelings, for fear of seeming or feeling weak and opening themselves to being trodden upon, destroyed, depleted, OVERPOWERED. This is an illusion, for only when you reveal your true Self, with all its strengths and weaknesses, are you truly empowered. This however is only a reality when the imprint is released, let go of and destroyed in a sense, out of the human conditioning into which it has ingrained itself. This is the key to how many things become stuck on the 3D. Not many have the courage or strength to look into it. We are giving you more the overview so you can see how life beyond your own individual experiences is affected by this.

The issue of appropriateness is important here. Inappropriateness is rife on Earth. Look at how inappropriate it is to destroy the Earth as it is being destroyed. Look at how power is used inappropriately to suppress, to keep under control those who try to break free from the constraints on the 3D. See how apparent this imprint is if you really look for it in your lives. Our warning is, do not see this as more clearing, more therapy, more dross to let go of. It is not so, it is deep work, a deep release, which has ramifications on many levels. It should be seen as a joyful process, from the point of overviewing the situation, for you will be releasing shackles that have been in place for many aeons. There will be some people/energies however who may not be a hundred percent happy that you are ready to leave this behind. Do not be frightened by this, for it does not need to be a problem. Simply be aware that the effect will be felt on many levels, so take care, take strength, and let go with love and without fear, then all will be well. The imprinting is deep, one you all hold on Earth, one of the Fallen Light, the lost promise of love that went away, and the struggles to escape from the fact. Now it is time to return to where you belong, so the old fears and needs have to be looked at. The need for security, the need for power, these two run hand in hand. Only when you let go of one can you let go of the other. The emotions of hate and fear for all those who have pressed you down, oppressed you and caused you pain, lie in the arms of this statement. All that have hurt, hurt, so the cycle goes on and on. To break it takes courage, for you will need to go through a wall of fire and protection around your innermost being that has been tampered with long ago. To free yourselves you have to feel the internal fire and fury, release it slowly and gently as it comes up, and complete on it all with a statement:

It is my intention to be free of the past needs for love and security from outside myself. I now hold the power of my true Creator Being and trust that it will guide me and love me all the rest of my days on Earth and beyond. I feel free to express my truth, knowing that others too need to feel this pain, for only with its acknowledgement comes the freedom of spirit so needed on Earth now.

IMPRINTING IN THE WILL

Can you tell me about the Will and the imprinting from the Mother, both in this life and in emergence?

The Will is an energy of movement and change, fluctuating at all times to accommodate to its surroundings, to its energy fields within and without. It is a barometer, a measure of fearlessness and love, of hate and warmth and closeness. The Will is lost on Earth, unable to forgive, unable to forget, unable to move on, so its very nature and instinct is threatened by the held back, repressive control and structures imposed by the mental patterning of centuries of conditioning.

The Will too wishes to control in one way, to let the feelings go. This is its aim and its motivation. It has lain dormant and stuck for so long and now the freedom of the Mother/Will energy on higher dimensions seeks to reveal and repeat this process all the way down to the origins of Densities, dimensions and time. This process is happening, is approaching its point of departure. The springboard to a new way, a new way of being, is through the unleashing and banishing of the stuck control mechanisms within the Will energy. This is only safe with the energy of love, the energy of the heart guarding and guiding the process from a higher level.

Now you seek to free yourselves there is an opening for movement. This is not wrong, not pleasant in many ways, but necessary. You know this integration of the spirit, mind and Will and heart is important, but do not see quite how strong this process will become over the next few years. Those that live in denial will pay the price now for this in discomfort, in fragmentation, in unease and imbalance. There is no changing this fact from the outside; only from the inner, conscious choice to explore this realm can a change come and take place within every individual.

Many will claim to feel but touch only the outer edges of the Will energy. It takes courage to enter the Gap, a place of no return, no reason, no meaning and no help. Only when this energy field is entered will the space become clear and dynamic for the spinning wheels of change to start to move. You cannot do this alone with ease. The warrior is a little stuck in this realm. Only with help can this be an easy journey.

Tell all who wish to know that this path is a path of love and Light, and can free you further as human souls to your true purpose on Earth and beyond. We love you. The Angels of Light and Love.

DENIAL OF THE WILL

All of humanity in existence at this time is a part of, has manifested the Fallen Light in varying degrees. It would, therefore, be a misconception to think that reclaiming your Will, your emotions, your denial, all of which has been denied by that energy, can be left aside and forgotten as part of the ascension process. It is not possible to truly ascend to these higher realms of existence, to the level beyond the Creator Being, without first going down into what has previously been left behind.

These denied emotions, the denial of the Will energy, has kept humanity stuck in the karmic wheel, has perpetuated the cycle so that reincarnation has been necessary to keep repeating the lessons that will teach us this very basic rule: that you must go down in order to go up. The chance now, the big change in energy progression on one level, is that you no longer have to continue in this cycle. You can jump off the roundabout now, but to do this takes a great deal of energy, not on the physical but on a deeper level, to release the charge of the weighty, heavy, sticky emotions that have kept you on this wheel.

RECLAIMING LOST WILL

The highs, the lows and the gaps in between, how to balance on all levels, that is the problem here. The Will energy is one vast pool of moving, enervating and depleting energy that is swirling around at this time, looking for nooks and crannies, looking for spots to move in, release in. Every one of you has issues with the feeling mode, the Will, female, energy. This is a time for balancing this, for without this there is no steering, no rudder, in the material world of form. All the denial, all the lost Will essence, needs to be collected, needs to be returned to each and every soul incarnate so they can fulfil their true purpose on Earth and beyond.

In a wider scale, the Will energy is expanding and contracting, expanding forth within humanity, contracting from the upper spheres and grounding downwards towards Earth. This is hard to understand but it means that all that is manifest has to stay in balance with this energy, and ground and hold it within themselves, reclaiming all the lost essence lost from before, whether it was here or in spirit.

CLEANING THE 3RD CHAKRA

Washing the 3rd chakra at the waterfalls up the track.

As the Light body develops, the feeling body becomes more sensitive, and the 3rd chakra can go into overwhelm when faced with denial or inappropriate discharge of emotion. It is easy to pick up unwanted energies, and until the inner strength and clearing of resonance is complete, this method of cleaning and purification can be helpful.

We ask you to be aware of the fact, of the meaning of the places you visit, you come to. They are great energies, great focuses for energy of the Earth for you, and can help you to balance, not only now, but in the future. The places you find yourself in are given to you to aid your processes forward, and to leave the fears of the past, the connections of the past. Then the way forward will be easier for all concerned. Let go of your fear, wash away your fears, let them go now, see them go and clear away. Let them go gently down the streams you visit, let them go and wash away further the energies you do not need. This is not for now, for today, but for the future. We ask you to take time to do this for much can be cleared by this act of purification. Wherever you feel it appropriate ask the Earth, the Devas of the Earth, to clean and heal the rifts in your own energy fields, and then your Earth-based systems will function more correctly, more easily than before, and aid you more easily in your work and life. We love you. The Angels of Light.

IMPRINTS OF WEAKNESS AND POWER THAT AFFECT MEN AND WOMEN ON EARTH

On Earth both men and women hold on a deep level within the Will, the imprint

WHEN I AM WEAK I AM NOT POWERFUL

How each sex manifests this imprint is different, but its effects are huge, keeping both trapped in a karmic wheel that becomes harder and harder to break. Around the Earth there is a web, a tightly woven mesh that holds us all within its grasp, the matrix of the 3rd Density experience in form. As we attempt to break free on our individual ascension process this particular imprint, backed up by many thought forms and cultural beliefs, causes much suffering and subconscious misuse of energy. 95% of women and 98% of men hold this imprint so it is hard to imagine a reality not held within its grasp. To make the attempt to be free of this is the missing key, the reason for so much clearing work with acucords, for only when this clearing of karmic ties, feeding cycles and need for others' energy is cleared can the real release from this resonance be accomplished.

Women have within their outer energy fields an egg-shaped layer of misplaced protection from the dominance and abuse of men. This shell or skin needs to be removed now, but this healing and clearing can only be successful when all cording has been cleared. It is worth remembering, while looking at this imprint, that we have all experienced incarnations as both men and women. So if in this incarnation we are shocked at what is uncovered around this issue, remember, no one is blameless. If we acknowledge the suffering of both sexes we may yet break free and live in a happier union of male and female, both within our bodies and in our relationships with others.

So, around 14 inches (36cm) from the body there is an energy field that needs to be cleared from many women. This bubble-shaped energy field is a thought form that invites towards it abuse from men and their unconscious need to feed from female strength. Men hold the same thought form about weakness and power but manifest it differently. They believe they have to be strong and need to take energy from women, because if they are not top dog in a relationship they will be weak and lose all power. This belief resonates too with the deeper split between Spirit and Will, the feeling, female Will energy being seen as chaotic, dangerous if given its freedom, so needing to be controlled, the male, mind, spirit energy being seen as logical, cool, rational and right.

On Earth, men hold a subconscious belief that their vertical connection is not strong enough to hold them. Some have a vertical connection but doubt their own power and, feeling a lack of true inner strength, look to feed from powerful women, entities, mind structures and hierarchy. Because of the hidden fear men become 'hungry ghosts' and deny their need for women, and so feed unconsciously

and create millions of acucords which entangle them further in the
3D experience. Meanwhile women invite this abuse and draining of
their energy by their belief in their own weakness and imprint: I am
not powerful. Women hold more trust and belief in their vertical
connection but do not believe they hold strength on the 3D level.
There is also a misplaced belief that women need men to ascend.
This is not true, they do need men, but only as a catalyst for growth.
We all ascend and go through energetic gateways alone, we can
only point the way to others.

The mesh around the Earth is created by the tangle of cording
connecting human beings together. So this male/female dilemma keeps
humanity stuck on Earth, and is the reason why we have to cut and
work with so many acucords. When the cutting of cords is complete,
women can then shift the energetic structure.

**Two people at least will need to help in this removal. It is best
done outside in a place you dowse is appropriate. Protect
yourselves well. Using your hands locate the energy field
above the person's head, around 14 inches (36 cm) from the
body, sweeping downwards on either side until the person being
healed can step over the lower part of the bubble and walk
free. Ground the energetic charge into water or the Earth
and check everyone involved is O.K.**

This is where trust needs to be developed so you can walk into the unknown territory that extends your experience beyond the logical boundaries of what you think you can achieve on Earth.

The work you do uncovers the deeper meaning of the needs and wants, the cording, and the inadequate protection of the hard shell of bitterness that constantly attracts more and more abuse from men, and mental reasonable energies, against the soft, melting energy of female love. Here there has to be an understanding; for if men are to move on, are to move into this new work, they have to let go of much fear, become vulnerable and weak to their mental-thought-formed, structured selves. They can then discover their truth within this. Sometimes, by accident, those that are old or infirm stumble across this truth of reality, but many do not and remain rigid and stuck, embittered and hungry for the energy of others. We love you. The Devas of the Trees.

FEMALE IMPRINTS

If I move and it sees me, it will come down harder than ever and I am so HURT I cannot survive such an attack. So I must lay low and offer what peace-meats I can to keep him at bay and acquiescent. I will never challenge him again, for to do so I will lose all, everything I love here and in the future. For those I love, they will pay for my release and so I have to suffer, forever alone.

To approach the gapped anger around this imprint you have to open out on one level and feel all the pain a little more clearly. Many women hope it will go away, and it will, but the truth has to be faced and it is a little hard to look at. There is much fear around this anger. If you can feel this and let it go with the breath, or with any way you can to let it go a bit, then the anger will surface, but not until you look at the fear, and this is true of you all.

Somewhere deep inside there is a fear of men, of the hurt they can cause, the damage they can do to you against your will, and look at the statement, AGAINST YOUR WILL. Here is the key, to stay afloat you have to deny this part of yourself to stay secure in society. In the home no woman likes her lover sleeping with another, but somehow will have to circumvent these feelings to stay put as the wife, the mistress, or whatever. A man will dominate, has called the shots for centuries to hold a woman in place, because he is frightened of her truth and strength and so this statement holds strong. It is the feeling of every woman with a child, wronged by a man, will he disinherit her baby, will he pass the wealth and goodies on to another and leave her child out of the picture? A true story all down the ages, a reliance on meekness, good will and a blind eye have led the way into this state of affairs. Now it can change, in some parts of the Earth there is a push for freedom on all levels. Many houses resonate on this male/female dilemma too. We love you.

THE MALE / FEMALE DILEMMA AND 3D EXPERIENCE

Channeling for someone who felt violated by an entity and could not understand the resonance

It's time to leave the past behind in all ways. You have been violated for so long, cannot feel any other way yet to be, do not know what is real and what is fantasy. You doubt at times your ability to cope and take in these new concepts and ideas. So for now, rest and let it be. The 6th Density negative being waits, and will do so for a while yet, you cannot be free of the invitation, you can be free of the violation once the old energy block around male/female is cleared.

This male/female dilemma is basic to duality, is the building block of 3rd Density and has to be transcended to be free. You need the two halves of the totality to be whole, but these two halves cannot be found without in a partner, they are within. The male, spirit, mind energy and the female, Will, feeling energy, have to be found, balanced, loved and worked into a total being, a total mass of energy to move. Once this is in place you can transcend and ascend, for you are free of this old division into being one or the other on an energy level. This is not about gender or sexuality or nice, fulfilling relationships, it's about bringing the energetic force of male/female together and locating the clue to the positive, loving path. You need to be aware that the Dark is not wrong or out of place, just offering you a choice. You do not choose this path and it would not be good for you to do so; the way would be long and hard and against the truth of your totality, which is orientated to the Light path. Can you see how denial takes you on this Dark path: you deny your truth, your ego makes you more or less, but you are not in harmony with your total being, and are therefore vulnerable and open to the energy of others. Some have sussed this but will find it hard to break the habits of a lifetime, and indeed many lifetimes.

We love you. The Angels of Light and the trees.

PULSATION BREATHING AND REICHIAN WORK

In the 3D world all energy follows a simple formula:

charge - tension - discharge - relaxation

From the simple movements of a single cell amoeba to the complex fight and flight response of a human being, this formula holds true. Wilhelm Reich discovered that deep breathing in the belly charged the energy body so that held emotion and tension from past incomplete cycles could be released. The blocked energy or armouring can be located at any point or segment in the trunk of the body. When human beings are unable to express the emotions they feel, especially as children, the energetic cycle is broken. The charge is not able to be released, so tension builds and is stored within the body. The unacceptability of a child's rage to adults often causes armouring, and grief at feeling separated from loving acceptance. Our very real separation from Source lies at the root of all negative human experience.

The emotion needs to be felt and expresssed through the body to move beyond it. The habitual repression of emotion is the building block of conditioning. Reich classified people into three main types: pain, fear, and anger, each type developing a habitual response to energy blockage and a corresponding physical form that expressed their type.

Pulsation breathing follows the basic energetic formula and very quickly brings to the surface blockages that restrict the rhythm and flow of movement. The rhythm of breath and resulting movment in the cerebral spinal fluid create a gentle wave-like motion within the human body. Pulsation work emphasises this movement so the body becomes charged and can release the blocked tension and armouring through a natural process. As deep emotions can be released during these sessions, make sure everyone is willing to stay in the room and go through the process. It can be helpful to dance or move, to loosen and charge the body before you begin. Latihan can also be helpful here. This work is done lying down. When the body is horizontal it is easier to access the body's emotional/animal energy. To sit up is helpful for meditation, and communication through the vertical connection. Work in pairs, one of you breathing and the other sitting alongside, watching and providing a safe space for the person breathing to let go. Support is helpful, as this technique can be used to release the hidden, charged emotions of the Will.

If you are the person breathing, lie down on a thin mattress on the floor and place your feet about shoulder width apart, where your knees would be if you were lying flat. Keep your feet on the ground while you breathe. As you breathe in, hunch your shoulders, clench your fists, tip your chin down towards your chest, and tilt the pelvis down so your back is arched. Take a deep breath, and as you breathe out tilt the pelvis upwards, relax the shoulders and hands and let the head roll backwards. If you push against the floor gently with the feet, this movement is easy to achieve, so that the back is flat against the floor. Continue the deep breathing rhythm. To express anger beat cushions with your arms and legs, and scream and shout if you feel the need. The movements of a young child's temper tantrum are helpful, with your head moving from side to side as opposing arms and legs hit the mattress. If there is fear, try to keep the movement going so you don't go dead and stop the breathing. Although it is advisable to keep your eyes closed during pulsation work, when strong emotions are discharged it is good to open the eyes and look directly at the helper or therapist. To show negativity to another being who is non-judgemental heals the unacceptability of negative emotions.

The guide should watch carefully for counter-pulsation, where the body moves in disharmony, the diaphram being the centre point for the breakdown. You will see the top half of the body moving in a different rhythm to the bottom half: shoulders up and in charge position whilst the pelvis is lifted up in the relaxed position. This means there is blocked energy trying to surface into consciousness, but the feelings are threatening, and the body unconsciously tries to protect and avoid. Gently help the body back into synchronisation and encourage them to keep breathing. If you are not sure what to do, do nothing and observe.

Twiddle and see what is happening so you can be aware of the process you are assisting. Pulsation can be used to feel orgasmic and ecstatic, so don't view it only as a clearing method. It can also release the joy felt within the breath and the body. This is powerful work, and can often give a strong sense of freedom, joy, and awareness of life.

RAISING THE FREQUENCY WHILE CLEARING IMPRINTS IN THE WILL

Is the frequency all-important to unlock these imprints, these sessions seem much more direct and easy than other emotional work I have done before?

The frequency is all-important, is the key to the success of this work. As you have seen, if you work within the correct band of vibration you will release the imprinted matter much more easily. It is on a higher frequency from your normal life and this is why it is so hard to access normally from a therapy perspective, because it does not lie within 3D existence. These experiences on Earth only mirror the realities laid down in other Densities and dimensions. You can never totally re-create the Density of imprinting, but you can effect a facsimile that is near enough to trigger the unwanted material into action, and gives the intelligence of the Will energy a chance to move and free itself. It is not all over in one session, the work is to bring down to Earth level a different reality, with the Will energy moving and feeling freely: a hard task on a negatively orientated planet at times. The whole planet is not moving negative, but much is being pushed in this direction and it is hard to watch. The Light is not extinguished and a mixed Harvest will follow, but keep it clear in your minds now that you have to face what is Dark, not ignore it, for it is very dangerous now to be Light and unaware of what you walk amongst. To hold strong you need to keep your Light shining brightly within the honesty of your feeling body. We love you.

Will imprints are one way of clearing the past on a deep level. To begin you need to make sure the frequency of the space you are working in is appropriate. If the frequency needs to be raised, breathe upwards on the in breath bringing energy up your spine with each breath, as if mercury is moving up a thermometer. When you reach the top of the head check if your work is successful. You can also twiddle the number of levels you need to rise by, this will give you some idea of where you need to pitch the frequency. Remember when the session is completed to lower the frequency again, by reversing the process and breathing down the spine on each out breath, until the energy is centred in the first chakra.

So when the process has begun be creative; along with the breathing healing may be needed, and structures from the past may be found in the energy field, both in and around the body. These can be cleared with visualisation. Many sessions may be needed to clear a deep imprint and afterwards work with the mental patterning caused by the imprint may be helpful. We love you.

WORRY, WORRY, WORRY

Fear, how to let it go and stay free of worry.

Enlighten the crystal grid system, bring blue from the core of the Earth to hold it in Loving Light.

For you, you need to breathe down, connect to the Earth, to the core of the Earth, and anchor your own Light firmly into this consciousness of love. The Logos of this Earth is of the Light, of love and acceptance for all. It is being corrupted in many ways and needs strength and support, and can also offer strength and support. It can be contacted most easily at night; in the day the energies are stronger from the outside of the Earth, at night stronger from the Earth upwards to the sky. This is the time to bring the energy up to hold the Earth in love and to do both: give and receive.

As to the worry, it is deep, it's personal and it's particular, each day, each moment brings forward a new focus for you to focus on, but the real focus is hidden from you. It is the corruption of your being, of your Source, by another. This you have to look at squarely and you have to connect with the parts of yourself, your being, that are not corruptible. The Creator Being level of each one of you is contacted now and then – not on a day to day basis, not on a moment to moment basis. You have to make room in your lives for this energy to inhabit what you do on the everyday level. This bringing of the higher into the lower will give you the distance, the overview you crave and need, to hold strong when all looks so chaotic. You will need time to tune in, it is not complicated: you need to invoke the Light and love of the One to inhabit the many parts of the Self - the intention followed by the time and space to do this. You could listen to something to distract the mind, you could focus on the breath. This is merely a way of distracting the mind, not an end in itself, whilst the process takes place. It is not a big deal, just a process you need to go through and to make firm. Don't go back to the ways of the past, move on to ways that will suit you NOW and you may make progress with this.

The Earth is dark at this time, it's heavy with fear and blame. Do your best to shine brightly and give love to those around you and the Earth itself, that so needs it; others can join in this and work individually, or in groups, to help this process along. Those of higher frequency will make more impact but love is love, and even the intention will help. We love you, The Angels of Light.

Why do we worry so much, logically it seems unnecessary and I felt it was worth checking some of the most obvious reasons to see what was happening, and if changes could be made. We looked at the following:

DEATH URGE

PAST LIFE

MIND IN CONTROL

LACK OF MEDITATION AND CENTERING

UNSEEN PATTERNS

SURVIVAL FEARS

HABIT

FEAR

Fear was the key, and channeling led us to look at the issue around the corruption of your being, of your Self by another. My colleague had constant worries about work, of making a mistake or the wrong decision. She needed to uncover the energetic dross from two past lives before uncovering a third life where her decision-making had resulted in the death of a brother in battle and a lonely life, ostracised by her peers. The release of the emotion around this life and the bringing forward of the heart energy made her ready to begin the work with the Creator Being level. For myself there was a hidden pattern that was holding me back, so it is worth checking if one or more of these areas needs looking at before you begin the invoking of your Creator Being level. So to work with this method, twice a week take time to:

Breathe down and connect to the Earth, anchoring your own Light from your body into the core of the Earth. Use whatever colour you twiddle is appropriate for the day.

Invoke the Light and Love of the One to inhabit the many parts of the Self, and sit for approximately fifteen minutes. If you need to distract the mind you could listen to music or watch the breath.

For the Earth it would be good after this process is completed to bring blue light from the Earth's core up to the crystal grid that lies beneath the surface of the Earth. It is being corrupted and this clearing and cleaning is a help. Visualise the core of the Earth as a bright blue sun radiating outwards to the crystal grid and see it lighten and brighten; this could be done about once a week.

THOUGHT FORMS

What are thought forms, are they energy structures created by our minds that exist independently of their originator? How are they attached to people?

The thought forms are efforts, are tries, are experiments of a human mind, they are creations from within that exist without, they are the stuff too of the astral plane. The projected thoughts are fixed and frozen in time, unable to move on, frozen. Like fragments these energies are hard to move, are dense, heavy and weighty, and cause much pain to their adherents, these can be many or few. There are mass thought forms, beliefs held by a nation, a religion, or a political party, or they can be small, shared amongst a family, a friendship, or a tribe.

Most dangerous of all they can be created by intent. Those who have delved into magic hold within the power to create on this astral level, then thought forms stay stuck on many places on Earth and on many people. They disrupt the free flowing of energy, contain all within a vortex so it is frozen, it too cannot move to free itself. This is why the energy is so sticky and heavy, for to uncover it you have to feel it and uncover its structure or mental patterning, the original thought if you like. There is much fear of change that comes from the drag of thought forms; freed from this you can move on. When you understand the dynamic you will feel and see these energies, then they can be lifted and removed.

Where there is resonance you have to be careful. You have to check for this, for when present-time resonance exists with past-time-created thought forms, you have to undo the present before you can undo the past. You cannot undo the past belief if the present emotional charge is strong, so it is always best to start with the emotional body and then free the energetic structures later. At peace with themselves, the strength can be found to clear this drag and weight, and all will move on. The fear around these energetic structures is great and usually has ramifications with the Will and its imprints.

The feeding cycles connect across the horizontal plane between people. The linking creates a circuit, an energetic field, that makes these thought forms more powerful, they too feed off this energy system to exist. The stronger the need and dependency, and pulling on the energy systems on the horizontal plane, the greater the potential strength of the thought forms' energy and power to disrupt. Thought forms left in particular places on Earth are often the creation of a group consciousness with this strong feeding-cycle energy of dependency and need in place. To break these you have to undo the mental energy carefully. It can explode in your face and you need to know how the wiring, the connections, move across the Earth, how the pattern configures, how it is tied in on the map, on the land, and then you can move easily, undo the points, and move the whole. It is like a ship with several anchors, you have to undo them one at a time to get the ship moving again.

HOW WE USE SELF-INFLICTED THOUGHT FORMS TO STOP MOVING FORWARDS

These are indeed self-inflicted wounds. You allow these ideas, these thoughts from others to penetrate, and you believe them, test them out for size to see if you are found wanting or lacking in some way. This is O.K. to a point but not when you feel one thing and consciously go on thinking another. Do you feel to blame? No, you know of your intentions and these are honourable, so what is the problem? The whole world can think what it likes. If you waver, the energy of the hate, or whatever, finds a mark, a home, to stick the energy into.

Either you block your expression, your thinking, your feelings, whatever, it all amounts to the same: less energy, more fragmentation, and a slowing down of the whole process of change. Which is where we came in on the subject of change and the fear of loss of security. The willingness to change must be acknowledged now or not, and the process looked at of confusion and fuzzy thoughts and thinking.

The thought forms are expanding on the Earth, holding sway, this is why so much is so hard; so many are plugged into one belief system at once. This is something new, it has a power that is hard to match on any level. The thoughts are of repression, destruction, at times of self-destruction, of inner turmoil, and yet here on the outside, good intentions. None can understand the paradox: the internal unrest, the good intention, the internal turmoil and the lack of rest outside.

COMMON THOUGHT FORMS

What are the most common thought forms in the world and how do they affect us?

The thought forms, they are ones of greed for the self, of need for something or someone that has to be satisfied - needs that are not real, needs of the mind to have or get what it wants instantly. The mind seeks excitement, distraction, diversion, and all these get funnelled into these primal needs (survival, that is an issue on the 3D) that are distorted and become out of proportion. To a degree shopping mania is part of it all, the instant gratification to fulfil a need, a hole that seems to get filled when such and such is acquired. Now there are other needs as well: to belong, to feel loved; and these needs, when directed outside of the self, fall into a huge category of human endeavour and time-wasting. The lessons that can be learned in relationship have become side-stepped into mental ideas, a treadmill that has no end to it because the lesson is not directly seen, let alone resolved.

So many of these thought forms are communal, are driven by this unfulfilled need, are strong and have much weight on Earth. They hold people enslaved to a continuing circle of experiencing, like a tape loop that is not bringing them out of this and into something new. Again the same experience is repeated and repeated, and the hidden frustration this brings is denied and channelled into more need for distraction and diversion etc. etc. on and on. Can you see that this wheel is hard to break. Only with a great deal of inner soul searching will the truth of this habitual process come to Light. It does not mean you have to live frugally, but you do have to be aware of what is appropriate, what is need and what is distraction. If these become disentangled all shall run smoothly and easily.

A common thought form on Earth that affects many people lies around the issue of work and earning a living. Not surprising that it is difficult for many to live the life they would like to create. The restriction of this thought form holds strong for many employees who earn their living. It may have been created in past lives, held in the energy field to recreate the resulting misery over many lives.

Work is not enjoyable but I have to do it

Energetically this is seen as a black hood that fits closely over the head, down to the level of the nose. Bring blue light up from beneath you, from the Earth to lift this upwards and off your head.

This thought form was uncovered working with an intention. It became clear that I too was affected by this thought form, and checking later, it seems many are in a similar position. So it may be worth checking if this is true for you.

I choose to be relaxed about work and the people I work with.

A THOUGHT FORM HELD BY ANYONE WITH RELIGIOUS CONDITIONING, ALMOST EVERYONE ON EARTH

This thought form has its root within the first chakra. From this root grow five threads that connect upwards to the second, third, fourth and sixth chakras above. Each thread has a particular emotion attached to it. These threads lie latent, waiting to be catalysed in each lifetime. Once activated they effectively stop you creating for yourself and feeling good about yourself. Although not exclusively Christian, this thought form is especially strong for those with a Christian or Judaic religious conditioning.

I WILL BE JUDGED AND PUNISHED IF I DO WHAT I WANT AND GO OUTSIDE THE BELIEFS OF SOCIETY

The thought form is immense, is a pin for much negativity to be stuck on Earth, for much that is negative to work on. For within each person there is this hidden root, this hidden blame that fits so well with the anger of the Dark that works on blame to catalyse the fear and change through lashing out, through power over - the victim who at last fights back. Blind to the feelings of others and the feelings of the self because they are so heavy, so hopeless, for the victim there is nothing to lose by struggling to change, and to dominate others seems the only way out.

Those that refuse this option stay poor, stay weak, and hence you are so leery of money, so fearful of success because it seems it cannot be achieved cleanly, with love, with care for others. Some DO achieve this but it is rare, and they tend to share, to work in the path of the Light either consciously or unconsciously. Contact with this thought form can corrupt those innocent of its true meaning. So simple people, primitive cultures, have been overwhelmed and lost in their simple structures of sharing. It is not money that causes the change but this thought form. So its effects are vast on this planet, and it is time it was released.

To be yourself, to be free, to be clear of all indoctrination, is important for you to be authentic and true to yourself. When this happens you can pick up and create with any tool that feels right, but this is not out of belief, out of need for a crutch to hold onto. We love you.

This thought form was uncovered while working on an intention, looking at my own personal needs and wants and my discomfort with having things for myself. When you try to create something good for yourself, this thought form is activated and stops you. Survival fears rooted in the first chakra become an issue, and the emotions connected to the first through the threads become the major internal focus. The distress can be part conscious or unconscious. This thought form was instigated by Christian and other priests who believed you had to fight your true nature, in the form of enjoyment in sex or personal possessions, to be saved. They also wished to hold power for themselves and keep people in their place. Poverty, and the idea that this was somehow holy and would be rewarded in the future in heaven, makes those who are loving uncomfortable now with money and power.

To clear the religious thought form

If the thought form is deeply entrenched you may have to work with silver, or another colour, first. Bring the colour up through the body from the first to the sixth, in a gentle anti-clockwise spiral to bring light into this area. Find a place outside to work. You will need a laser crystal and a candle. Check which threads are catalysed for you, these will be especially strong, and will need more work to feel and loosen.

Starting from the bottom up, feel the emotion in each chakra and how it relates to your life. This will loosen the threads from the chakra concerned. Check this is complete.

Unsexy in the second

Atonement in the third

Stagnant in the fourth

Bothered and Blame in the sixth

Loosen the thought form in the 1st chakra with a laser crystal, pointing it upwards, into the 1st chakra.

Pull the crystal downwards towards a candle flame, the threads within the energy field of the body will follow so the whole structure comes away cleanly.

Fill the space within with a colour from the Earth, breathing it upwards through your body. Silver or the blue from the earth may be appropriate. Move the energy upwards to the 7th chakra and on to the Higher Self.

WHAT IS GOING ON AT THIS TIME ON EARTH

It is so easy to slip into a feeling of overwhelm and confusion on how to proceed in life. It seems so hard to live now in this country. However much effort you make it does not seem to work.

There are pieces of the jigsaw you cannot see or understand just yet because there is a shift and change going on now, so the aftermath of this is to a degree unknown. There are little inner reserves at this time, it is one of the facts of life that there are waves and surges of negative and positive energy. Like with a magnet, there is a movement first to the one, then the other. Overall there is balance but at this time there is much negative energy, and much suppression of those that choose to look within. It may not seem like that, so much channeling and weird and wonderful things, but also many are stopping, giving up, and this you can see.

Do not fear, over all there is balance here on Earth, it is not so bad in truth, just a hard patch. In the future it may be harder physically for many, but this can be more bearable without the weight of hopelessness and despair on all levels. The Angels are not at one with all of creation, there are areas of negativity they cannot touch, cannot perceive, cannot go within. These are pockets hidden from view, as much as that which lives within bright Light is hidden from those in the Dark. The movement now of these negative energies is great, and it does impede progress on Earth at this time.

Do not fret, keep on with your own contacts, keep on with your own knowing, and keep in touch with the energies of nature that are less affected by mental thought forms and means of oppression. We love you. The Angels of Light.

CUTTING CORDS ON 4TH DENSITY

People able to reach this fourth Density level of consciousness are able to create with thought. They may be unaware of the power of this ability to create, and have no understanding of the damage and karma they create through thinking, but not expressing, negative thoughts about others, and blaming them for their own problems. Blame that resonates on your own self doubts and personality weaknesses opens the door to a more subtle form of cording. These can be seen as empty tubes, transparent and shining, waiting to be used when the person sending the blame thinks of the person concerned. Elementals can also use these openings to approach you.

To disconnect, you have to tune in and raise the frequency at least two to be on a frequency higher than fourth Density. Check you are on the right frequency and bring pink light from the Earth upwards to the chakra concerned, and see the tubes that radiate outwards from the chakra. Push them back gently with the pink light, and follow it with green light, also from the Earth.

Intend out loud or within:

No more, no more opening to you at this time, I wish to be separate, clear, clean and completely free from all energetic interaction with you.

The cords can be in the outer energy field of a particular chakra, or actually embedded into the body. You may find thin filaments that follow the cords as you push them away from you. These thin, trailing filaments may come from other chakras inside the body. Make sure all is clear when you are working and that the whole connection is broken. These cords have some connection with the deep thought forms held on Earth, particularly the thought form anchored in the first chakra concerned with loving the Self. (See Thought Form from Religious Conditioning, page 434)

THOUGHT FORMS PROJECTED BY NEGATIVE BEINGS ON 4TH DENSITY

I cannot change anything I want to change.

I am not free to change my life.

I fear being trapped in relationship.

I am not able to express my grief, hurt and sorrow.

Those in the Light are targeted by negatively polarised beings on the 4th and 6th Density. The Dark, seeking to pull others onto this path, jacks up feelings of separation in the Will energy when they occur. If the normally open and loving relationships of those on the Light path can be corrupted, the group loses its strength, and if internal fragmentation follows, the individuals concerned become slowly weaker. If communication breaks down between people and they experience feeling **tired, frozen, vulnerable** and **horrible** and do not address this problem, the tendency is to lift off the uncomfortable feelings in the Will, and resort to the mind and ego's offer to work out how to proceed in life.

The weak point of all humanity is the structure that exists in the mind. In an attempt to deal with the 3D problems through the mind, grounding through the Earth Star chakra can get blocked and support from the Earth is lost, overtaken by doubt and confusion. The resulting lack of internal integration makes life confusing and fearful, with any issues of survival and relating becoming the main focus.

Unaware that any outside influence has occurred the real problem stays hidden, and the strength of the Light is weakened. The emotions of separation are a key to a possible poke from 6th Density negative and a check on the following statement will start a process of healing the situation.

THE EMOTIONS OF SEPARATION ARE PRESENT

If this statement checks positive break the energy, have a cup of tea and come back to the situation afresh. Be honest and gentle with each other, and if working with others consolidate the group with a visualisation of Light before you all leave. It is wise to remember that this offer is always present, in the supermarket as much as anywhere else, and that with awareness of this fact we are less vulnerable to disruption in future.

If the Earth Star chakra beneath your feet has become blocked through this interference, Light will need to be taken from above down into the Earth. Check the colours to use: they may be on the pink, orange, gold spectrum.

HOW THOUGHT FORMS ARE CONNECTED TO DENIED WILL

Thought forms fuel the strong rage and then fragmentation that happens when denial is to the fore in anyone's system. It is as if we say 'I cannot now but I will' and we leave a spark of energy to make it happen somehow. Later when others try to move/lift the thought and it is shifted and lessened, the perpetrator of the thought form will feel a tug on the other end of the string and may reclaim the denied Will by healing their own current reciprocal situation or may drop it, in which case all will heal. If the same situation just continues, it continues but unattached, it is a story unfinished for the perpetrator but ceases to harm anyone else.

Thought forms can be felt, can be seen sometimes. Acts of vandalism are thought forms, they are fairly weak because they explode on the surface of something, and the seeing of this damage creates the problems in other humans.

Other more energetic thought forms are very strong and Dark pieces of energy, they have no outward sign, but they are felt and they burn those that come into contact with them, or are in their influence. They are heavy and hard to shake off.

THE OFFER OF THE DARK TO THOSE ON A PATH TO THE LIGHT

On a spiritual path you will encounter offers from negatively polarised beings. They will offer knowledge, wisdom, and the familiar security of a hierarchical structure. The consequent use of your energy and loss of free Will, as you are likely to be used by this being, is not obvious at first, or openly expressed. These invitations will not stop happening, even when you are polarised to the Light. The balance of duality rests upon equal opportunities for both Light and Dark to offer guidance to those on Earth who wish to communicate with higher Densities and dimensions. From this interaction we can develop our potential as human Creator Beings. With awareness of the choices offered we know that the only true method of discerning Light from Dark is through feeling, and the only real protection for those on the Light path, love. Negatively polarised beings are not fond of being offered love, and will tend to withdraw to regain polarity. It is worth remembering that to open the heart and give love to a being that may invoke fear in you needs an open, moving 3rd chakra, so you can process the fear, understand the situation and be loving, both to your own fear and the negatively polarised being. The Will is a powerful ally on the path to the Light, minimising the dangers of exploring unknown territory.

The Dark path offers, on the surface, an easy path to enlightenment. Wisdom without love, the idea of progressing or learning without the hard work of looking at oneself, is very appealing. To look at the past with all its pain and hurt, and understand and accept all parts of the Self, seems like a long, hard slog compared to exciting adventures into Spiritual knowledge. We all long to drop the past and move on, but if parts of the Self, usually the body and feelings, are left in denial, unattended, unloved and unaccepted, this is a ripe ground for the Dark energies to pull on through resonance later in your development. With an expanded awareness everything happens so much faster. If then the mental structures and avoidance patterns of the personality come back into play, the truth of the fear around the attention of the negatively polarised being gets denied. These warning feelings of fear around an opening experience, maybe with channeling, meditation or healing on a high frequency, are then ignored.

To be familiar with these personality structures is essential, for with awareness the realisation of being off-centre, disconnected from feeling and stuck in the mind, is easy to see and the internal fragmentation can then be remedied. At this point, if you lose awareness of your inner being and stay fragmented, you are vulnerable to the invitation of the Dark, for you cannot feel clearly stuck up in the mind. The personality is built out of duality, with hierarchy, fear and blame inherent in the system, so in many ways the invitation to forgo responsibility for Self and rely on another to lead the way feels familiar. To stay strong, and stand alone in your own vertical connection and source of your own Light, is hard. The invitation of help from another being that looks so exciting and seductive is hard to refuse. Through feeling you can sense the truth behind the offer.

To look at the truth with love, at all costs, is the path to the Light. This can be hard, especially at first, and results can appear to be slow in coming viewed from human ideas and concepts around the meaning of success. If circumstances throw you back into depending on your own vertical connection for support, it is hard; those in the Light naturally wish to communicate and melt with others. However companions on the path may fall by the wayside and the emotions around this loss are strong, for this feeling of separation is a deep wound within the human personality, mirroring the separated state of 3D human reality. To repel the invitation from higher frequencies of the Dark, and stand alone on Earth, needs courage. The Earth and second Density beings can lend support and stability in such a situation, offering a loving connection when the human connections are shaky.

To want to progress and not look at the uncomfortable truths about oneself can unintentionally lead to the Dark path. So an important step in spiritual growth is the understanding of the human personality structure held in the mind, and a willingness to feel the denied feelings of pain and anger that are held in the body and Will. When accepted, all these levels of being are then approached with love. The Dark sees higher as better, lower as less, Earth as gross, spirit where it's at, negativity and fear as feelings to be moved beyond by mental discipline, so rising above the emotional turmoil. The door to freedom opens downwards, the energy to move on lies within the lower chakras. For so long we have looked up, wanting to be redeemed from the pain on Earth. Our freedom will come from the integration of Spirit and Will within the body, so all of our being, accepted and loved, moves on to the next stage of evolution. Loving the physical body while we live within it and letting it drop back to the Earth when we die fulfills the potential of an incarnation on Earth.

The search for wisdom without love easily becomes the search for power. The fear is provoked by an encounter with a negatively polarised being from higher Densities, making it even harder to drop back down into the overwhelmed Will energy of feeling. Take care you progress on the path you intend to follow so you do not find yourself unintentionally in a hierarchical power structure, through fear of your own inner being. Loving Light has made a promise: if we are willing to go back and look into the Gap, the place where we feel alone and frightened, feeling overwhelmed by emotion, there will be a hand to hold, a loving presence to keep us safe. The feeling of being alone is an illusion, but we have to step over the edge and into the void to feel this loving presence. It takes courage to do this but a spiritual path was never easy, and to balance life in the world with this inner work is sometimes hard. So little time to sit and just BE, to sit and feel. The high-frequency energies present on Earth now mean change happens fast, and you need to be nimble to turn the catalyst of everyday experience into loving Light, a loving understanding of the truth of reality.

MEDITATION TO INTEGRATE THE MIND

It is hard to see clearly now, so much fog and uncentred turmoil where no clear messages can come through. Many are in great fear but are unwilling to admit any loss of control, although they display it constantly.

To relax, to feel the place, to explore the land and find a place by feeling, to drop the mind, to sit and gaze, to feel the fear that comes up if there is no structure. Structure keeps you in a state of mental balance but disharmony elsewhere. The heart and Will are not fed by this, are not acknowledged, as there is a constant override mechanism in place of great strength, that leaves no room to even feel what is truly there. When you are busy you are focused outwards 100%, the mind is keen, receptive, active and strong, this helps greatly in all you do but now you seek another dimension, one of inner strength and peace, and here you will have to explore and pick up the parts of yourself you have denied. Your mind will resist and make it hard to do this, it does not wish to lose control over your totality; but to move on, this is the next step.

So take care, relax and feel where you need to be here, and watch. Watch the mind and how it chatters on, how it moves into past and future, how it moves into judgement of others and Self, how it moves in time and space, anything to avoid the confrontation with the heart and Will's feelings. The mind threatened by your feeling body: a loose, disorganised maniac that will upset all your plans, cause you grief and distress and make you unruly, uncontrollable, and even mad. This is far from the truth, but these are the fears of the mind and you need to be aware of this: that this is the game plan, the structure of the mind to keep you in one part only of your being. You long for the freedom of movement within your true, real, total Self, and this is right, is a real step forwards, is a real movement to the Light and to fulfilment in the life on Earth and beyond.

So how to do it, sit quietly, rest and relax, and allow the mind to wander knowing what you do; watch and observe unconditionally, give it no restrictions but just watch and observe. You will soon see its structure and games if you allow. Look at what you think, maybe note it down for 5 to 10 minutes. You will be surprised at the repetition and the fear the mind holds around all this. Look at it and feel it deep inside. The other parts of you long to be free, so take the key now and unlock the door that fits the key.

We love you. The Angels of Light.

6TH DENSITY BEINGS AND THEIR EFFECT ON EARTH

The Higher Self cannot affect where a human moves to after death. Those who live in a mental, structured reality are already at death moving to 4th Density. They are vulnerable to influence from negative 6th Density through the structure inherent in a mental reality, and can also influence the thought forms on Earth and the mental structures within the human mind, thus increasing their negative potential. 6th Density negative is affecting life on Earth through 4th Density and the thought forms and mental structures that already exist on Earth. The push is to fragment internal integration of heart, Will and body through the mind.

This effect on human life from the 6th Density goes unnoticed by humanity, for the mind still feels emotion, although this is a different form of feeling from that felt in the Will. It is shallower, less connected to the body, and can mirror the internal fragmentation within the body. This very confused and incomplete emotional expression can lead to mental fragmentation and madness. When trapped in this mental emotional turmoil it stays stuck, trapped in a recurring pattern with no end or peace of completion. Only connecting to the Will and grounding into the body can bring relief and internal integration.

There is a negative interaction between 4th and 3rd Density that is connected to the fragmented Will on both these Densities. Negativity on 3rd Density is fed by the negativity on the 4th Density, by pulling the 3rd to a more mind-structured reality as the Will becomes even more denied. It cannot affect the physical body. Those who are connected to the Will energy will reincarnate on Earth to continue the process of integrating and reclaiming lost Will. Beings who deny their Will on Earth at death move to 4th Density, which is a more mental reality.

Those in the Light are very vulnerable to this 6th Density mind interference. Doubt and confusion coming from 6th Density negative beings corrupts the anchoring of the Light into the Earth, not the body, on the lower frequencies of the second chakra. The Earth Star chakra is blocked, so a true, anchored connection to the Earth is not possible. Light and a symbol projected from above down into the Earth can rectify this. The human being involved is lifting off from the pain of the Earth and so becomes more and more vulnerable to input from negative sources and attempts to rely on the mind to survive and relate to other human beings. This weakens those in the Light. This problem is not going to disappear, and awareness of this possibility needs to be kept in mind by all people seeking the Light.

SYMPTOMS OF INTERFERENCE FROM 6TH DENSITY NEGATIVE

The Light path works through open, trusting networking between people, within ourselves, and with other dimensions. When this breaks down in any way you are vulnerable to interference from those polarised to the Dark path on 6th Density negative. An attempt is made to increase the emotions of separation in the Will. The feelings of being tired, frozen, vulnerable and horrible are all keys into separation, the energy of the Dark path, and as the feelings intensify we tend to retreat into the mind and focus on our own survival and relationship issues that are around at that moment in time. Confused and unsure of how to proceed in life we begin to panic and become even more vulnerable to the 6th Density interference through the structures in the personality and mind.

If you feel these emotions of separation:

TIRED

FROZEN

VULNERABLE

HORRIBLE

check on the statement:

THE EMOTIONS OF SEPARATION ARE PRESENT.

The same advice is given when dealing with thought forms projected by 4th Density negative beings. (See page 442)

If this checks positive, take a break, change the energy for a while and then come back to the problem. Understand you may be experiencing interference from those on 6th Density negative, and be honest about the situation as you see it. Be gentle and work to heal the feelings of separation, tuning in and anchoring the Light to regain a supportive and loving contact with the feelings in the Will and each other.

THE GREYS

The greys do have prominence at this time. They seek to keep the status quo, the turmoil and troubles alive on this Earth, and they will force many situations so that they can keep the triangulation of power between them and us and humanity alive. They are open to change, but only changes they can perceive as fruitful for the race as a whole. They fear too the destruction of humanity, so want to keep in check the total destruction here on Earth but see it as inevitable that you as humans will do this yourselves. So they seek to salvage genetic material, keep it safe for future generations of beings as a cross, a watermark of the three races that can hold a positive vibration on 3D and feel what is needed for individuation. Fear stops many of them from accepting the positive aspects of humanity, the totality of expression of the human being.

In time the threat of these energies will not be a problem for humanity, but now they do seek to keep the vibration low and static. Static is important, the lower the base note the deeper the penetration they have to your field of reality. As the vibrations rise and you move with it they will not be able to touch you, and you can protect more easily the places you all live and work in. For now be aware of this and take care to check the vibrations, before you start any major work, for faults or delays in contact with us. This can be caused by interference of a different nature than you are used to, and you need to be aware of this. Clean the head and shoulders with light of palest blue and pink and silver and work with sound; this will help too.

MOVING BEYOND THE LIMITATION OF THE FALLEN LIGHT

Open the pages of the mind, the heart, the feelings, all these combining together can bring focus to human existence. Now is the time to blend and melt all that is lost, is forgotten, is forsaken, into a new whole, a new being of love and acceptance. This new being is a trophy, is a peak, a pinnacle of human existence, that is so needed by all of creation to fulfil its part in the scheme of things on Earth and elsewhere.

One small step for one race has repercussions throughout the universe. This is hard for humanity to fathom: in some ways it's so proud and in others so unaware of its significance, its point of reference to the whole. Here there has been an experiment, an experiencing of the Fallen Light that was needed to prove the pointlessness of isolation, the pointlessness of a fear-based civilisation and culture. Only slowly will these new possibilities dawn and open out for humanity. It's your job, those of you who are aware of this potential to be, to beam the strength of this connection and love that comes from beyond this limitation, into a world that is still in chaos, that is still to a degree undecided on its material fate.

On a deeper level each human being is making a choice. Many have chosen, but on the lighter levels of your human experience there is little actual awareness of these choices. Slowly they will manifest and come to fruition, and as these paths and pathways broaden out and open, you and those that can walk them will grow wise of the ways of this world and many others. Complete now all that needs to be completed on your karmic paths, so you can run free unfettered by the bonds that have held you still for so long. Now you can move, so take this grace, this dispensation out of the endless wheel of karma, and move; but remember, only by involving your Will will it happen. Only your choice to move will provoke this new step. You are choosing and looking, so hold strong and abate the fears of the night with the inner feelings of strength you can now all contact.

IMPLANTS AND ENGRAMS

The implants are means of expression, means of letting go of one whole area of reality and creating another. This is the positive side of them, the other is the negative aspect and use of these: they are infiltrated and used by many different energies. One implant placed in a being can corrupt and open the door to many resonant energies that can use this original, placed, energetic structure. On Earth there are many, both within the Earth and its people. This causes many difficulties for you and for others when you try to clear your way through to the core, the original nature, the true face of a being that lies beneath the conditioning, the energy structures, the beliefs and implants and engrams. All these are layers; one after the other they have to be peeled away to reveal that which is of you, of your reality. This can then be used to create again a reality from the Source, from the correct vantage point of the vertical connection, not from the implanted and encoded materials of another's ideas and beliefs.

This will come clearer in time, but for now seek for the idea behind the implant, the energy that is suppressed, and the form or structure this suppression takes. Also look for the meaning of this in a person's everyday life, how it manifests now in life. If you can undo the deeper levels and layers, and attend and be aware of what lies nearer the surface, you can carry the project through.

Many have engrams, many do not, it is not that everyone holds the structures of an implant within an engram. An engram is a belief, an implant is a placed structure that sits on top of the belief and holds it in place. Engrams are unfolding now, the belief system can move easily, be seen, but the work to clear these has to be done by the individual concerned: the witnessing, the watching of the many feelings and thoughts that pass through your being. The reality you create on a day-to-day basis can give you a clue of what lies underneath, and from here you can see and understand the dynamic.

So look for the beliefs and see them in life. Look deeper for the constricts and structures and see if these are Self-placed, an engram, or put there not by experience of reality but by another, an implant.

Implants are open to be changed more easily now. The higher frequency of the Earth helps in this release work and makes it easier to undo the bondage. Those that have these structures within their energy fields have a very deep level of hopelessness programmed into their systems. This mental conditioning will take time to release, longer by far than the removal of the energetic structure, so do not be surprised if this work seems to go on for some considerable time after the removal of the implant. We love you.

EXPANDING AWARENESS

An expanding awareness, what does this mean, how does it fit into the scheme of things and where do you all fit into this puzzle? This is something you look at, and tussle with, and try to come up with a satisfactory answer. This is not possible because you all operate on all levels, and when you can see this as a fact, communication flows more and more easily between levels. This does not mean that the mind and conscious thinking patterns of all that is around you are like an open book to be scrutinised. This is a distorted idea of communication. It is more that there is a feeling of empathy that surpasses the known energies you are familiar with.

When lovers meet there is a palpable feeling in the air, a combining, a melting, a longing for completion. Exaggerate or enlarge on this feeling and you can begin to see the true meaning of communication between dimensional spaces. It is a resonance of love and Light: love as the pulse, the beat, the rhythm, and Light as the coding, and the expression of the knowing held within this pulse beat. You, as humans, rely on the heart energy to provide the pulse beat. Out of form there is another deeper pulse; the relationship between atoms more clearly mirrors this 'out of form' communication. There is an on/off switch too, not only between dimensions and forms, but between the synapses of a deeper communication between levels. This can in humans be opened gently, and a little more deeply now, to form a bridge to the higher Light consciousness that encircles the Earth. This Light cannot enter into a human form without the permission, without the longing, without the resonant heartbeat of love, and acceptance of All that Is. This provides a real, open, communicating network between dimensions, where all is of importance, and all information has relevance and space to expand and contract. To grow and deplete, this is the rhythm of nature on this 3D level, and it too is mirrored in higher planes, in cycles, in openings between dimensions, in the movement of soul forms beyond the known territories. This is the process you are involved in: the movement of the gateways here on Earth. We are involved in the saving of those souls on Earth that wish to evolve and move on. There is a harvest in process, a gathering in, a change in the flow from contraction of all that you can see on Earth of beauty, of love.

So remember, when you doubt and see so much in turmoil and in chaos, that the resonance to the new is opening apace if the beings wish this, want this, love this as a process, as an adventure. What you stand to lose is your security, your fears, your fretful needs on this 3D plane. On other planes the openings bring love, Light, acceptance and the dance of movement between dimensions. Old scriptures tell of this but do not give the keys in a way you can all understand. Follow your hearts and minds on a deeper level and then, when you can communicate personally, trust the process you are shown and follow it lovingly, feeling your way into every step, until the Light glows strongly at the end of the tunnel, then you will see all in its truth and beauty. We love you.

DIFFICULTY IN SLEEPING AT NIGHT

Why is it so hard to sleep between 11pm and 3am, the energy seems very electric and the mind active, wanting to keep going and not rest. We get it is connected to the meridian cycles, the gall bladder and liver being active between 11pm and 3am. Is denied anger pulling us up into the mind?

There is much opening at this time of the many layers and levels of a human being. As these levels come to the surface there is often fear, fear of the unknown, fear of the denied, fear of the impasse this new energy system will create within a structure. The mind is a structure and one that holds strong against all new energies it does not recognise, understand, and place within a structure. At this time much is moving on and much is being brought to the surface. You cannot let go of much of this; it is a contained inner energy and has to work out within the being. It cannot be so easily thrown off, it has to be internally processed. Many are not used to this concept and have no idea how to react, or to act to change an energetic reality, therefore they feel stuck and need to repair and retreat back to the security of the mind base.

At this time of night there is much coming to the surface through the meridian peaks, highs and lows of energy that carry with them the energy of the channel concerned. So gall bladder and liver are both wood energies and have a lot to do with internal balance - with anger and peace, fear and warlike actions, or not. So these energies are triggered by the new frequencies within and are activated. If you are in denial of anything around these issues it will force the energy up into the mind, and here you will try to escape from the discomfort.

Many will suffer in this way. You need to let go, to go within, and feel on a daily basis, and this will help to keep this internal energy moving and free around the 3rd and 4th chakra. As time goes on other energies will also be more active, and will pull you further into the mind, or not. Humanity has a huge fear of change. The new holds much terror and yet there is no stopping this, only acceptance of change will help at this time, and acceptance of all that is within. We love you.

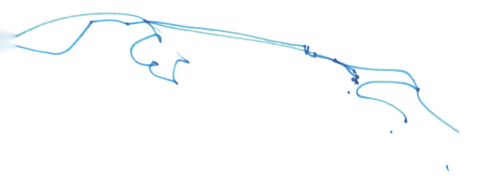

INTEGRATION OF THE SOUL INTO FORM

The release of the past, the genetics of the past, is one thing you all need to look at. The resulting mismatch on a DNA level is partially rectified but not completely. A visualisation for the body will help.

Connect to the body, it needs to be held in white and green light and then lifted and placed down in a circle of blue.

You visualise yourself doing this. This will open and connect to the body's growth and transformation that will take a time yet to achieve. It is on its way, the integration of the soul into form, on a more complete and clear level. Let go to this and all will be well.

PATTERNS AND STRUCTURES

The patterns are a process of growth, of uncovering the depths of the programming and conditioning you are all trapped within. Slowly you will see more, and feel freer to act in the here and now. With this awareness comes clarity, and with this, enlightenment. It takes time on the Light path to move. Sometimes the opening can happen in an instant but before this there is much to do, and this is a part of the process you often wish to hurry along, not understanding that it is all a part of the totality that is you, that is All that Is.

So take care, you do not need to dwell on your problems and issues, but you do need to deal with them. There is a difference. Dwelling on things of the past makes you inward looking, makes you dead, makes you stuck in your past, looking at the issues from the past. If looking makes you move on, feel more alive, more free, more aware, this is the measure of what you are aiming for.

So, look at these patterns and see how, and if, they relate to you, look at the structures and the ways they manifest within you, and clear them gently from the path. We love you.

DNA CODING AND THE PATTERN THAT PINS US INTO DUALITY

UNCENTERED

NOT BOLD

LOST

FRIGHTENED

This pattern comes from Orion and pins us into 3D reality. It manifests as a thought form in the heart and is implicated in heart attacks. When we feel discomfort in our energy field we move to the periphery to feel what is happening. To stay connected to the core of our being is often difficult so we lose touch with the love at our core and become uncentered. The end result is fear, and the inability to stay connected to the truth of our being, one of love and contact through the vertical connection to the Higher Self. This pattern is lodged in our DNA coding and the process we used to release it was as follows:

Sit in the sun and allow this energy to touch the heart. Open to it and sit for fifteen minutes asking within for this clearing process to happen now. Centre your consciousness in the heart, and see the black, pea sized ball lodged at the back of the heart, and project it outwards back to Orion. Check, there may be more than one. See the double helix strands, nine are already active and 12 need now to be activated. Work first with the nine already active strands, one by one pour white light upon them and see them unravel from the double helix and become 18 single strands that will move away when the process is completed. There are now 18 free moving strands. Next repeat the process with the 12 double helix strands that need to be activated. Undo them one by one and activate them in the white light, each one will move away when it is activated. Then see the DNA strands, nine are active, 12 need to be activated using white light, they need to unravel from the double helix pattern so they are straight lines, then activate them by shining white light on them and see them move as they need to.

The DNA, the coding, is crucial to the freedom of the Self, it's the key to the prison of 3rd Density. It is the ultimate pattern that has been placed in humanity to stop it easily finding the door to its own power, its own salvation and freedom. You are not free, and every human being has to realise this fact before you can open this door.

All energy rubs off, one against the other, so freedom has to come from some other avenue, some internal avenue that is not tainted by the outer energies of love, war, or want. Can you see that it is a prism, a stuckness that revolves around and around, never coming clear but encapsulated into its glass prism. Colours flow onto the walls but the prism remains the same, a solid immovable structure, and you will have to see the structure in the heart, the revolving prism, to be free. It is not only a pea implanted but this is a start, it's how the whole mechanism of duality works, and colour is one key you can use to get to its root and its freedom. Duality is a mechanism to help you to push forwards on your paths to the Oneness, the unity of All. It is meant to be there, it's an expression of love for this to be so, otherwise there would be no movement, no push to move on. Like the leaf turns to the sun, so the human soul searches and seeks love, first outside itself and then within. The deeper point comes to a level, a feeling, of dis-ease, of discomfort with the suffering and the unnecessary challenge put upon humanity. To find the key that fits the lock, to be free, it has become a deep yearning, almost an obsession in those that look deeply into this reality. Now you have come to a point where you and others long for this overview, the contained and expanded experience both of love and connection to All.

You will have to go through the fire of duality, it's like a sword that cuts into two parts, one side from the other. It is mirrored in your brain, your hands, your heart, this two-ness, this double sidedness, to make the being able to work, able to operate on the 3D. You long to hold the higher energies that are not divided, you need to burn away the dross, the fear of this unity in its negative aspect. There is a fear of the emptiness, the void, it's inherent in all beings within 3D, this too is coming to the surface. You will have to face the fear, but not its expression, not the negativity of the void. You have to acknowledge it and let the fire of love burn away the fear that is there, it is deep in the heart and soul level of all who enter this 3D realm. It has to be seen from a higher perspective and walked through, up the frequencies, through the fear levels to the One. It's a conscious choice to do this.

It will take time, you will need to be in the open. You need support from crystals, from the sun, from trees, from light, from love within the Self to do this. Do not rush at it, find your moments, choose your times well, and it will happen but only when it's right to do so. It will take time and be all in an instant, it's a paradox.

Do not be frightened of the fear, it's always there, not something new, but certainly something you attempt to distract yourselves from. It is a step on the path, one that brings joy and fulfilment on this level. Go slowly and all will be well. Take refuge in the love of the One for All that Is, and remember you're not special, just one part of the whole finding the key back home. Once obtained it's available to others, in this way you can serve in whatever way you choose to live. We love you.

PATTERN THAT MAKES IT HARD TO STAND ALONE

NO VITALITY

DRAINED

DENIAL

VULNERABLE

DARING

CONSPICUOUS

FROZEN

GULLIBLE

People will play out this pattern in different ways; the following examples are firstly from someone in a demanding job who tries hard to fulfil her employer's demands, and second from someone who finds it hard to stand alone, outside of the consensus reality.

How the pattern works for someone in a demanding job.

No vitality, overwhelm, so much work to do.

Drained, tired and exhausted.

Denial, fed up with no support but I can cope even though I feel tired.

Vulnerable, I cannot cope anymore, I may be seen as a failure in my work.

Daring to ask for help from those in authority.

Conspicuous, noticed but there is no relief, no real support.

Frozen, need to keep going so freeze all feelings and get on.

Gullible, I am exhausted again and for what. They are taking me for a ride, What have I done to deserve this? I don't know what this is and I feel trapped. It is horrible down here on Earth.

How the pattern works for someone who finds it hard to stand outside the consensus reality.

No vitality to stand on my own.

Drained, it is hard to be out of the system.

Denial that if we do not fulfil the criteria of the world we are still valuable human beings.

Daring to stand up for yourself, your knowing and the truth.

Conspicuous, you are exposed and the private becomes public.

Frozen, I am not certain of myself and my truth, I don't fit in so maybe it is me.

Gullible, I am only being myself, what have I done to deserve all this anger and sadness.

No vitality, overwhelm, hide, not processing the emotions society wants us to repress.

A deeper level of the pattern and how we can fall prey to Sirius energy.

No vitality in the body.

Drained and not enough energy to keep going.

Denial that I don't want to do this anymore.

Vulnerable, as the need to conform to society means you have to keep going. A split between the Will and mind happens within.

Daring, ignoring true feelings and mentally override them to keep going.

Conspicuous to Sirius and other negatively polarised, predatory energies and now resonant to a negative input from Sirius, Orion or others.

Frozen, as the Will is blocked both internally and possibly now externally, there is no feeling and the body suffers from the internal repression and the drain of vital life energy.

Gullible, fear of the repercussions of what is happening and lack of feeling any vitality in the body.

PATTERN SHARED BY WANDERERS WITH MANY PEOPLE ON EARTH

Pattern held in the third chakra around being out in the world, making friends.

TORTURE

HOSTILE

NOT EXCITED

HOSTILE

WOUNDED

This is an example of how this pattern was played out in the life of a wanderer who felt alienated from the people around her. We talked through how these emotions were working in her life and muscle tested when we had the correct interpretation of the pattern. When understood we could release the emotion that so often hides the energetic structures that lie beneath the surface. With intention the structures can then be removed from the body.

Torture, feeling on a different wavelength to these people around me.

Hostile, I feel fed up with this situation I cannot listen to the same old crap anymore.

Not excited by the people around me.

Hostile, feel grumpy with them because they won't face their own denials and truth.

Wounded, do I want too much out of life, I should be happy with my lot in life, it is hard to keep going and keep facing this situation again and again, I would rather hide alone.

Torture, I am a sociable person, I don't want to be all alone all the time.

Hostile, how did I get into this mess, all alone, I do not want this.

Not excited, I cannot be bothered with what's on offer.

Hostile, with my own life and the place I live in.

Wounded, others' ideas of friendly behaviour hurt me, I do not want to be noticed in this way, gossip seems just nosy to me.

Beneath this pattern in the third there is another layer in the second chakra, the pattern here is

FROZEN

NO VITALITY

FROZEN

HOSTILE

Frozen, people would be shocked if they knew how I felt and saw reality. The expression of my truth is held back, not expressed, because I will be judged and the situation will get worse if I do say what I really feel.

No vitality, it never seems to work out that I can be myself, on and on I go with disappointments and half cocked experiences.

Frozen, who I am is hidden, others will not understand what I am feeling or being so there is a gap with people and inside myself also.

Hostile, I feel hostile with myself for being so unloving, this is not how it should be, I should be open, there is something wrong with me. This does not feel loving to be so separated and stuck

The following structures were found relating to this pattern for this individual. Energetically there is a 2 inch (5 cm) wide triangle in the second chakra of a dirty green colour with a dirty yellow in it, this needs to be removed out of the front of the body and sent with intention into blackness. In the third there is a circular disk of dark grey metal with a clear, see-through tube stretching upright into the heart chakra. When triggered into the pattern the feelings of being unexcited about life overflow into the heart. To remove the disk, intend it forwards out of the body and dissolve it into blackness. The clear tube will trail behind the disk so it all is cleared together.

A PATTERN AROUND THE MEANING OF YOUR LIFE

DISGUSTED

FURIOUS

NOT ESSENTIAL

This pattern affects your ability to see the overview, the meaning of events in life that happen around you. It also stops you seeing how you fragment internally when challenged by unloving events going on around you in the world, whether personal issues around your job or the wider issues of world politics.

The pattern's structure lies in the 6th chakra and looks like a dark grey ball with sharp triangular shaped facets sticking off its surface, like some rather ugly christmas decoration. The bauble is about 4 inches (10 cm) across and needs to be sent to the black to be dissolved by intention.

ADVANCED CHECKLIST

I AM 100% HERE NOW

MY CHAKRAS ARE IN BALANCE

MY VALVES ARE OK

I AM FREE OF UNWANTED ENERGIES

EMOTIONS

HARDWARE

SIRIUS ENERGY

ENTITIES

THOUGHT FORMS AND PATTERNS

FEEDING CYCLES

CORDS

ZIZZY ENERGY

ELEMENTALS

FEAR

I AM IN A BUBBLE WITH

PROJECTED ANGER, BLAME OR HATRED

ENERGY OF A PLACE OR SITUATION

WILL IMPRINTS, IMPLANTS AND ENGRAMS

I AM CENTRED IN MY HEART

I AM CENTRED IN MY WILL

I AM GROUNDED

I AM PROTECTED

I AM ON THE RIGHT FREQUENCY

**To contact Linda Christie
or visit the Centre of Light in Scotland**

write to Linda Christie,
The Centre of Light, Tighnabruaich, Struy, Beauly,
 Inverness-shire IV4 7JU Highland, UK

Telephone +44 (0) 1463 761254

email Lindachristie@ecosse.net
website www.centreoflight.co.uk